A Saga of Tolerance and a Legacy for Posterity

CATHOLIC VISIONARIES AND WOMEN'S EMPOWERMENT IN NORTH INDIA

A Saga of Tolerance and a Legacy for Posterity

CATHOLIC VISIONARIES AND WOMEN'S EMPOWERMENT IN NORTH INDIA

Molly Abraham

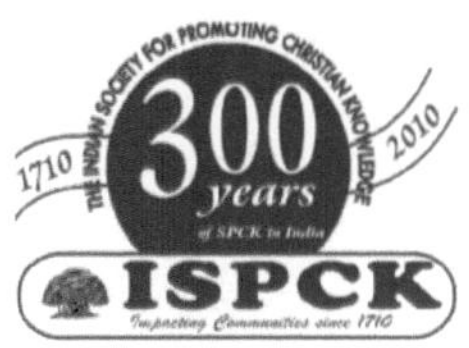

2021

A Saga of Tolerance and a Legacy for Posterity: Catholic Visionaries and Women's Empowerment in North India - Published by the Indian Society for Promoting Christian Knowledge (ISPCK), Post Box 1585, Kashmere Gate, Delhi-110006 under Women's Empowerment Programme (WEP-45).

Online order: http://ispck.org.in/book.php

Also available on amazon.in

ISBN: 978-81-949231-0-7

Laser typeset by

ISPCK, Post Box 1585, 1654, Madarsa Road, Kashmere Gate, Delhi-110006 • *Tel:* 23866323

e-mail: ashish@ispck.org.in • ella@ispck.org.in
website: www.ispck.org.in

Contents

Acknowledgements

As a member of the Congregation of Jesus and Mary and as a faculty member at Jesus and Mary College, Delhi I am passionately interested in the questions and issues related to our ministry of education. For more than 150 years, Jesus and Mary educational institutions have offered thousands of students, Catholic education within the JM tradition. Hundreds of JM Sisters have taught in its classrooms, laboratories, and lecture halls. The legacy of the Congregation of Jesus and Mary charism is not just a museum piece; it is a dynamic tradition that is lived day in and day out in our educational institutions.

Besides serving on the faculty and in administration, the most important dimension of the JM presence, in my opinion, is our witness of prayer and living in community. And it is this prayerful presence that is the spiritual foundation of our campus communities. This wellspring of spirituality and scholarship is the source of our inspiration as we engage in a post-modern world. As a JM member, my personal responsibility is to learn and hand on the great Catholic intellectual tradition of the Congregation of Jesus and Mary. And in this context, I deem myself so privileged to do a study, the first of its kind, that throws light into our charism and educational apostolate. First of all, I express my gratitude to the Almighty for His blessings and grace all throughout my academic journey.

This book would not have been possible without the assistance of many people. I extend my gratitude to the Librarians at St. Patrick's Junior College Library and Archives, Agra, St. Joseph's Inter College Library and Archives, Agra, CJM Library and Archives, Waverly (Mussoorie), St. Joseph's Library and Archives, Sardhana, CJM Library and Archives, Chelsea (Shimla), CJM Library and Archives, Dehra Dun, CJM Library and Archives, Ambala, St. Antony's Library and Archives, Agra, St. Bede's College Library and Archives, Shimla, CJM School Library and Archives, New Delhi, CJM School Library and Archives, Hampton Court (Musoorie), HP University Library, Shimla, Indian Institute of Advanced Study, Shimla, National Museum and Archives, New Delhi, CBCI Library and Archives, Delhi, Cathedral Library and Archives, Agra, Cathedral Library and Archives, Chandigarh and Arch Bishop's House Library and Archives, Mumbai. I record my special gratitude to the Librarians at CJM Generlate Library and Archives, Rome and CJM Angelic Library and Archives, Lyon, France for unstintingly ordering dozens of books, journals and articles.

I am very much indebted to my Provincials, Principals and the members of the congregation who encouraged me in every respect. My deepest appreciation goes to JMC community members and my friends for their valuable suggestions.

Finally, I do appreciate the love and support from my mother, family members and friends. They helped me through it all, over these years working to get this done. Their support has been invaluable, and their love has made it all make sense.

Sr. Molly Abraham

Foreword

"To strive towards excellence in all spheres of individual and collective activity so that the nation constantly rises to higher levels of endeavor and achievement" is one of the most important Fundamental Duties of the citizens of India, under Article 51 A of the Constitution of India. I am extremely delighted to present this book to all those who would like to know the models of excellence in the field of education, and the history of women empowerment in North India. History is much more than the path left by the past; it persuades the present and shapes the future. The past decade witnessed a proliferation of excellent research studies on very important topics concerning women— their education, their roles and relative status, their participation in work force, in politics and their contribution to economic development and so forth. Such scholarship is rich and highly relevant for understanding the significance of education to women's lives. We learn a little from this body of knowledge about why women attend Christian schools, what they learn in school, how education received in Christian institutions affects them, or whether education makes a contribution to improve their lives apart from class, ethnicity, and other social factors. Therefore, in this book titled 'Catholic Visionaries and Women Empowerment in North India', Dr. Sr. Molly directly addresses the contribution given by the Jesus and Mary Congregation and the missionaries in the field of women education in North India. The book also has highlighted the quality of education girls receive from the educational institutions founded and run by the Congregation of Jesus and Mary. This historical scholarship focuses on the content of the education, their contributions towards women education and their efforts to remove the structural barriers to women's full participation in social and economic life. It also identifies a number of trends that provide a useful basis for raising questions about women's educational patterns and contributions made by the Congregation of Jesus and Mary towards women education in North India. Thus, this book assumes importance and relevance in illuminating the issues related to the field of women education.

The focus of this book is on how education impacts women and improves women's lives, recognizing the educational mission of the Congregation of Jesus and Mary in North India in the context of social systems that oppress women. It maintains that the mission need not merely reflect or reinforce such systems, but rather that the education institutions can be made instruments for transformation of the society. The pioneers of JM institutions were visionaries and had a far-sighted mission. When they responded to the persistent request of the people of India to open schools for the children in the far-flung areas in North India, they realized that this was the best way of leading young minds from the darkness of ignorance to knowledge and wisdom. They had an unshakable conviction that education was the most effective means of transforming a society from within.

Since the main focus is on the contributions towards female education, it introspects whether education indeed enables women to mediate the impact of the family on their economic and social roles, and whether education substantially affects women's lives in the family. It has been oriented around the question of how education changes women's lives in the gamut of roles women assume. The book is a resourceful reference and I am sure it will serve as a source of guidance for women involved in the ministry of education, to achieve excellence. Dr. Sr. Molly has undertaken a strenuous and praise worthy task in focusing on women's education in North India. The author has done an excellent job. I wish the author and the readers all the best.

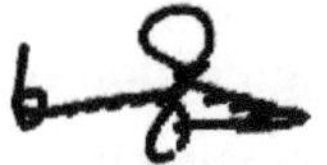

Justice (Retd.)Kurian Joseph
Former Judge, Supreme Court of India

Chapter 1

Catholic Visionaries and Women's Empowerment in North India: An Introduction

While adopting the theoretical formulations of scholars including Sabyasachi Bhattacharya, Hayden Bellenoit, Tim Allender,and Krishna Kumar, this work uncovers the complexity of Catholic missionary education in North India suggesting how women Catholic missionary educators in a Protestant setting were able to thrive in knowledge production transcending the spatial metaphor centre periphery binaries (Allender 227). This is to suggest that the Catholic visionaries,[1] well engaged with communities of different cultural traditions, by teaching the economically disadvantageous sections, could transcend the deeply embedded formal colonial divisions of caste, class, gender, and race.

Exploring the implications of French revolution on women, interconnections between Catholicism, education and other aspects of modern society in North India, it explores the role played by Catholic women missions and the ways in which they influenced many aspects of traditional ethos, gender and literacy through women's education. It argues that the educational obligations were not so explicitly pronounced on the socially disadvantageous sections as they were on the higher castes of Hindus until they had multiple visionary encounters (Leitner iii).

Theoretical Implications of Catholic Visionaries

Recent historiography of Christianity resolutely suggests that Christianity in India is neither a current contingency, nor a by-product of British colonialism, but can be traced back to 52 AD in Kerala, where a very early Catholic Christian community began to emerge (Panikkar 15). These are traditionally known as Saint Thomas Christians or Syrian Christians of India. They are considered as an ethno-religious community of Indian Christians from the state of Kerala, and a few scholars claim that the coming of Christianity to India is clearly explained in the opening chapters of the *Acts of Thomas*, written in the third century AD in Syriac (Neill 26).

The European expansion and consolidation in India were largely accompanied by visionary activities in the sixteenth century after Vasco Da Gama's discovery of the sea route and the arrival of Jesuit visionaries in Goa in 1542. Dissemination of Christianity and spreading of western knowledge through education during the early modern period demonstrates that there was a strong relationship between these two main actors –colonialism and missionaries (Kumar 4). Portuguese patronage to missionary work in the sixteenth century, anti-slavery movements, and religious revival in Britain in the eighteenth century continued to resonate visionary movements in Asia and India in particular for both colonialists and missionaries felt the need for Europeanization, standardization, and civilization through politics of representation (Nag xiv). Sanjay Seth (2007) argues that the nineteenth century missionary activity in India had been intimately connected with the British empire as the powers of the East India Company to allow, limit and prohibit missionary activity were exercised with discretion, though the colonial government resolutely refused to champion Christianity in its official capacity (28). Nevertheless, with the rise and growth of British power under the East India Company, both the Catholic and Protestant missionaries made India one of their largest areas of activity for religious preaching, education and medical mission (Bellenoit, "Education, Missionaries" 177).

As British India made every effort to delink the nexus between education and politics through various initiatives such as Risley Circular and so on, but they feared that students' activities would lead to sedition; hence, colonialism buttressed missionaries'religious education through grants-in-aid system. Recent scholarship on missionary education, especially Hayden Bellenoit in his *Missionary Education and Empire in Late Colonial India, 1860-1920* argues that European missionaries welcomed the imperial British presence because it gave them adequate protection, public space, and maneuverability (Bellenoit, *Missionary Education* 34).

The colonial schooling in the early eighteenth century emphasised traditional methods of learning and Section 43 of the 1813 Charter Act declared a respect for Sanskrit ethics as a part of its strategy to keep the educated elite Indians loyal citizens. Similarly, early orientalists in 1820 such as H.H. Wilson, H.T. Prinsep and others made every effort to advocate Eastern Algebra, Geometry, and literature. It was during this period, leaders of Indian enlightenment like Rammohan Roy urged the colonial government that Indian education should be based on European Enlightenment with the idea of western learning (Allender, *Ruling Through Education* 6).

Similarly, Arya Samaj became more aggressively anti-missionaries and anti-Christians and even began to reconvert those who had converted to Christianity and Islam. The transition from idolatry to Christianity through missionary teaching was interrogated by social reformers such as Keshab Chandra Sen who lamented that old faith was gone and no new faith was established in its place (Seth 31). Nevertheless, influenced heavily by the utilitarian ideology, Anglicists like Alexander Duff, C.E. Trevelyan, and others advanced English language while preserving Indian classical languages including Arabic, Persian, and Sanskrit (Allender 17). The missionaries viewed western learning as a 'steppingstone' for promoting Christian faith (Bellenoit 184) and perceived it as an appropriate instrument to prepare children for overall development through English education. It should be noted that there was a great demand among the elite Hindus as English became a precondition for government jobs (Seth 31).

While some Governors General such as William Bentinck supported the expansion of educational infrastructure for the education of the children of the peasants, others like Auckland opposed the very idea of educating the children of farmers as it would lead to an unhappy life with their cottage. He even asserted that the policy of the government was to educate only the 'respectable natives' not the children of peasants. This attracted a great deal of attention of elite Hindu organisations like Dharma Saba, founded by Radha Kanta Deb, who vehemently criticised that the 'insensible introduction of education' to the children of peasants would only underestimate the plough, the axe and the loom (Rao 177).

Missionaries considered that education was one of the most effective means to reach the young girls of Hindu population, which faced a series of challenges due to caste, and class restrictions, which questioned their participation in the public sphere (Johnston 70). In girls' schools, apart from formal education, missionaries felt that plain sewing, knitting, spinning and embroidery should be taught (Leitner 108). The elite Hindus, on the other hand, contemplated that the so-called unselfish interests of European ladies were merely for the sake of their religion, which actually retarded the progress of western missionary education in India. They even asserted that if these ladies would have excluded religion from their course of teaching, Indian women would have been attracted towards them in large numbers with greater attention and exceptional earnestness (Leitner 109).

Religion and Education

The mission of any Catholic educational institution flows from the very mission of the Church itself. The biblical text says that Christ, the glorious rebel, wanted the Church to be his presence in the world until he returned, and sought the Kingdom of God amidst temporal affairs.

The mission of all Catholic educational institutions is education based on the presuppositions and principles that the Gospel of Jesus Christ provides. God's Word is the light of the world that enlightens everyone. The educational enterprises of the Congregation of Jesus and Mary, therefore, find their genesis in the rich Catholic intellectual tradition. All the educational institutions run by the Congregation of Jesus and Mary in India have a charisma and centuries-long tradition that inspire and motivate their mission. As the mission of the education ministry of the Congregation of Jesus and Mary goes all the way back to the 19th century in France, this study throws light on the origin of the Congregation in France and the establishment of educational mission in India.

Tradition of Christianity in India

Tradition found in the West, in agreement with the tradition of West Asia and India, says that St Thomas, one of the twelve closest disciples of Jesus, came to India in the very first century, perhaps even less than twenty-five years after the death of Jesus. The 'Malabar' or 'Indian Tradition' specifies that St Thomas landed in Kodungaloor near Cochin in 52 CE, and that he was martyred in Mylapore, now part of the city of Chennai, in 72 CE. Many of the ancient writers mention India as the place where Thomas brought the Gospel of Jesus after preaching to the Parthians somewhere in modern day Iran (Fernando and Sauch 59-60).

The Apocryphal Gospel of St Thomas,[2] possibly composed in the middle of the third century in Edessa, says that Thomas came first to the land of Gondophorus, a Parthian, whose numismatic and archaeological evidence shows that he ruled over parts of modern-day north-west India and Pakistan. From there he went to Mazday, interpreted as Mylai or Mylapore. The stronger tradition of Kerala, however, affirms that following the maritime trade route he came to Cranganore or Kodungallor. Kerala was at that time a commercial centre in contact with West Asia and the Mediterranean world. Thomas would have preached first to the Jews settled in Kerala, and then to the indigenous population (Cherian, "Kerala Empowerment" 129).

The tradition of Kerala affirms that he started Christian communities in seven places: Maliankara, Palayur, Cranganore, Kokamangalam, Niranam, Chayal and Kollam. It also states that he appointed elders (priests) to look after these communities. His death in Mylapore is an accepted tradition. Kerala and Tamil Nadu were at that time one entity called Tamizhakam. Whatever be the traditions, we know that historically it is in Kerala that a Christian community existed from the very ancient times to the present. This community keeps the memory of St Thomas as their apostle and identifies themselves with legitimate pride as the 'St Thomas Christians' (D'orsey 63). There are many other traditions also regarding the origin of Christianity in India. A scholarly Brahmin, the then Chief Secretary of the Government of Travancore, on special assignment to complete a state manual, wrote in 1906 about the Apostle as follows: "There is no doubt as to the tradition that St Thomas came to Malabar and converted a few families of Namboodiries some of whom were ordained as priests, such as those of Shankarapuri and Pakalomattam... This is a valuable piece of evidence of conduct of the community, corroborating the early tradition extending on the coast" (Aiya 122). From the early centuries of the Christian era we have evidence of various Christian communities living in South India, whose traditions refer back constantly to St Thomas. The St Thomas Christians must be considered the first community of Christians in India, at least among all the communities presently alive (D'Souza, *Growth and Activities* 102).

Whatever be the traditions, the Church in India is not of recent origin; nor can it be looked upon as an exotic plant to be tended and nurtured in the hothouse. In many parts of the country, particularly in Malabar, the faith has taken deep roots in the soil and has all the vigour and vitality of spontaneous growth. The 'Travancore Government Census Report' of 1941 points out that the Church in Travancore is one of the oldest Churches in the world, older than that in any part of India and most parts of Europe. It was introduced into the country "straight from the land of Jesus Christ, not long after his crucifixion" (Thomas, "The Advancement of Christianity"2). But isolated and tucked away in a corner of our vast country, the Christians of Travancore were not known in other parts of India, nor were we aware of any effort on their part before the modern period to spread the light of the faith.

With the arrival of Portuguese missionaries in the 16th century, a new epoch began in the history of Christianity in India. This began after the arrival of Vasco de Gama in Calicut in 1498 A.D. His arrival in India was not only the beginning of Western domination in the political field but also the beginning of expansion of Christianity in India. In 1516, Alphonse de Albuquerque, the Portuguese Governor, found 25,000 Christians settled in Kollam, a town in southern Kerala. St Francis Xavier's arrival in 1542 A.D. opened up another chapter in the history of the Church in India (Panikar 56).

Christianity came to North India during the reign of Akbar, the great Mughal Emperor. Akbar was a man of natural curiosity and was anxious to know about Christianity and the traditions they followed. For this reason, he learned the Portuguese language from a Catholic priest. The first word the priest taught, and later Akbar pronounced, was 'the sweet name of Jesus'. The king found such a pleasure in the Holy name that he repeated it at each step he walked up and down his house (D'Souza, "Influence of Catholic Women" 7). And not long afterwards he sent an ambassador to Goa with a letter addressed to the Portuguese Fathers residing in Goa:

Be it known to you, that holding you in great esteem, I am sending you my ambassador Ebadola, and his interpreter Dominique Briz, to beg you to send to me two Fathers learned in the scriptures, who shall bring with them the principal book of the law, and of the Gospels. I have a great desire to become acquainted with this law and its perfection.... I shall dispatch them with great respect and honour. Let them not hesitate to come, for they will be under my care and protection. (Du Jarric16)

The ambassador and his interpreter arrived at Goa in September 1579 and were received with great honour. The Father-Provincial chose the following priests: Fr Rudolfe Aquauiva, then thirty years of age, the leader of the mission; Fr Antoine de Monserrat, a scholar, and a man of letters. In addition, Fr Francois Henriques, a Persian convert, was selected probably for his knowledge of the Persian language. On 18th February 1580, after a long journey, after passing through many difficulties and dangers, they arrived at the Imperial Court of Fatehpur Sikri (Du Jarric18). The priests presented two beautiful portraits to Akbar - one representing Jesus and the other the Glorious Virgin Mary, His mother, along with the Holy Bible in Hebrew, Chaldean, Latin, and Greek languages to Akbar (Du Jarric22).

Plurality of Faith

Akbar always held the Christian faith in high esteem, and many of his acts show this very clearly. He gave permission for a certain Portuguese who had died, to have public funeral with Christian rites. The priests were given permission to convert as many as they could. He gave them permission even to build a hospital for the sick, out of the charitable offerings of the Portuguese. Moreover, Akbar allowed the Christians to build two churches: one at Agra and another at Lahore. Jahangir who succeeded Akbar was still more favourable to the Jesuits.[3] The most fascinating part of the argument is that even today, the Agra Church is being identified as Akbar's Church. These and other means adopted to advance the glory of God, together with the King's affection for the priests, and his favourable treatment of Christians, aroused in many of those who served his majesty a desire to embrace the Christian faith (Du Jarric32). Through all these, Akbar tried to make a synthesis of the various religions in his empire in order to unite the people of the widely different religions of his vast domain.

The latter part of the 18th century saw the suppression of the Society of Jesus in Europe. As a result, the Apostolic Vicariate [5] in India passed over to the Carmelite Fathers. They found it impossible to govern such a large territory committed to them as they lacked the required number of missionaries. Therefore, they petitioned Rome to hand it over to the Capuchins who had been working in Patna. Rome, by a decree issued on 17th May 1784, attached the northern part of the Vicariate to the

Prefecture[6] of the Hindustan-Tibet Mission. It should be noted that the territory comprised the whole of North India including the mission stations of Delhi, Agra, Sardhana and Gwalior (Du Jarric 32).

This was the early stage of the settlement of Christians in the northern area of the Indian sub-continent. With the coming of the Protestant missionaries, after Henry VIII's break from Rome and the Lutheran Movement, the Christians got an easy foothold in India because of the East India Company, and the patronage and support of the English Queen. The first motivating impulse of the Europeans was trade, especially spices. Later on, however, there developed in them a desire to share their Christian convictions with the people among whom they lived and moved. These pioneering missionaries also saw the urgent need to impart quality education to the new Christians of their flock, especially those not of the Brahmin caste. The Brahmins were the educated members of the Indian society at that time. Thus, began the educational history of the Christian mission, which has been continued to this day (Du Jarric33).

The advent of Christianity was a crucial turning point in the history of modern Indian education. Whoever came to India and opened educational institutions - whether any Religious Order or individual missionaries - followed Jesus as their teacher par-excellence. Jesus says, "For this was I born, and for this I came into the world, that I should bear testimony to the truth".[7] Jesus taught people through parables, and illustrated his practical wisdom as a teacher. Christ's mission as a teacher did not cease when he left the earth. He handed over this special charisma to his followers, "Go, therefore, teach all nations …and I am with you until the end of the world".[26] These words of Christ are the characteristic features of the Christian Church as a Teaching Institution.

In the early Church, the form of education was ecclesiastical[9] by content, for they considered divine knowledge as the best knowledge since it led people directly to God and to the ultimate end. They were anxious to impart it to the new recruits who wanted to embrace the new religion that was brought to this country. The early missionaries had to undergo many hardships in India. They left their comfortable existence at home, and suffered the tropical heat, tropical sickness, and hardships of the Indian climate. Since then, the Christians have played a significant role in the field of education in our country, especially after the introduction of education as a national system.

In a multi-religious culture such as that of India, any national system of education has to be religiously neutral and secular. However, the system allowed and encouraged private participation and initiative, and this made it possible for various churches to start schools and colleges. In the process of initiation, development, and growth of modern system of education in India, individual Christians and different churches and religious Orders have played a significant role. It was with the coming of the Portuguese at the end of the 15th century, and the establishment of some territories under their rule, especially in Goa in the 16th century, the Christian Church could be said to have undertaken educational apostolate for the people.

Catholic Women Visionaries and Education

When Protestantism arose in Europe, the Reformers occupied the universities founded by the Catholic Church. This forced the Catholic Church to start new Congregations for men and women who devoted their lives to teaching. The institutions formed by them had the common purpose of teaching the religious truth along with secular knowledge among all classes. These institutions, namely, the Society of Jesus (SJ), the Congregation of the Religious of Jesus and Mary (RJM), Institute of the Blessed Virgin Mary (IBVM), Presentation Sisters, Apostolic Carmel (AC), Clarist Franciscan Missionaries of the most Blessed Sacrament Sisters (CFMSS) etc. were some of them that came to India (D'souza, *Growth and Activities* 33). They started several centers of education, where they began to impart secular education along with religious instruction. The spirit of dedication of these visionaries and the quality of training imparted in their institutions were well appreciated, and people preferred them to institutions run by others. This trend has continued even to this day, and people take pride in saying that their children are studying in convent schools run by visionary Christian educationists.

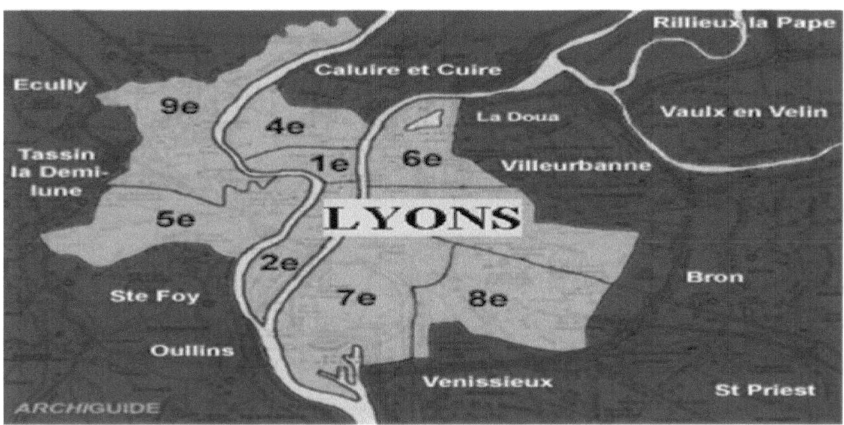

The humble origin of the Jesus and Mary institutions is linked to the greatest ever social and political upheaval that shook Europe in the last quarter of the 18th century - the French Revolution. One of the bloodiest chapters in the history of those times was the revolt of Lyons, the second most important city in France. Lyons was known as the 'Silk Capital'of the world. There was no city, not even Paris, where social contrast was as evident as in the industrial capital Lyons. On the one hand, there stood the proletarian working-class, and on the other, the royalist and capitalist-minded industrialists – a fertile soil for the rise of the most fanatical of bloody conflicts. Many French Catholic families in Lyons were helplessly caught up in the turbulence. One of them was the Thevenet family, made famous by Claudine Thevenet, who founded the JM institutions.

Claudine Thevenet, later the Foundress and the first Superior General of the Congregation of Jesus and Mary, was born at the Rue Neube in Lyons on 30th March 1774. She was the eldest daughter of the Thevenet family of seven with three boys and four girls. Her father was a prosperous silk merchant in the city of Lyons, known predominantly for silk industry. Therefore, the child was born surrounded by peace, comfort and affluence, characteristic of so many of the affluent Catholic families of Lyons during this period.

French Revolution, Claudine Thevenet and Women's Education

From her earliest years, the Catholic faith to Claudine was a living-breath reality. The Benedictines of the Abbey Royale des Dames de Saint Pierre carefully instructed her in its tenets. At her home, the practice of Christian faith found ample expression in all aspects of deeds including love, kindness and charity. Claudine imbibed these splendid qualities from her own family members. In the contemporary writings of an anonymous nun, her outstanding qualities are praised thus: "Her greatness of heart, her perfect tact, her total honesty, her masculine determination, her living faith and her uncalculating generosity are the gifts which heaven pleased to bestow on the destined one to found a great religious family" (Maria 241). Such qualities were, indeed, important for the restoration of a society devastated by revolution and the reign of terror that began in 1789 and continued for the next ten years. Like many other reformers of the world Claudine can be aptly called as one of the first women reformers in France.

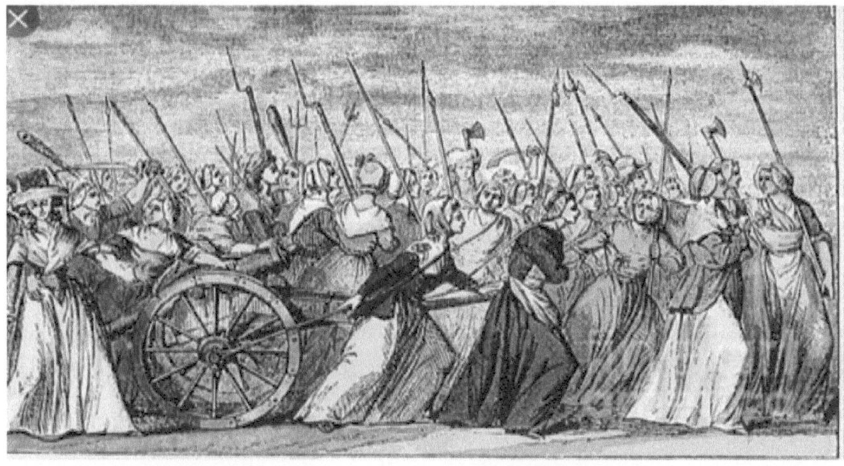

As a mere child Claudine was remarkable for her peaceful and charitable disposition. She was aptly termed 'the Angel of the Home' in the domestic circle. The youthful rashness and impetuosity of her brothers always yielded to the mild and courteous kindness of their much-loved sister 'Glady'as she was affectionately called. The peaceful spiritual atmosphere of this truly Catholic home was not to last, for those were difficult days in the history of France and Europe. On 29th November 1789, the Constituent Assembly passed a law nationalizing all ecclesiastical property, and in the following year all religious Orders were suppressed labelling them as useless to society. Both these laws naturally affected Claudine's schooling at the Abbey, which now ceased to exist as a religious institution. Therefore, her peaceful years ended abruptly (Maria 242).

At first, the assembly had acclaimed Lyons as the dawn of a long promised and much needed reform, but a sad disillusionment was in store. The revolutionaries started abandoning those principles and institutions on which all social order rested. Things finally reached at such a phase in that the law-abiding, liberty-loving, and peaceful people of the city, exasperated by the menace of the clubs, the searching of private houses, arrests and murders, rose with the cry of 'Down with oppression'. The result of this rising in self-defense was that Lyons was condemned as a rebel city by the Convention. The so-called 'National Army' was commissioned to subjugate the city. However, the people of Lyons were determined not to submit to this tyranny. An army of volunteers was quickly enrolled under the gallant General de Percy. All considered it an honour as well as a duty to defend their native city and its liberties. Among the first names to enlist for the noble cause were Claudine's two brothers, namely, Louis, aged twenty and Francois, aged eighteen. Before the city was completely besieged, Monsieur Thevenet, the father of Claudine had taken the four youngest children for safety to Belley, a town some miles away, from where he was unable to return until the siege had been raised (Maria 243).

During the horrors of the two-month siege, Claudine, the young girl barely nineteen as she was then, devoted to the task of comforting and consoling her mother whose heart was torn with anxiety about the safety of her loved ones. Claudine's charity was not confined to the home circle alone. The city presented a sorry spectacle: houses were crumbling like matchwood before withering shellfire; conflagrations were raging on all sides. Soon famine was rampant everywhere. In the midst of this diabolic scene, Claudine was seen day after day in the company of some young brave daughters of France who regardless of danger to life and limb flitted through the ruins and skirted among burning buildings. It was a routine work, especially on their way to the hills of St Irene and St Justin from where they returned with food and alms for the sick and the wounded of both the armies (Maria 244).

The raising of the siege was followed by a night of heart-rending anxiety caused by the uncertainty of the fate of her brothers. She was not sure whether their bodies lay stark and cold amidst the ruins of the stricken city or, worse still, they were among the doomed prisoners whose blood alone could save the thirst for revenge of the Convention's commissioners. She was not daring enough to hope that they could have been among the few to reach the friendly shelter of the woods. Claudine comforted the mother the best she could when the anxiety grew intolerable. She donned her hooded mantle and accompanied by a faithful manservant made her way to the 'Quai de Retz' where she knew that her brothers' columns had been engaged. There, with trembling limbs but resolute heart, she reached for Louis and Francois among the fallen, breathing many a prayer for the souls of those brave men cut off in the prime of their manhood. Her search was in vain. With an appeal to Heaven for courage and fortitude to face the future, she returned home to find that her brothers had already reached there in safety under cover of darkness. Nevertheless, the joy at their safe return was destined to be short-lived (Maria 245).

Religious Persecution and the Crucible of Faith

Lyons, a city destined in the designs of Providence to be the cradle of so many Religious Congregations, had to pass through the crucible of suffering. In that city, the reign of terror began in deadly earnest. All who had a share in the defense were tracked down mercilessly and handed over to the Revolutionary Tribunal that they might be shot or guillotined. An amount of thirty to sixty Francs was the price offered for the betrayal of each defender. Soon Louis and Francois were among the proscribed; they were arrested and placed with others in the revolutionary prison that had earned for itself the well-deserved name of the 'Mauvaise Cave' [10] (*Life and Work* 27). During those dreaded days of imprisonment, Claudine was indeed a ministering angel in her home to her grief-stricken parents and an angel of comfort and consolation to her young, imprisoned brothers.

Claudine considered no price too high, humiliation too neither much, nor any self-sacrifice too great a price to pay for the happiness of seeing her dear ones. Under disguise, she managed to penetrate into their prison cell and to bring the much-needed relief not only to her loved ones, but also to their fellow prisoners among whom was a sick and aged priest. Often times she had to pay dearly for the privilege of being allowed to visit her brothers. On one occasion, when she sought admission to prison disguised as a peasant girl, the rough guard handing her a goblet invited her to drink to the Republic. The very soul of this sensitive girl revolted at such a deed. A blush of indignation mantled her cheek and brow, but the thought of her brothers pining in their dark prison helped her overcome her natural repugnance. She took the cup and swallowed the contents. This proved to be her last visit to the 'Mauvaise Cave' (*Life and Work* 28).

Day after day during the next few weeks, she set out for the prison, only to find that all attempts to gain access to her loved ones were made in vain. On a bitter morning early in January, Claudine accompanied by a faithful servant set out as usual for the courtyard of the prison. They had proceeded about halfway when they came face to face with a melancholic procession of the condemned, setting out to face the firing squad in the ways of 'Les Brotteaux'.[11]

Eagerly scanning the faces of those marching to their death, Claudine was horrified to find her brothers among them. Stifling her grief and emotion, she forced her way through the jostling throng and came nearer to her brothers. They recognized their sister and made signs to the aged servant who stooped down as if to pick up something and took from Louis' shoe a note, which proved to be a farewell letter from both the brothers to their dearly loved parents. This farewell message, written by Louis and Francois only a few hours before their execution, was certainly a balm upon bruised hearts, for it bore witness to their deep faith. One could not read this farewell note without emotion. They both wrote and, in addition to signing their own, they signed each other's letters. Louis wrote:

(Letter from Louis Thevenet (File No. F/ III [73] Archives CJM Generalite, Rome)

**Letter from Thevenet (File No. F/ III [73]
Archives CJM Generalite, Rome)**

Father, mother, sisters, cousins and friends, Good-bye! Good-bye for the last time. Good-bye, my dear, good father, good-bye. You did all you could to save us, but to no avail. Our fate was decided! My greatest sorrow is having involved my brother; if it had not been for me, his age would have saved him. Do not reproach anybody with my death; I am alone guilty, if anyone is. Do not grieve too much.... We have only four hours left to live; we are trying to make good use of it (Chiasson 29).

As they passed close to her, Louis murmured in low tones to his heart-broken sister the memorable and beautiful words: "Forgive Glady as we forgive" (Chiasson 36). It was a faint echo of similar words uttered by dying divine lips on the peak hill of Calvary in Palestine more than seventeen centuries before, which had inspired through the ages many such deeds of heroic sacrifice and charity. More dead than alive, Claudine followed them. The fatal shots rang out. Fervent prayers ascended to the throne of God from the soul of that young girl, while in the intensity of her sisterly love, she knelt and prayed for her young brothers as they passed from life to death.

Worse was yet to come. When the last shot had been fired, Claudine joined by a few sad figures, moved stealthily among the dead, seeking to recognize the well-beloved features, and to imprint upon them one last farewell kiss. She had not far to seek; a horrible sight met her gaze. The brutal soldiers were crushing to death the poor victims who had survived, and among them were her two brothers. The heroism of her great soul enabled her to live their last words beseeching for forgiveness, as with horror-stricken eyes she gazed on that horrible scene. It was a ghastly sight even for angels to behold. Perhaps, the vials of God's wrath were withheld from falling on those brutal members of the human race by the prayer of agony wrung from the soul of that brave young maid of France, as she knelt with clasped hands (Chiasson 37).

Raised to heaven uttering that cry for mercy, once so long ago wrung from the noblest and the most loving heart that ever beat in a human frame: "Father, forgive them for they know not what they do"(Luke 23:34). The memory of the dreadful moment caused a shock to her nervous system from which she never quite recovered. Heart-broken with grief, she traced her steps towards the city bearing the precious note which the faithful old servant had received from Louis, and pondering in an agony of grief and anxiety over the tragic news which had yet to be broken to her parents. Such was the hard school in which the future Founder of JM institutions was suddenly initiated, and in which she proved herself an apt pupil. Here she laid deep down the foundations of sanctity that expresses itself in an abiding confidence in an ever–loving providence, an utter selflessness, Christ-like charity, and sympathy with others. These virtues were outstanding characteristics of Claudine Thevenet's life and work. Her task was not an easy one in the sorrow-stricken home. Now, more than ever she had to be the 'Angel of the household', to whom all turned for help, comfort, and consolation. She had generous love and affection for her dear ones, especially for her beloved parents who would have been the support of their declining years (Chiasson 37).

The fury of the revolution had spent itself, and with the death of Maximilien Robespierre, the architect of the French Revolution, on July 28th 1794 the reign of terror came to an end and with it also set in the inevitable reaction against the terrorists. In Lyons, the thirst for revenge was widespread among those whose loved ones had been so cruelly ill-treated and slain. This unchristian reaction did not find favour with the Thevenet family. The name of the man who so treacherously played the part of Judas, and in doing so sent Louis and Francois to their death, was well known to them and they could easily have denounced him. However, they refused to do so. Claudine guarded the secret of the name of the traitor and his family till she died; it lay buried with her in the nameless silence of eternity. The request of those young dying heroes had been nobly and generously fulfilled in her life (Chiasson 38).

The evil effects of the revolution did not end with the cessation of hostilities. Poverty, wretchedness, and misery in every shape and form were its sad aftermath. Stark materialism and insane hatred of God had fallen like blight upon the fair land of France. Ignorance of God and of eternal values prevailed among the people in cities and towns, where vice and brutality were rampant. Claudine was concerned that in her native city thousands of little ones were brought up not only with the minimum of this world's values, but also with little knowledge of God and the world to come. One of the area's most seriously compromised by the French Revolution was the education of the children among them, specially the girls. The young in France were sadly neglected. Inspector, Jacques Sellier, thus described the situation:

The young no longer considered any moral code, and they lived in utter dissoluteness. Children insulted honest men and old people.... They learn nothing and accepted no discipline whatsoever.... The girls, not knowing how to work, spent their time in suburban eating-houses with soldiers. They blasphemed and used obscene language as would have caused the grenadiers of my time to blush.... Unless prompt remedies were applied to such evils, the future of the nation was truly in peril. This sorry state of affairs was caused by the unrestrained liberty in which children were allowed to grow up without any education whatsoever (Chiasson 36).

In addition, one of Bonaparte's ministers expressed himself in much the same way:

> For ten years, education has been entirely neglected; religion lies at the base of all good education. Children are victims of the most dangerous idleness and given to alarming delinquency. They have no idea of God, hence wild and barbarous customs, and a lawless people. If one compares education today with what it really should be, one cannot but be apprehensive for the present and future generation (Chiasson 37).

The innocent people are put to suffering for the guilty. It had become imperative to heal the wounds of the past. The absence of priests and the religious was keenly felt. The men and women of Claudine devoted themselves generously to education of the young, of both sexes and of all social classes.

Claudine's apostolic zeal was stirred to its very depths by the sad plight of these little ones. She longed to teach them about their kind Father in heaven who loved them so much. Her prayerful soul soon found inspiration and courage. She devoted herself to the spiritual and temporal welfare of these little ones. Her charity towards her neighbour was heroic and constant. The forgiving love, borne of the painful experience of her brothers' death, impelled her to love God and to reach out to all who suffered because of man's sinful lust for power and possessions. Thus, her charism, expressed in the goodness of God, began to pour out on all those poor and marginalized souls whom society refused to help in any way. The love of God and the labour for his glory was the pivot on which Claudine's whole life turned. In these neglected souls, she saw his image, and she used unstintingly her strength and money to meet their spiritual and temporal needs. Claudine's example of charity soon attracted others to her side (Chiasson 37).

French Revolution and the Congregation of Jesus and Mary

No other time in French history have political movements got intimately associated with the outstanding lives of inspired men and women, and their works of courage and self-sacrifice as the era of the French Revolution. It occasioned to give birth to many great foundations. The Congregation of Jesus and Mary is one of them. Here we note that a simple, humble middle class woman was able to rise above the disasters and calamities of her time to initiate, with and through her God given charism of love to all, a tremendous work of education for the young unfortunate girls of her day. Claudine was one among those great ones. During this period of national upheaval, while the foundations of society seemed to rock and reel, she displayed extraordinary courage in spiritual matters (Maria 94-95). In our world down through the ages, when society was rocked and was on the verge of self-destruction through anarchy and immorality, God inspired charismatic leadership through specially chosen people. They have done marvels at the times of crisis. Ancient India too witnessed an age of religious ferment of the same kind in the 6th century B.C. At that time, Gautama Buddha and Vardhamana Mahavira came proclaiming various ways of deliverance from spiritual ignorance and suffering.

The Vedas and Brahmanas had developed at the hands of priests into a burdensome sacrificial and ritual system. The theories of caste and karma crippled people socially and spiritually. Escape from evil consequences of deeds could come about only through the performance of prescribed ritualistic acts performed by the priests. As a reaction to these, some formalized mechanical practice was inevitable. The Upanishads had already begun the revolt, and Buddhism and Jainism were a culmination of it. Buddha's stress on right consciousness, renunciation, brotherhood, and non-violence initiated an era of peace, and society was thus reformed through his leadership (Maria 95).

Jesus came as redeemer of human beings in the world and he too found none of the humane ennobling laws in practice. The spirit of the law had vanished in the course of time. Piety was paraded in the marketplace. The Jewish religious leaders paid lip service to Moses, and indulged in narrow formalism, unbridled pride, and scorn for the masses. Jesus proclaimed liberty of spirit to everyone. The law, he stressed, was made for man and not man for the law. Consequently, the spirit of peace continued to resonate in the political and social struggle for freedom in different parts of the world. Interestingly, during the struggle for independence even Mahatma Gandhi appropriated the legacy of Christ and contextualised it in the political discourse. Gandhi even asserted that 'an eye for an eye' only makes the whole world blind. He took up the peaceful means of Satyagraha and dialogue in the political front, and equality and brotherhood in the social arena to achieve the end - freedom from colonial rule.

Claudine Thevenet: A Prescient Leader

Similarly, hundreds of men and women, both great and small from the East and the West, have taught that prosperity, peace, goodwill, and hard work can make our world a better place to live in. There were many such people of good will in France after the French Revolution and among them was Claudine Thevenet.

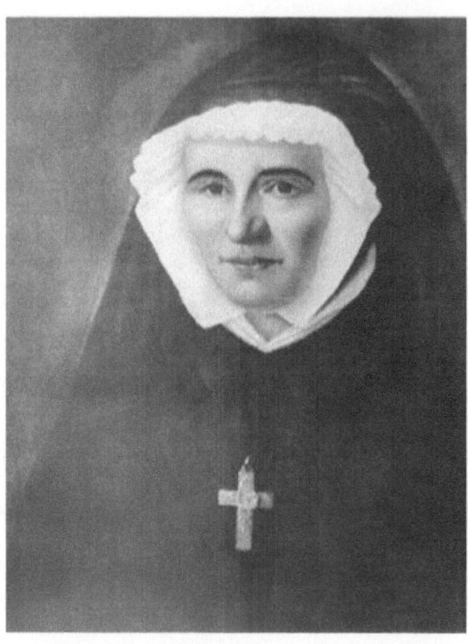

Claudine Thevenet (1774 – 1837)

Her ideals are lived to this day by the members of religious family she founded, namely, the Congregation of the Religious of Jesus and Mary. Though no international awards and memorials have publicly acclaimed Claudine, she has contributed significantly to the betterment of the society through the Congregation, most especially through the system of Christian education followed in her schools and colleges. Following her inspiring example, several young women of her social class began to devote themselves to works of charity among the poor and the unfortunate. Claudine had a wonderful way of infusing some of her zeal and enthusiasm into her friends and colleagues (Maria 94-95).

Instruction in the truths and doctrine of the Catholic faith and exhortations by word and example were the principal works of zeal engaged in by Claudine's young women. Each of them, although working on her own account, looked up to Claudine as their model and leader. For nearly twenty years, Claudine devoted herself with untiring zeal and selfless charity to the apostolate of education. Soon her very name was held in benediction in the poverty-stricken areas of her native city. Claudine often said, "God will provide" (Barrel and Carlos 281). Alms arrived just when needed, as if measured out by the all-knowing hand of God. Works multiplied, companions increased and for eight years Claudine was Director of the charitable works.

A new stage in Claudine's life was beginning; an important period between twenty and thirty in the life of every young woman. One bleak December evening in the winter of 1815, Father Andre Coindre saw two shivering little girls crouching on the ground in the church porch of St Nizier. Sad indeed was the tale unfolded to him of these two little waifs abandoned by both the parents. They were left to starve on the streets. In their short span of life of four and two years respectively, they had already seen much of life's woes. They had experienced cruel treatment at the hands of those who should have been their protectors. Instantly, he recalled the name that he had so often heard in his daily ministrations among the poor and the needy. It was the name always spoken with love, and reverence in every humble home –the name of Claudine Thevenet.

Lifting the little ones in his arms, Fr Andre Coindre proceeded towards her home, where he was certainly not disappointed. Claudine welcomed the good priest and, with hardly a moment's thought for a solution, relieved him of his charges. Such was the meeting of two great souls, both aflame with love of God and Christ-like charity for all. The meeting of these two souls, Coindre and Claudine, was a momentous event destined in the designs of God to have far-reaching results and to bear fruit both for the time and for eternity (Barrel and Carlos 282).

Fr Andre Coindre was an educator, not just a preacher. He valued people and knew the importance of development. When he found orphans, he placed them carefully with people who could provide care for the whole person - people who could provide for the children's material needs, most importantly, and who recognized the dignity of children, the value of spirituality and the values of the Gospel. Despite the fact that Andre Coindre had done a tremendously rich contribution for the establishment of educational institutions, he was not able to dedicate his whole life for education on a regular basis. He was not interested in developing highly educated learning machines. He saw the value of educating the whole person, of recognizing the person's need to be accepted and loved, and of educating a person for life. He emphasized the need for teaching one how to learn, providing an atmosphere of intellectual and spiritual growth. He was also keen on recognizing and developing the spiritual dimension and providing a chance for a better quality of life through education (Barrel and Carlos 281).

Perceiving how much good work Claudine was doing by word and example, Fr Coindre conceived the idea of forming the group of young women into an association, so as to give the work the benefit of firmer organization. This step was taken on 31st July 1816. The principal aim of the Association was the sanctification of its members by the practice of Christian virtues and evangelical counsels,[12] together with the exercise of charitable works. The pious union was to give a new and deeper apostolic impulse to the activities of Claudine and her companions (*Life and Work* 112).

Fr Coindre drew up a framework of the regulations they were to follow, based on the Rule of St Augustine and the Constitutions of St Ignatius. "To form souls for Heaven by means of a truly Christian education"(Barrel and Carlos 225), was their ideal and their constant effort, while working unremittingly at their own sanctification and of those committed to their care according to the ideals he presented. On 6th October 1818, Claudine left her mother and the home she loved so much. With one companion, she went to the desolate place they had secured for their orphans. God blessed her sacrifice; the modest orphanage grew and prospered. Later, it was shifted to Fourviere in France, where she bought the property from a dear collaborator of the Association, Madam Pauline Marie Jaricot.

Claudine and her companions were warned of the many hardships they would have to face in future, and many had criticized the bold endeavor. Claudine experienced conflict in her own self and she always referred to the night of 5th October as the 'most dreadful one'. Laurentine Chiason writes about Pierres-Plantees at the end of October 1818, three weeks after the memorable night:

> What does one find at Pierres-Plantees? The weaver Jeanne Butty, a brave pioneer, five candidates for religious life, twelve orphans, two looms, a few pieces of furniture and an abundance of faith, hope and charity and animating all this, a presence, that of Claudine, whose persuasive kindness and reassuring strength won by all hearts (Chiason 63).

Within two years Pierres-Plantees was too small to house the growing number of students. Therefore, they started a new establishment at Fourviere by November 1820. After serious reflection, it was decided that girls of bourgeois families would also be admitted. A Secondary School with a boarding was opened. Claudine's preference was always for the poor. She refused admission to many rich girls, but never was a poor orphan refused for lack of space or provision. Along with her companions, Claudine sought new homes to establish orphanages, schools, and boarding houses (Barrel and Carlos 256).

The associates, in the section for instruction, were to teach the Christian faith to those who would otherwise be neglected. They had to prepare children for their first holy communion,[13] and provide good literature to those who were unable or unwilling to procure such for themselves. Soon many pious women of Lyons sought the privilege of participating in this effort. On 31st July 1818, the divine call "Come, follow me,"[14] spoken so long ago on the shores of Galilee, re-echoed in the hearts of these young women. Generously they responded to the divine invitation, and her chosen companions resolved at once to form a pious group apart and led a kind of religious life while remaining zealous members of the 'Association of the Sacred Heart of Jesus' as it was called in the beginning. Later the name was changed to the 'Congregation of the Religious of Jesus and Mary'. On that day, it first conceived the idea that has since been the aim of the Congregation of Jesus and Mary: "to form souls for Heaven by means of a truly Christian education" (Barrel and Carlos 225).

It was not a light burden that was laid on the willing shoulders of Claudine Thevenet who was then forty-four years of age. Her preference had always been for the poor. Therefore, she decided to serve the educational needs of these children, whose parents could not provide for them. They would, first of all, be taught the truths of their holy faith. In addition to receiving an elementary education, they would also be instructed in the profitable trade of silk weaving, which would enable them to earn an honest livelihood when they left Pierres Plantees. With this end in view, one room was set aside for this work. A loom was installed, and an excellent young woman was employed as an expert at the trade. The first little one to be received was an abandoned child. Surely, it was a modest beginning: One child, one loom, one room, and one work woman (Barrel and Carlos 225).

By the beginning of the 1820s, the community had increased considerably; so, had the orphans. In 1821, Claudine was given the opportunity, which she had long desired, of putting in practice on a wider scale the motto which she had chosen for her Congregation: 'To form souls for Heaven by a Catholic education'. So far, this had been accomplished only among the poor and the destitute. The need was equally great among the children of the better off families. To meet the requirements of this class, a boarding school was opened in 1821 at Fourviere in France. In the same year, she and her companions adopted a black costume as a religious habit. This outward token showed their renunciation of the world. Henceforth Thevenet was to be known as Mother Mary St Ignatius. And on 25th February, 1823 Mother Mary St Ignatius with a large gathering of her spiritual daughters from the houses in Fourviere, Belleville and Montréal, consecrated themselves to God forever by the religious vows [15] of poverty, chastity and obedience (*History of the CJM* 133).

In 1823 itself, Claudine was elected the Superior General of the Congregation, and she continued in this position until her death on 3rd February 1837. Her last word, pronounced with a tone of conviction, was "How good God Is" (Chiasson 216). She was a woman of good judgment, loftiness of soul and robust virtue, capable of enduring all the trials which the Lord did not fail to send her along with the works that He wanted her to do. This humble beginning made rapid and quite remarkable progress among the works of our epoch. This was evident in its prompt approval of the Church given to the congregation to be an International one, especially as missionaries to India with a noble cause and sole purpose to devote themselves in the education of girls by the then Holy Father Pope Pius IX on 21st December, 1847 (Chiasson 36).

Arrival of Women Visionaries to India

In 1841, four years after the death of Claudine, the young Congregation which had established its mission of education in Lyons and at Le Puy in France, was invited to India by Monsignor[16] Joseph Antony Borghi, Vicar Apostolic[17] of the Hindustan-Tibet Mission. It was found that the building of a humane and just society in North India was being impeded due to the lack of opportunity for education of its people and widespread illiteracy in the country. The Bishop wrote: "One of these days, I was talking to a man, and asked him what he expected after death. He did not seem to know because of his misguided religious belief and extreme poverty" (Cuthbert, *Echoes of a Century* 151).

The worst of India's problems in pre-British India was the stifling caste system. Brahmins had the exclusive right to preach religious doctrines, to officiate as priests, and to function as teachers. As such, they alone had the privilege to study religious and secular knowledge. The other castes were debarred by religious edicts and denied the access to higher studies. The medium of instruction was Sanskrit, the sacred language of the Hindus.

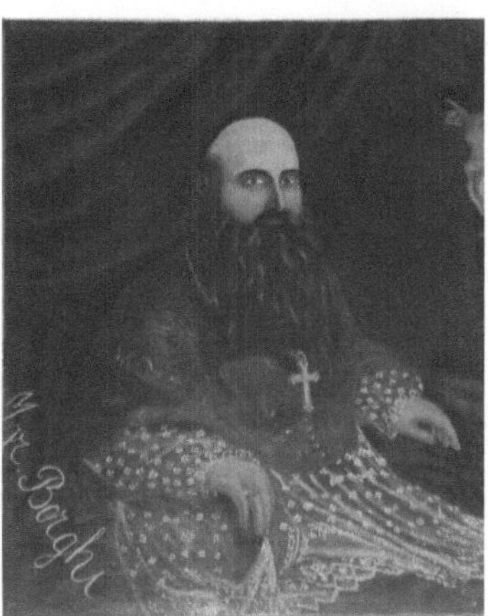

**Rt. Rev. Joseph Anthony Borghi OFM Cap.
(Vicar Apostolic of Agra, 1841-1849)**

For the common people, there were vernacular schools in some villages and towns that taught them mainly reading, writing, and rudiments of arithmetic, besides imparting religious instructions to the pupils. Generally, these schools catered to the needs of the children of wealthy merchant class. Women and members of the lower castes hardly received any education. Thus, education among the Hindus, in pre-British India, was restricted predominantly to elite sections of the society. The Brahmins enjoyed the monopoly of higher education. The laws of Manu laid down all what a woman could or could not do. As a result, she was left totally in the background, and subjected to all rules that assigned her a lower status. Manu said, "By a girl, by a young woman or even by an aged one, nothing must be done independently even in her own house" (qtd. in Dass 2). Therefore, in such a milieu, there was no question of a woman being educated.

The colonial government initiated a systematic study of the caste system in ancient India. The foremost among the early works was by an educator in British India, namely, J.C. Nesfield, who wrote *A Brief View of Caste System of North-western Provinces and Awadh*" proposing that occupation was the basis on which the edifice of caste system stands in India (65). Similarly, Herbert H. Risley, the colonial administrator who carried out the census in India, argued that racial factor was one of the predominant factors in the evolution of the caste system. He even used the nasal index by which the length of nose was used in order to differentiate between the Aryans and non-Aryans (241).

Nevertheless, there were some contradictions and exceptions in ancient India. Women were eligible for the study of the Vedas and the performance of sacrifices. Upanayana, the Vedic initiation of girls, had been as common as that of boys. There were women scholars who remained unmarried for a long time devoting themselves to higher studies. It seems they even composed mantras for the Vedas. For example, Gargi, Vishwara, Apala, Maitreyi etc. were jewels among women. They were highly educated and were perfect scholars of the Vedas (Agrawal and Aggarwal 16).

There were instances in ancient India when women were so advanced in learning that they challenged men of learning in public discussions on philosophical and metaphysical subjects. Brihadaranyaka Upanishad gives an instance of Gargi and other women who had a revered memory, taking the place of Rishis. In an assembly of thousand Brahmins who were all erudite in the Vedas, Gargi boldly challenged Yajnavalkya in the court of Janaka, King of Videha and made him accept defeat with the words, "Oh Gargi, do not ask me too much"(Agrawal and Aggarwal 18). It is written in the Satpatha Brahmana,

> If you do not raise the women who are living embodiment of the divine mother, do not think that you have any other way to rise. All nations have attained greatness by paying proper respect to the women. Those countries and nations that do not respect the women have never become great, nor will ever be in future (quoted in Agrawal and Aggarwal 45).

After the Vedic period women's education received a setback due to the deterioration of the religious status of women and the lowering of the marriage age. Marriageable age was lowered to twelve from seventeen years. Girls in rich and aristocratic families, however, continued to receive good literary education. Percentage of literacy among women went down very rapidly during the Muslim rule. The society as a whole became prejudiced against women's education. The 'pardha system' stood on the way of girls being sent to school beyond a certain age, though very young girls had some schooling where it was possible. Sultana Razia who ascended the throne of Delhi Sultanate was an educated princess. Similarly, when Akbar was the Mughal ruler, he set apart certain chambers in Fatehpur Sikri for a girls' school. During this period, some prejudices against education of women through schools prevailed among the people. However, David Hare established a school for girls in Calcutta in 1820 (Agrawal and Aggarwal 21).

Touched by the work done by visionaries and philanthropic Englishmen, several great Indians lent support to the opening of girls' schools, braving the popular resistance against women's education. Among them, Pundit Ishwarchandra Vidyasagar, DayandaSaraswati and Swami Vivekananda played an important role (Chaube 122). By 1850, the stage was set for a change in the state policy. Lord Dalhousie, the Governor General of India, took the lead for this change. He declared that no single change in the habits of the people is likely to lead to more important and beneficial consequences than the introduction of education for their female children. He wanted the government to give its frank and cordial support to the cause. The Educational Despatch of 1854 later on confirmed these orders. The University Education Commission noted the importance of women's education and stated that there could not be an educated society without educated women.

During the rule of Lord William Bentinck and Lord Dalhousie, there was little improvement in the education of women. The Christian visionary associations had started many educational institutions. In fact, these were the visionaries who gave importance to women's education; the result of their effort is seen only today. Before they came to India, no concerted effort had been made in this direction. During 19th century, they made greater efforts for the cause of women's education in India than anybody else. Addressing the Indian Women's Conference, Dr. Muthu Lakshmi Reddi said, "I honestly believe that missionaries had done more for women's education in this country than the government itself" (Agrawal and Aggarwal 56). In 1923, the Church of England Missionary Society alone ran twenty-three girls' schools in the country. Girls of lower classes attended most of the mission schools.

Seeing the sad state of affairs of women's education in India, Bishop Joseph Anthony Borghi, one of the great Bishops that Agra had, felt it was high time that something had to be done about it. He, being a man both of vision and of action, laid down his plans for education in his diocese. He knew that unless children were properly educated, a well-developed society could never be established on a sound footing. For this, he did not have enough personnel. So, when he was on tour in France, he invited the Religious of Jesus and Mary (RJM) in Lyons. They had been recommended to him, by the Vicar General to come to his diocese in North India, to take over the education of the poor children, especially the under privileged girl children. The Religious of JM, a Congregation with a visionary thrust, was ready to respond to his plea. He found benefactors to aid him in his work, not only in Europe but also in India.

The 19th century marks the beginning of a New Era in the Indian History with the emergence of reform movements. Missionary (Western) education and industrial revolution brought about a new awakening in the minds of Indian intellectuals. The enlightened and educated Indians became conscious about the richness of Indian culture and realized that the existing social evils such as 'purdah system', untouchability, ban on widow remarriage, infanticide, devadasi system, gender inequality and a host of other evil practices were leading to human degradation. Under such circumstances, various social and religious reformers rose to meet the challenge of the times. Raja Ram Mohan Roy, regarded as the Father of Indian Renaissance, is the fore-runner of all reformers in the galaxy of such social reformers and Bishop Borghi is considered as the first social reformer among the Catholic Bishops who thought of bringing some women religious missionaries to North India, especially to his jurisdiction, the Hindustan Tibet Mission, for the education of young girls.

Bishop Borghi knew that the only way to dispel fear, superstition, casteism, etc. was through education. The schools would give light of knowledge that in turn would dispel all the darkness of ignorance, fear, and superstitions, and bring about social and gender equality in North Indian society. He wrote a letter to Monsignor Rossat, Vicar General of Gap, France:

> I ask you to find me six European Religious devoted to the education of youth. Here is my plan: Every other means has been attempted and has produced only unsatisfactory results. Education offers a longer road, but surer one. Numerous families would give us their children if only we would feed them and take entire charge of them. A rich Catholic, a General in the army of the King of the Marathas, whose capital is Gwalior, has given me a beautiful house with a large garden for the purpose of securing Christian education for a certain number of children. This mission, I propose, has two objects in view: the education of European girls, and the education of native girls. (Mitra 135)

When Archbishop Borghi invited the Sisters of the Congregation of Jesus and Mary to North India, not much headway had been made in education on a general scale. Only upper caste families and those who could afford it gave their children, especially the boys, the benefits of formal education, but that is not to say that sporadic efforts were not made by good people.

Transcending Boundaries: Education for Girls in Agra

In the long-neglected field of women's education, the Catholic missions have noticeable achievements to their credit. In India, the privilege of education was confined to men. It was enough for the girls to learn domestic chores, which would qualify them to fulfill role of good wives and good mothers. With the entry of nuns into the educational field, the situation changed. Even the most orthodox found no difficulty in entrusting their wards to the Sisters' safekeeping. They taught them not only lessons from books but also good manners and right living. Thus, the secular ban on women's education was broken (Sores 239).

Under such circumstances, concerned with the formal education of the orphan girls, Bishop Borghi requested Mother Andrew, the second Mother General of the Congregation of JM, to send Sisters to help in such a great need. The Jesus and Mary Sisters' special concern for the little ones, especially if they are left through misfortune or callousness without parental love and care, is shown in the number of orphanages they run. Apart from the orphanages, the Congregation maintains hostels and boarding establishments, sheltering a large number of students, and looking after their welfare and progress. The JMs believed that every child has the right to learn. No wonder when the Council of Instruction expressed the opinion that "only the missionaries can educate the lower classes" (Maghew 165).

Though efforts were made in the field of women's education, it was hardly a drop in the vast ocean. In such a situation, Bishop Borghi's concern was great when he asked JM Sisters to help him with personnel. Bishop wrote a letter to the Sisters of the Congregation of Jesus and Mary to motivate them, so that they could prepare themselves to come to India with the proper disposition for the education of girls. He wrote to them thus:

> My very dear Sisters.... I come to ask you to make the sacrifice, parents and fatherland and of all you hold dear, to take up your abode in India with the sole intention of winning souls to God.... All the means except education have almost completely failed, and you alone can impart such a benefit to daughters of India (History of the CJM 136*)*.

It could be seen from the letter that the aim and purpose of the Bishop of Agra was absolutely the same as that which had guided Claudine Thevenet to start the Congregation of Jesus and Mary. It was the same motives and intentions of Mother St Andrew, the second Superior General, who saw that the work they were being called upon to undertake in India was absolutely similar to what they had already been doing in France, namely Christian education. After nine days of prayer, the General Council of the Congregation unanimously accepted the offer to work in Agra as a part of their mission. Fearlessly they took up the challenge to work in the distant and distinct land of India. It was an answer to the fulfillment of the visionary spirit which had burned so ardently in Claudine Thevenet, a spirit which she had handed down to her successors (*History of the CJM* 136).

The invitation came at a critical moment of the history of the Congregation when the Church in Lyons attempted to merge it with another Congregation. Thus, the Congregation owes its preservation to the Indian mission and to the intervention of the Foundress who continued to protect it from heaven. Six Sisters were chosen from among the many who volunteered for India. It was a number specified by Bishop Borghi. The batch consisted of five French nuns and an Irish novice. Mother Theresa Motte, Assistant General and Novice mistress at Fourviere, was named Superior of the little group and she served in India for the next twelve years. She was capable, devoted, and full of energy, truly humble and a good model religious. She had a warm heart and a sense of humour even in the midst of difficulties, and a wonderful submission to the will of God. Her energy and enthusiasm led her to believe that the work of the congregation should be focused on missionary activities like education, especially education of girl children (*History of the CJM* 136).

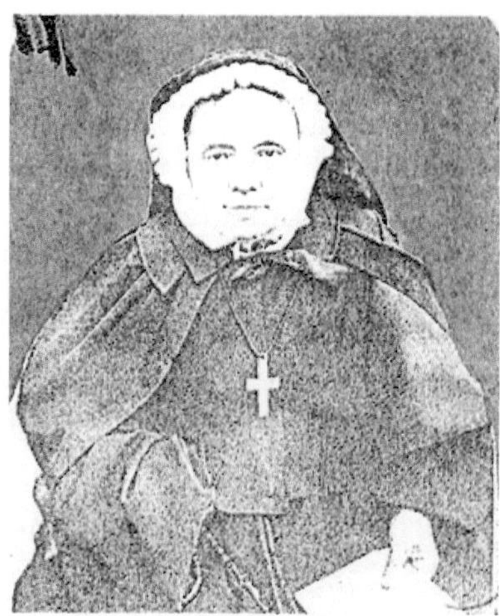

Mother Theresa Motte

The other four professed religious were the following: Mother St Ambrose, a kind and gentle soul, a musician who was later the Directress of the Cathedral choir at Agra; Mother St Paul, a distinguished artist and a saintly religious whose paintings can still be seen both in the Cathedral at Agra and the Convent of Jesus and Mary, Agra. Apart from them there were Mother St Augustine, a lover of the poor and an excellent organizer, and Mother St Joachim, whose cultured and dignified bearing made her devoted work for souls more effective. The novice Madame St Vincent De Paul was gentle, unselfish, and fervent. She could not withstand the extreme heat of Agra; it snatched away that young life within two years. To minister to their spiritual needs on the journey and to conduct them in safety to their destination, Mgr. Rossat gave one of his best priests' Fr Caffarel as their chaplain (*A Missionary Epic* 251).

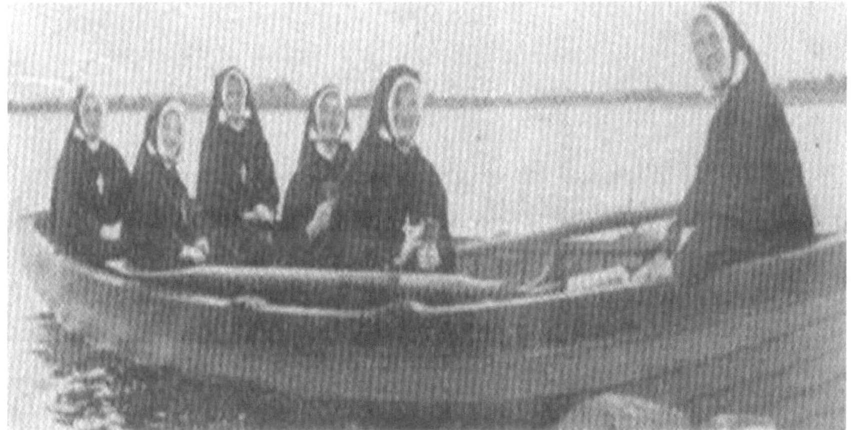

The Visionary Voyage

They set sail from Marseilles on 27th January 1842, amid the tears of their families and the holy envy of their Sisters at Fourviere. The little band of six young religious women with a chaplain left their homeland for ever and never to return to their place, transcending boundaries of nation, language, culture, and identity. It was a long and difficult journey in those days. The boat stopped at Leghorn, Civita-Vecchia Naples, Malta, Syria in the Grecian Archipelago and finally at Alexandria.

Then they went up the Nile in a boat to Cairo, and from there to Suez by a caravan. They travelled by a boat from Suez to Aden, and by steamer from Aden to Bombay and on to Calcutta. The journey from Marseilles to Agra, their destination in India, lasted ten whole months due to several mishaps. They arrived in Agra on 11th November, 1842 (*A Missionary Epic* 251).

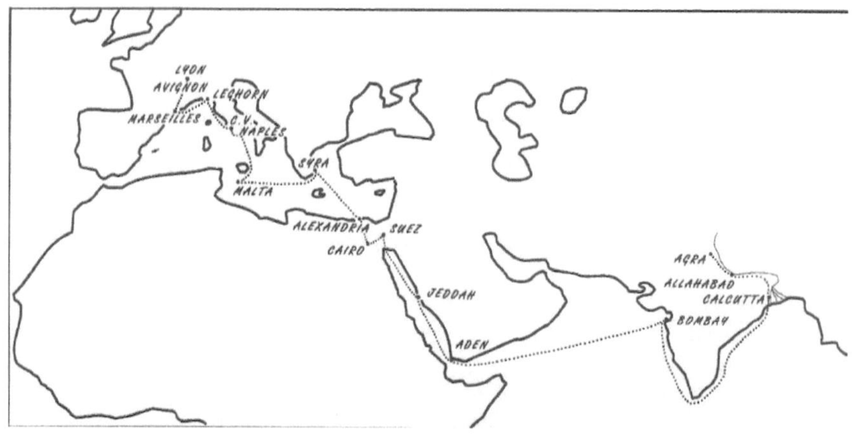

Route followed and stopping places during the journey

Departure from Lyon: 27th January 1842. Arrival at Agra: 11th November 1842

In an extensive enclosure of the Sisters of JM, there were three large schools quite separate from each other. Each had a fine house with its surrounding buildings and offices. The first of the JM schools at Agra was a boarding school with the number of children varying from ten to fifteen. The majority of students were from Protestant families who demanded not to interfere in the least degree with their children's religious ideas. But as one could well imagine, those dear little ones who were educated in these educational institutions were impressed by the ideals of those nuns, who's impeccable life-style changed a considerable number of students (De Cesinale 2). This excellent seed bore fruit in its own time, for a large number of them embraced religious life.

The second school was an orphanage and a Secondary School under the patronage of St Patrick. The daughters of soldiers of English armies, who were mostly orphans, were admitted in this institution along with the children of European origin. The work engaged in was one of the most beneficial in the Agra mission, for the dangers to which the young girls were exposed were extreme. It was beautiful to see the angels of mercy (nuns) devoting themselves with angelic zeal and motherly love correcting and training those poor little ones (De Cesinale 4).

The third school called St. Joseph was for Indian orphans and poor girls of India. There were already twenty-two girls looked after by Bishop Borghi with the help of a woman. Mother Theresa added two Muslim girls to it. Indeed, this was really the apostolate of a religious visionary. Some of these children were from Christian families and the others from Hindu and Muslim background (De Cesinale 5). A few months later, a day-school was temporarily started in the cantonment area called Numila, near St. Patrick's church. The three separate establishments gradually grew up on the spacious grounds provided by the Bishop. Besides learning literature, music, art, and good manners, the salutary influence of Catholic education and solid virtue spread and bore fruit among the girls of all classes from every part of India. After a period of more than one and a half century, these establishments are still flourishing. They have been giving solid Christian education and the formation suited to their state of life from generation to generation (De Cesinale 5).

Bishop Borghi and the people of Agra received these Sisters with great joy. These five French sisters and the Irish novice were the first religious pioneers of Jesus and Mary women to respond to the call of Christ to work in the Vicariate of Hindustan and Tibet Mission. At fairly short intervals other religious sent by the motherhouse at Lyons joined them.

JM Congregation, right from its beginnings in India, gave due importance to both English and the vernacular languages along with skill-oriented education. In fact, St. Joseph's School, Agra was opened first as an Urdu medium school, and later on after independence, Hindi became its medium of instruction. All these schools catered to the children of different religious beliefs and social status. Mother Theresa's letters tell of the joys and sorrows experienced by the nuns of the first Indian foundation. She wrote, "The boarding school which opened with twelve pupils, soon numbered thirty children. Among them there were Hindus, Muslims, and Protestants" (Motte, Correspondence, 1843).

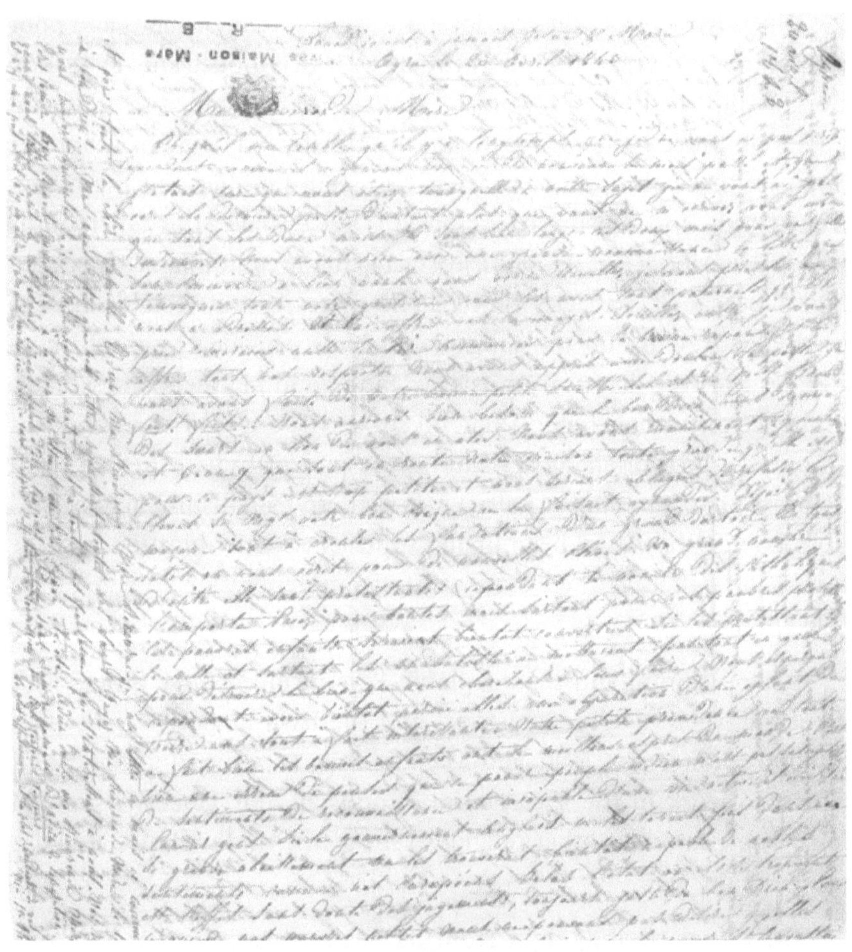

Letter from M. Theressa to M. France 1843
Dated Agra 20 April 1843 (File No. II S/1a Archives CJM Generalite, Rome)

By this time, the Congregation had been established as a Religious Organization for the service of the Church and humanity at large. Ever since the foundation of the JM Congregation in India, it began to expand all over the world through hard work and relentless efforts of the pioneer members. Today it has become an international one, with hundreds of institutions educating girls in every continent, as a global affair indeed. As far as the functioning of the Jesus and Mary institutions are concerned, it is remarkable that the Congregation is systematically well organized with its solid foundations rooted in the values of Christ and the special charism of Claudine Thevenet. The Congregation has its own written Constitution with its proper rules and regulations. The Constitution underlines the structure and organization of the Jesus and Mary institutions and the lifestyle of its members (Motte, Correspondence, 1843).

Any discussion on JM educational mission and their contribution towards women's education in North India must be in relation with the different organizational aspects of the agency which provides education with certain emphases on the role of governance, management and leadership. Most of the key issues deliberated so far, focused on the origin of JM Congregation and their unique historical situations in India. Developing a relevant strategy for women's education and the JM's educational leadership for women in India must be linked to the understanding of the structure of the organization and the authenticity of its mission. "Structure and Organization of the Congregation of Jesus and Mary Educational Institutions" explores the charism of the Foundress and the organizational mechanism of the administrative policies with which the educational institutions operate. It also looks into the Constitutional provisions and the structural framework that give stability to the smooth functioning of the institutions.

Endnotes

[1] The period under study deals with the educational contributions made by the Catholic visionaries in between 1842 and 1968. They established their first ever school in Agra in 1842. Their contribution continued even after India's independence. This

study will also explore the institutions of higher learning including Jesus and Mary College, set up in New Delhi in 1968.

[2] It is not a Gospel, but an apocryphal collection of sayings of Jesus in 114 verses.

[3] Members of the Society of Jesus.

[4] A Christian religious order of men under the Roman Catholic Church.

[5] It is a form of territorial jurisdiction of the Roman Catholic Church.

[6] The office, seat, territorial circumscription of a Prefect.

[7] John 18:37.

[8] Matt. 18: 19-20.

[9] Belonging to or connected with the Christian religion

[10] The basement prison cells near the city hall in Lyon. Literally, the translation is 'the Bad Cave' or 'the Dungeon'.

[11] The area situated near a large plain —where Claudine's brothers were taken to be shot. It is now one of the more elegant neighbourhoods of Lyon, but in the 19th century, it was outside the city and served as "killing fields" during the Revolution.

[12] The three evangelical counsels or counsels of perfection in the Church are poverty, chastity, and obedience.

[13] A person's first reception of the sacrament of the Eucharist in Roman Catholic Church.

[14] Luke 5: 27.

[15] A promise made to God to live in poverty, chastity, and obedience

[16] A form of address for those members of the clergy of the Roman Catholic Church holding certain ecclesiastical honorific titles.

[17] Usually nowadays a titular Bishop who has power over the territorial jurisdiction of the Roman Catholic Church established in missionary regions and countries which do not have a diocese yet.

Chapter 2

Organisational Structure of the Jesus and Mary Educational Institutions

Women's education in India is linked to social reform movements, and as such it is intended to create fundamental changes in the structure of the social and family organisations. The Jesus and Mary [JM] Sisters, who pioneered education in Agra during colonial periods, thought that the best way to cater to the educational needs of the people would be to undertake first a survey of the families in the area, and then to see how they could serve the people of the place effectively in the field of education. Therefore, the education mission of the JM has been focused from a number of related perspectives such as its administration, organisational structure, strategic planning, resource allocation, management of the personnel, innovation, and entrepreneurial enterprises.

In the light of the survey, the JM Congregation realised that many children and young people were orphaned and left to live by themselves away from their families. So, they started organising these children and their families, and they became their focus of attention. In order to reach out to these orphans, they were offered a place of shelter by Bishop Borghi [1839-49] of Agra to begin their work of formation, and the pioneering works were rather strenuous. This is largely due to the fact that the language of the local people had to be learnt by the members of the JM Congregation in order to interact and communicate with them properly. Once the Sisters, the little band of six, had a clear vision and understanding of what they were supposed to do with the people of the area, they began to organise themselves according to the instructions received from the Generalate[1] of the JM Congregation in Lyons, France.

Claudine Thevenet had believed in 'being all things to all people' (Theresa 7). So, she had formed her Sisters into groups known as communities. In the forming of this community, she had also been helped by Father Andre Coindre, founder of the Brothers of the Sacred Heart congregation, devoted to elementary and high school education in France. It should be noted that the first group of secular women was formed in 1816 before the religious community was established (Cuthbert, *Echoes of a Century in India* 3). Two years later, after the annual general meeting of the Association, on 31st July, Father Coindre made an announcement to the effect saying: "You must unite and form yourselves into a community at once, without hesitation or delay"(Barrel and Carlos 118). Then turning to Claudine Thevenet, he suggested her to be their leader and Superior. She fell on her knees as crushed, but he exhorted her: "Heaven has chosen you, be faithful to the call" (Smith 5). This resulted in the formation of the Congregation of the Religious of Jesus and Mary on 6th October1818 at Pierres Plantees in Lyon, France (Theresa 108).

Consequently, in February 1823, Claudine and her first companions had the happiness of making the vow of poverty, chastity and obedience and of receiving each one a religious name and wearing the religious habit; a simple black dress according to the custom for women at that time. Claudine chose the name of Mother Mary St. Ignatius, as she was devoted to St. Ignatius of Loyola, the Founder of the Society of Jesus. Claudine's zeal and enthusiasm were appreciated from all sections of society, despite the fact that her preference was always for the poor and the marginalized. She continued to be passionate towards the orphans, who were considered to be the lowliest creatures, as they knew nothing of the mother's love. Claudine said empathetically and with great passion: "We must be mothers to the children; real mothers, both of soul and body. We must love them all equally, but if we ever have a preference, it should be for the poorest, the most miserable, the least favored" (Chiasson 78). Many a times, there was a question of giving up well-advanced educational establishments for the privileged sections in order to cater to the needs of the underprivileged. In fact, Claudine did not hesitate when she publicly pronounced: "Let us give up the well-established boarding schools and keep our orphanage" (*Horny* 92). When the tradition of the Congregation was established, she emphasised on hard work, commitment to the children, and forgetfulness of self and resolute faith in God as the outstanding motives of the Congregation.

The Constitutional Framework

Once the Congregation was fully established, it called for a proper structure and governance to make its educational work effective and efficient. Its innumerable institutions spread through different parts of the Asian, African, European, North American, and South American continents. For administrative purposes, the Congregation was guided by a group of unwavering, relentless, and ardent Sisters. They were usually appointed or nominated after much reflection and prayer with the consultative votes of the Sisters of the Congregation. Claudine, the Founder of the Congregation of JM, was a woman of great foresight and clear vision with exceptional qualities of administration. She wanted that her Congregation should function systematically and to that end, she had given special rules and regulations to make it systematic and strategic. Once being aware of the decaying of all the best values in religion and society in the West, she emphasised the need for an immediate return to good spiritual values and a well-balanced society through the realisation of her ideals and ideas of education, especially for women (Poulin, 5-13).

It should be noted that all Jesus and Mary educational institutions are functioning as non-governmental and non-profitable organisations with its own well-defined constitutions and regulations. The whole Congregation follows a common code of law known as *The Constitutions of the Congregation of the Religious of Jesus and Mary.* The religious members of each community are strictly encouraged to study the constitutions and live accordingly. It has a well-organised structure with a clear vision of its mission. The Congregation and its institutions epitomise the Christian values of education, well marked by the special charisma, vision and ideals of the Foundress Claudine.

A Mission with a Vision

Following the commandments of Jesus Christ, the preeminent and unique teacher, "Go, teach all the nations" (Matt. 28:18), the Congregation of JM continues its vision bearing the light and knowledge of Christ. The institutions of the Congregation of Jesus and Mary, an expression of Church's presence in the world, aim to collaborate in formal and non-formal education at the national and international level. Since it has the Pontifical Approbation[2] of the Holy See[3] the Congregation is directly under the Holy Father and has now its headquarters or Generalate at Rome (Poulin, XXIX-XXX).

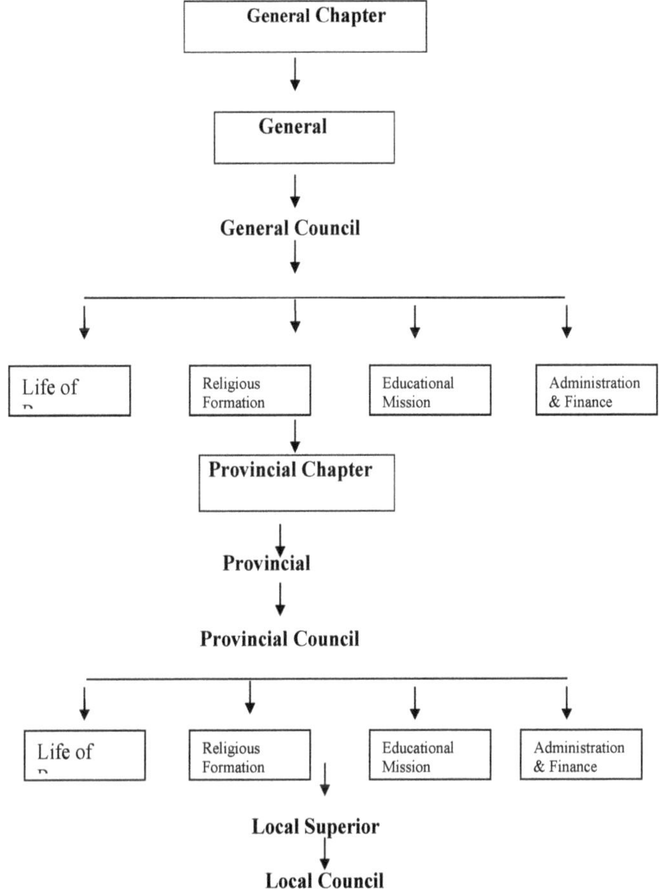

Figure-I: Policy-Making Structure in the JM Congregation

The Figure-I shows the hierarchical structure of the Congregation of Jesus and Mary, where the General Chapter is the final decision-making body in the whole Congregation. The General has a team of four Sisters who are known as General Councillors. This particular council of members would advise and assist her in all major decisions and in any other important matters related to the working of the Congregation, especially with reference to education. The General and her Council always reside in the Generalate at Rome, but at regular intervals of six years they visit all the Jesus and Mary institutions throughout the world and personally meet each member evaluating the various activities conducted in each institution (Poulin, 63-73).

Expansion and Mission

This administrative structure of the Congregation is further divided into Provinces. The number of provinces may vary according to the size or length and breadth of a given country and the number of institutions each country has. A Province is headed by a Provincial Superior and is aided by four Councillors. The pattern of government seen at the General level is continued on the Provincial level as well. The same is true of each convent or institution headed by a Sister Superior and her Council (Poulin, 70-73).

When India got independence on 15th August 1947 the Province of India was divided into the Indian and Pakistan Provinces in order to facilitate the transfers of the Sisters. When the number of institutions grew in India, it became very unwieldy to be managed by the same Provincial and Council. Also, as the language being different in every region, it necessitated to divide the Indian Province further. Accordingly, it has been known as Regions, namely the Province of Delhi (Northern Region), the Province of Pune (Central Region) the Province of Baroda (Western Region) and Kolkata vice province (North-Eastern Region).

Governance of the Congregation

The Superior General, the Councillors and the General officials constitute the General Government. They have the responsibility to keep alive the evangelical ideal, which gave birth to the Jesus and Mary Congregation, and to ensure that its work continues to bear fruit. They follow the spirit of the Church and the constitution: "In fidelity to the Church and in filial submission to our Holy Father, the Pope, the Congregation governs itself under the authority of a Superior General" (Poulin 67).

The General Chapter[4] is a collegial assembly of the government of the Congregation. The Superior General, who is its President, convokes the General Council every six years. It is conducted at the residence of the Superior General and the councilors in Rome. It is the supreme legislative authority in the Congregation. If anything has to be amended or changed, it can only be done by the General Chapter and the assembled members represent the whole Congregation. The ex-officio members consist of the Superior General, ex-Superior General, Provincials, and the ex-Provincials. The delegates are elected by the members of the Province. The preceding General Chapter determines the number of the participants in the General Chapter (Poulin, 62-64).

The General Chapter elects the Superior General and her Councillors for a period of six years. They may be re-elected for another six years more. It takes decisions on major matters of general policy for the entire Congregation. These formulated decisions are called Acts of General Chapter and it has a binding force on the entire Congregation. It revises the constitutions and has to be submitted to the Congregation of Evangelisation of Peoples, Rome for approval. The General Council[5] promotes the spiritual and apostolic vitality of the Congregation. It strives to examine and discuss the questionnaires proposed by the Provincial Chapters[6] and take appropriate decisions, if any amendments or changes are necessary. The position of the Superior General is that of a Constitutional President: "The authority of the Superior General extends over the whole Congregation and each of its members. She directs and governs with the help of her Council and according to the Constitution of the Congregation" (Poulin 75).

The Superior General is elected through a secret ballot during the General Chapter by an absolute majority of deliberative votes. The session for this election is presided over by the local Bishop or his delegate. The Constitution of the Congregation makes it clear that "if the first three ballots give no one the absolute majority, a choice will be made in the fourth ballot, between the two religious who have had most votes in the third ballot. If the votes are equal in the fourth ballot, the religious who has seniority of her religious profession will be considered elected" (Poulin 65).

The Superior General can be deposed before the end of her term of office for serious reasons. The General Councillors could be obliged to apply to the Holy See for permission for this, and act according to its decision. The Mother General should be a well-educated and mature Religious. She should be gentle and kind. At the same time, she should be firm and free from partiality as far as possible. She should be a person of prayer, a woman of sound judgment, a woman with a balanced head, perfect tact, and uprightness of views. She should be a person of vision to carry out the mission of the Congregation according to the values of Christ and the teachings of St. Claudine. The Superior General assumes authority confided in her as a service to the whole Congregation, promoting the common good and accomplishing Church's mission in the world. Her mission consists in animating, directing and unifying the whole Congregation, and in providing for the extension of the apostolate. (Poulin, 68-69).

A Community Animated by the Spirit

It is the Superior General's duty to keep the Congregation faithful to the Church, the Constitution, the charism of the Founder and the discussions of the General Council. She consults her Council, not only when she requires its deliberative votes, but also as often as congregational matters require this consultation. Here she also consults a group of 'Advisors Sisters' from all the countries called 'Permanent Commission'. They are consulted and asked for their vote on any important decisions, like closing an institution, starting a new institution and so on (Poulin, 67). The General takes an active interest in the different sectors of the government in order to assure it as an Apostolic Congregation[7] for the best possible service to the Church. She maintains the relationships of simplicity, charity, and mutual confidence with each one of her Councillors and officials. She listens attentively to their views and suggestions in order to reach the final decision, a decision that she takes in prayer and with the light of the Holy Spirit.[8] So, whenever it is required, she will also consult with the necessary Church authority.

The Superior General has to have a clear vision of the Church's mission. Every Congregation collaborates to fulfill this mission according to the needs and the Congregation on their part in accordance with the experience and the number of its personnel. So, with the collaboration of every Congregation or Religious, the Church is able to accomplish Christ's mission on earth. It becomes indispensable that each Congregation strives to give their maximum support to this mission within the framework and structure of their own constitutions. For example, a Congregation that has taken health ministry as their apostolate [9] would naturally work towards the up building of health without neglecting the spiritual needs of those who come under their care. The same applies to education as to any other field of service. The important decisions, when Bishops may ask for more definite terms of collaboration, will usually come under the jurisdiction of the Mother General and her Council, who will inform the Provincials concerned (Poulin, 66-67).

The General Chapter also elects the Councillors to assist the General: "The Councillors will be elected separately following the same procedure as for the election of the General except that in the fourth ballot, a relative majority will suffice" (Poulin 66). They also can be re-elected for further six years. For a better service of the Congregation, the Councillors and officials have the responsibility of at least one sector of work, under the direction of the Superior General. They strive to deepen their knowledge in their particular field, making it their duty to share information thus obtained, with the other members of the government.

The Provincial Superior assigns personnel to the different houses and directs its activities. At the head of every convent there is a local Superior appointed by the Superior General, who has the care of the Sisters in that convent, directs their activities and sees to the administration of the house. Individual Sisters are under direct authority of local Superior. The local superior is answerable to the Provincial, her immediate authority, and then to the Superior General who is the head of the whole Congregation. The form of government is hierarchical in authority descending from Superior General to Provincial Superior and from Provincial Superior to local Superior. The Superior at each level has a Council with the advisory functions (Poulin, 62-63).

The highest legislative authority of the institute resides in the General Chapter, a collegial body. It consists of the Superior General and her Council, whereas the Provincial Superiors and the delegates are elected from each Province. At the Provincial level, the highest sole authority resides in the Provincial Chapter. It is composed of the Provincial Superior and her Council and certain number of elected delegates from the Province as stated in the Constitutions. It makes major policies called 'Acts of Provincial Chapter', and it has to be approved by the Superior General and her Council (Poulin, 64).

The General Councillor responsible for any sector of works maintains a frequent and cordial relationship with those responsible at the Provincial level. It has been done by meetings organised either at the General or Regional levels, or by official communications and ordinary correspondence. In the same way, the Councillor responsible at the Provincial level regularly informs the progress in the life of the Province to those responsible at the General level and the community level. For a better co-ordination of effort in the whole Congregation, periodic evaluations are being made, which would enable those responsible to keep themselves informed of the work being done in the Provinces and the communities and the problems confronting each (Poulin, 69-73).

Consecrated Life –A Call to live in a Community

The Religious Sister who is responsible for this sector devotes herself to deep study of the religious vows of Chastity, Poverty and Obedience, prayer and community life in the context of the Documents of the Church, Canon Law[10] and the Rules of the Congregation of Jesus and Mary. She will keep herself informed of the general evaluation in the religious life and community life by means of lectures, seminars and contact with other people in a competent manner.

She proposes guidelines to the Superior General or Provincial for the on-going formation programme towards the orientation to be given to the communities in order that they should live a better religious life and deepen their own spirituality. The orientation may take place through study sessions with groups of Superiors, or with a particular community in order to help the religious to make their lives effective in the field of education. The Constitution says, "The role of the General government is apostolic as well as spiritual. The Religious are encouraged to live fully their consecration and to give themselves wholeheartedly to the demands of their apostolic work" (Poulin 73).

Formation: A Preparation for the Mission

The Religious responsible for this sector at the General and Provincial level works under the direction of the Superior General. She follows attentively the orientations of the Catholic Church in matters regarding formators and formation. This ensures the quality of formation offered by the Congregation in view of the true service to the Church. Responsibility for formation is of the utmost importance in any religious congregation. Every Religious in charge of formation is a person of intense prayer. It is her solemn duty, at whatever period or level, to be constantly attentive to the formation given not only in accordance with the charism of the Foundertogether with the constitutional texts of the religious congregation and the particular law of the Congregation, but also in conformity with the thinking and teaching authority of the Church and the State.

A candidate desiring of a membership in the Congregation is assessed by competent persons regarding her motivation and her moral, spiritual, intellectual, psychological, and physical capacity for a a life suited to the religious congregation and the society. A basic high school education with some professional training is needed. The person should be above seventeen years and preferably below thirty years of age. There is a period of initial intense training for three years during which the entrants are helped to internalise the spirit and values of the religious congregation, through talks, various activities, and experiences. They are helped to develop their human and spiritual potential through personal guidance by competent persons. This provides an opportunity for them and for the institute to test their fitness for Religious life. During this period of probation and training, they are gradually integrated into the life and apostolic work of the institute. A final decision, to become a permanent member through perpetual vows, is arrived at both by the Sister concerned and the religious Congregation. Since the decision to join the institute is voluntary, members are free to opt out, if for any particular reason they feel they cannot continue their Religious life in the institute.

Before being initiated into the formation groups, those young women who wish to join the Congregation of Jesus and Mary are invited to live in one of the religious communities in the Congregation. The response being always a voluntary one, the formator-in-charge will invite the young girls to active participation in their own integral formation in a spirit of creative fidelity and of generosity in response to the love of God. So, eight years of formation is given to each member with the intention of leading the young to become women of great spiritual maturity, generosity, committed to the apostolic work of the Congregation, and conscious of their particular mission. The Formation Mistress sees that the young girls receive necessary help for their spiritual progress and for the gradual integration of their consecrated life while joyfully devoting themselves to apostolic work or continuing their academic studies, so that they became effective educators to form the future generations (Poulin, 72-73).

Formation for Transformation

When a young girl has been accepted after the consideration of her background, qualities, potentials and studies, she is initiated into the first step of her formation as a Postulant.[11] There she begins to learn the significant aspects of everyday daily life as a Religious Sister. The prayers, spiritual reading, manual work, recreations, meals and the rule of silence and so on form an integral part of the religious life. After a period of one year if the institute feels she is ready to continue, and if the candidate feels she wishes to stay on, she advances to the next step and she is accepted as a Novice[12] of the Congregation of Jesus and Mary in a simple private ceremony.

The Novice deepens the above stage with a profound study of the three vows, its rules and the Constitutions, the Catechism of the Catholic Church, the Biblical and Church History given by formators. She learns to follow all the rules and their applications, and able to explain them like any full-fledged member of the Congregation of Jesus and Mary. At the same time conserving her simplicity and cheerfulness, living the common life in community in a simple lifestyle without any external force, she makes of her life a true imitation of Christ. These two years of religious novitiate[13] are given exclusively to deepen one's own prayer life in an atmosphere of prayerful silence and reflection. This period is also meant for acquiring of virtues necessary for an apostolic religious with a complete understanding of the all-round formation of a consecrated soul towards a better response to the needs of our world today (Poulin, 52).

It is the formator's duty to see and encourage the Novice to inculcate these virtues without losing her innate qualities and spontaneity and develop a dedicated religious life in order to please the Lord Almighty. At the end of this two-year term, duly being approved of by the Provincial Council, she makes her temporary vows of chastity, poverty and obedience for a period of three years. At the end of this three-year period she can renew it for a period of further two years. She now begins her secular and academic studies, according to what she with the Council has decided, for her future apostolate. During these years of training period, any religious is free to leave the Congregation completely and return to her home. Normally at the end of the training period, the religious is expected to make her Final Commitment[14] in the Congregation taking the vows of Poverty, Chastity and Obedience in a solemn public ceremony according to the directives of the Catholic Church. After the Final Commitment if a Religious wants to be dispensed of her vows she may only do so after making a formal petition to the Holy See. Once the Mother General dispenses of her vows as per her request, she is able to return to the secular state of life again (Poulin, 54-55).

It is important that the Sister-in-charge of the trainees helps each young Sister to grow in true self-knowledge and self-acceptance by gaining maturity through the experiences of her normal daily community life. Then she is able to carry out the undertakings entrusted to her by the Congregation. The religious formation given by the Congregation of Jesus and Mary aims at "the progressive integration of all the values of the individual towards a full-blown maturity. It develops the qualities of a mature woman, capable of adapting to life situations, strong in faith and forgetful of herself in the service of others" (Poulin 52).

After a Sister has retired from the normal work in any capacity as part of the educative community, she still enjoys all the benefits as a member of the Congregation as part of the religious community. She still continues to be an honorary member of the educative community till she is capable of continuing. Her life continues to be a spiritual support to the institution with her life presence and her prayers.

Apostolic Life and Educational Mission

A religious member, responsible for the educational activities at the General and Provincial level, has to be animated by an enlightened and dynamic zeal for souls. She should have sufficient experience of the apostolate of the Congregation in which she exercises her responsibility. The Councillor-in-charge of all educational programmes is careful to follow the orientations of the Church's Christian education and the social pastoral ministry. She should be able to motivate the young through lectures or meetings with international or national organisations, directly or indirectly concerned with the problems of education today. She keeps herself well informed of the evolution of thought in this domain in order to make the apostolate more actual, realistic, and dynamic. She seeks information on pedagogical methods and the educational laws of the countries concerned. In particular, the Councilor strives to develop distinguished characteristic traits needed for the ministry of education.

It is the duty of this Councillor to ensure that all the Religious of the Congregation have more than adequate qualification to carry out the state educational programme. She frequently visits the educational institutions and the ministry of the Provinces. During these visits, she stimulates the apostolic zeal of the Religious, staff and students. In spite of the complexity of the work of education in all its forms, formal or non-formal, it may help them to maintain the fervent desire of accomplishing the mission for the educational uplift of society, especially in those places rampant in poverty and misery. In such a way she helps them in their difficulties and encourages them to put in effort in the especially important and difficult work of Christian education in a secular world. She is also responsible for the organisation and direction of studies of the Religious who will be future educators (Poulin, 5-7).

The main function of the Director of educational programmes is to promote, animate and stimulate the religious educators. She promotes values of the pedagogy of Claudine, the Foundress of the Congregation. She encourages those involved in education to confront their difficulties, enterprising optimistic attitude. For Claudine, the imparting of education is the greatest service to society. So, the educator must be a well-balanced, well-disciplined, and well-trained person. Father Coindre, the co-founder of the Congregation of Jesus and Mary, expressed his views on their educational institutions:

> Their discipline, their zeal and their special God-given talents had enabled them to educate young people in the practice of virtues and to give them necessary knowledge to become exemplary mothers, excellent teachers, and outstanding human beings. We believe that by encouraging these establishments we shall be rendering the greatest possible service to nation and society (Barrel and Carlos 248).

The Congregation gives its first care for education in one's own faith, irrespective of any particular religion. The directress of education aims at arousing a great zeal among the Religious and their staff. She urges them always to love and to be attentive to the most abandoned and poorest among the young people as it was the vision of the Foundress. The apostolate of the Congregation of Jesus and Mary is "an ecclesial act which is integrated into the pastoral activity of the diocese the institution, therefore, works with the people according to its own specific mission under the direction of the Bishops who are in communion with the Pope, the head of the Catholic Church" (*Rule Book of 1843*).

Today there are varieties of institutions run by the Congregation of Jesus and Mary all over the world. The Congregation owns its own educational institutions along with schools and colleges aided by the state. The medium of teaching in most of the Jesus and Mary institutions is English, but from the beginning of the work of the Congregation schools were opened to cater to the various vernacular languages according to the educational programmes of each state. In the past, the Congregation of Jesus and Mary had several boarding schools, but their number has diminished because of the increase of the local population. Nevertheless, in recent times, JM educational establishments have many day-schools that impart transformative education to millions of children.

Organisational Structure of JM Educational Institutions

Each school normally is headed by a Principal, Vice-principal, and a well-qualified team of teachers to cover every subject and programme. According to the needs and programmes prescribed by each State Education Department, each instituation updates its programmes in view of the exigencies of the public examination at the final level. All the JM educational institutions in North India come directly under "the Societies Registration Act XXI of 1860". Under this Act, the Society will be named after the name of the particular institution. The Society is a Christian minority institution claiming rights and privileges under Article 29 and 30 of the Constitution of India. Under this Act, the institutions run without any profit to any of its members. It can function with the minimum of seven members. According to this Act, the institutions are exempted from income tax under Section 80 (c).

All members of the Society, including those in training, are divided for the sake of administrative purposes in the geographical units called Provinces. Each province consists of 150-165 members working in 45 convents of the Congregation. The members of the Province elect a Provincial Superior who is installed by Superior General as the head of the Province. Each religious community runs educational institutions such as schools, colleges and training colleges under their direct management and administration. Each educational institution appoints an elgible Sister to be the head of the institution. The sisters who are actively involved in the field of education, strive to disseminate the spirit and ideals of Claudine Thevenet to the rest of the staff and the students. This spirit is very evident in all JM institutions. The staff in turn transmits this great spirit of love, service, brotherhood, and idealism to the entire family of the academic institution.

Various Bodies in Educational Institutions

JM educational institutions also have its own hierarchical structures following an order of precedence (see Figure-II). The Governing Body is the statutory body where decisions regarding the educational institutions are made. It consists of the Provincial as the President, and Local Superior who is also the Manager of the institution, acts as the Vice-president of the Governing Body. The Principal of the institution will be the Secretary of the Governing Body. Similarly, the statutory body also includes two teachers as members, nominated by the management. In some cases, an expert in the field of education may also be nominated as the Chairperson by management. The Provincial, Finance Secretary, the Local Superior and the Education Secretary of the Province are the ex-officio members of the Governing Body (Poulin, 160-165).

With the support of this Governing body each institution functions under its own local bodies for its day to day running of each institution. The Principal has the execution power regarding the academic and the administrative offices of the institution.

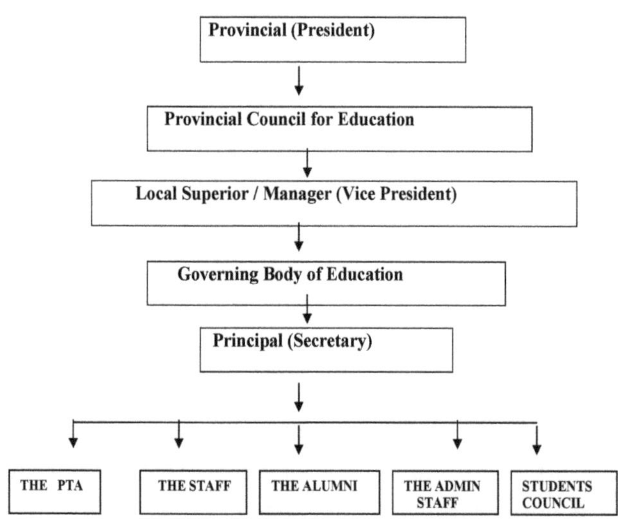

Figure-II: Organisational Structure of the JM educational Institutions

The rest of the functions are entrusted to different sections under the supervision of the Manager and the Principal.

a. The Manager and the administrative staff take care of all the administrative and clerical works.

b. The domestic staff takes care of the general cleanliness of the institution.

c. The Parent Teacher's Association ensures a fluid communication between the staff and the parent body concerning the studies of the students and the normal social activities of any educational institution.

d. The Student Council that has to keep a rapport between the students, principal and the staff representing their needs and problems whenever the need arises. They also participate and help to organize a series of extra-curricular activities.

e. The JM educational establishments have an Alumni association and keep a cordial and loving contact with all their past pupils often inviting them for special school functions.

Financial Administration and Management of Funds

The Bursar[15] at all levels of the government of the institution usually sees to the management and administration of the temporal goods of the Congregation, under the direction and control of the Sister Superior. She collaborates actively with the members of the General, Provincial, or local government, as the case may be. So, the Congregation may assure the continuity and progress of its educational mission providing for the needs of the members, staff, and students. They respond to the appeal of the Church in favour of the poor aiming always at a true collective poverty through a simple lifestyle, not above the one that of the ordinary middle class (Poulin,160-161).

The service entrusted to the Bursar is not merely an administrative task, but one which commits her to develop her apostolic and visionary zeal. The Bursar strives to exercise her authority in a great spirit of charity. She is a person gifted with solid judgment, prudence accompanied by charity and guided by justice, broad vision of the future supplemented by a spirit of dependence. She should have a practical intelligence capable of understanding problems and dealing with them clearly and of finding an appropriate solution.

Her responsibility further requires that she be orderly and precise in administration, prompt in managing affairs in exact and faithful in financial transactions. She makes herself familiar with the laws and social doctrine of the Church and the administrative regulations of the country and the state in which she works. She must carry out transactions in order that her administration corresponds perfectly with the civil and ecclesiastical laws, thus preventing the Congregation from being involved in lawsuits or loss of goods.

The Bursar prepares and concludes no contract of purchase or sale, no financial transaction concerning the goods of the Congregation.

She cannot dispose of any fund for extraordinary expenses without the approval of the Superior and her Council whom she will judiciously advise her in all economic affairs. At the end of the financial year, she submits to the Provincial Council the final balance sheet, the budget, the general accounts of all the goods entrusted to her with a detailed report of her administration. When all are verified, approved, and duly signed at its corresponding level, the Bursar forwards these documents for final approval to the Provincial or General Bursar, as the case may be.

The Bursar is responsible for keeping them up to date in the archives of administration. She has to conserve all the details of the property, the contracts, building plans, and every other document of an administrative nature in the archives. She forwards the copy of each of them to the Bursar at a higher level who classifies them in her archives. At every level, she also keeps the receipts carefully, as well as those of book–keeping. The Bursar is appointed for every community and institution of the Congregation. The expenditure and judicial acts of the ordinary administration of a bursar are valid. "For a more authentic practice of the vow of Poverty, Superiors and Bursars are advised to have only one common fund in the house" (Poulin 95).

The Accounting System

Each province may choose its double entry-accounting system and fix the dates on which the financial year begins and ends. In every house there will be separate accounting for the community and the educational work. They will pay a salary/stipend, according to the norms of the country, to all the Religious employed in teaching, administration, or any other work. Budgets are carefully prepared in all the communities, schools, or any other educational activities in the Provinces. These budgets will serve as the norm of administration for the whole year, and expenditure in excess of that foreseen should be avoided.

In order to provide information to the Provincial in connection with the decisions it has to take, each Province from an 'Economic Commission' whose vote will be consultative (Poulin 100). The role of the

Commission is to establish a plan for the administration in the province, to study plans and estimates for buildings, to attend to the purchase and sale of houses and properties, and to make sure that buildings are functional. The constitution clearly provisions that "the Congregation possesses goods only in function of the service to be rendered, namely, to assure the continuity and progress of the educational mission, and to provide for the need of the Religious. So, in the Congregation the ownership of current and fixed assets is subordinated" (Poulin 19).

Role and Power of the Secretariat

The Secretariat is the centre where all documents are received and kept, and from which information of a general or particular nature is communicated to the Provinces, the communities, the institutions and all the Religious. It, therefore, has an important role to play in the good organization of the JM institutions. At all levels of government, the responsibility for this service is entrusted to direct, precise, and methodical religious of great availability. She has the task of keeping in perfect order the filing-cabinets and registers necessary for the service of the secretariat. Secretaries should work with thoroughness, taking great care of correspondence, reports and other documents concerning the Congregation and JM institutions. The documents and copies of official letters are kept in the archives of the Secretariat. In addition, they are responsible for confidential documents and they send proper acknowledgement as the documents received.

It is their task to prepare customary letters, the draft letters of petition to Bishops, civil authorities, and official organizations, and to send them at the appropriate time. Before the date of expiry, they take care to inform the Superior of certain permissions due for renewal such as leave of absence of the Religious or authorization obtained from the Dioceses[16] for various activities. At the different levels of government, namely, local, Provincial, General, the secretary drafts the minutes of the various council meetings. Minutes will bear the date of meeting, number of persons present and absent, the questions treated, statement of the different points of view, and the resolutions taken, mentioning the division of votes. At the opening of the Council meeting, the secretary reads the minutes of the previous meeting. Once the Superior and the Council approve them, she writes them in the register and obtains their signatures. The secretaries of the General and the Provincial level are also responsible for the General or Provincial archives of the Congregation (Poulin, 62-65).

The General Secretary is responsible for the Mother General's correspondence with the Congregation and with people outside. She is available to the Superior General for the drafts of ordinances, circulars and other documents which are to be dispatched or promulgated. It is her duty to see that they are sent to the proper destination, after having had them signed by the Superior General, and after countersigning them herself. She co-ordinates the service of communication of the different sectors and is responsible for the information to be sent to the Provinces or institutions. Each year she draws up a memorandum of the state of the works of the Congregation and presents it to the Superior General and her Council (Poulin, 68-73).

All these well organized and well controlled sectors of work were precisely arranged in order that Claudine's vision of education could be put through and realized in a careful functioning of all her educational institutions throughout the world. It leads us to the broad vision of her educational mission and to the vision of education of the Congregation of Jesus and Mary as envisioned by its Foundress and reflected in the ethos and the philosophy of education in JM Schools and Colleges in Indian context. Being a woman of great vision, she was making sure that her charism lived through her Sisters and their educational institutions would never die but continued to have far reaching effects in the lives of those educated by them.

Endnotes

[1] The administrative centre of a religious Congregation where the Superior General stays.

[2] In Roman Catholic canon law, an act by which the Pope grants to an ecclesiastic the actual exercise of his ministry.

[3] The central government of the Catholic Church headed by the Bishop of Rome, the Pope.

[4] The upper collegiate body that has the ultimate power in decision-making in a Religious Congregation.

[5] An advisory body to each of the Religious Congregation.

[6] A decision-making body of the Province in a Religious Congregation.

[7] The Congregation under the Roman administrative office of the Holy See responsible foreverything which concerns a Religious Congregation.

[8] One of the three persons of the Holy Trinity who makes up the single substance of God.

[9] A ministry in cooperation with the Catholic Church.

[10] The laws of the Church; the chief governing document of the Church.

[11] The one who asks for admission into a convent/monastery both before actual admission and for the length of time proceeding their admission into the novitiate.

[12] A prospective member of a religious Order who is being tried and being proven for suitability of admission to a religious order of Sisters.

[13] The period of training and preparation that a prospective member of a religious order undergoes prior to taking vows in order to discern whether he/she is called to the religious life.

[14] The highest level of commitment that is exemplified by those who have taken their solemn, perpetual profession of vows.

[15] A senior professional financial administrator in a school or university.

[16] An administrative territorial unit administrated by a Bishop.

Chapter 3

Vision, Innovation and Strategic Planning

The Congregation of the Religious of Jesus and Mary can be assertively traced back to Claudine Thevenet's passion and devotion for Almighty and her passionate zeal in educational mission. In fidelity to the charism[1] received from what she called the Holy Spirit, she surrendered herself unreservedly to God's plan for her and for the good of the Church. Her heroic forgiveness, in imitation of Christ on the Cross, opened her heart to every form of human misery, and led her to dedicate herself for the betterment of others. This way of life helped her to lead the unfortunate and hapless people to be under the all-pervasive power of God and His love. Her experience of the goodness of Almighty urged her to devote herself to the education of the young girls. As the JM Congregation has been rendering their service in the field of women's education in India since 1842, this study attempts to explore the efforts of the members of the congregation of Jesus and Mary, who committed themselves in the promotion of a more just and humane society in our country through women education following the inspiring footsteps of ClaudineThevenet.

The education of the young generation, particularly young girls from the underprivileged and deprived sections of the society, is an exceptional and noble work. The congregation had a strong conviction that those who work for the poor, hapless and underprivileged should come to know and love Him; and should thus obtain eternal happiness. Truly it is a great and exalted calling to instill noble sentiments into the young hearts, to raise their low-esteem, and to inspire them with the idea of self-respect. The task is an extraordinary one, and the responsibility it entails is substantial. This is largely because education of children is, indeed, a task which requires constant care, supervision, and instruction on a full-time basis (Elise 34). Early childhood is the most critical years in a child's life. During this time, the brain is at its peak development stage and determines a child's development over the course of their lives. This period is extremely crucial because children develop cognitive, physical, social, and emotional skills. They are highly influenced by their environment and require utmost care by parents and teachers to ensure holistic development. Claudine was very particular about this and she asked her nuns and teachers to be extreme careful while teaching the little ones.

Charisma, Creativity and Nation Building

The vision of education of the Jesus and Mary institutions is based on the Christian vision of humanitarian values and the conviction that education has a unique role to play in an individual's integral growth as well as in nation building through sustainable development. JM institutions aim to equip their students with education that imbues in them deep spiritual, moral and social values along with environmental awareness. St Claudine Thevenet, the Foundress of the Congregation of Jesus and Mary, outlined her vision of education for the Congregation in the following terms: "Above all, let us train these girls that they may be able to deal with every domestic situation, and be regarded as a blessing in the homes, in the workplaces, and in the society they may enter" (Antonio and Paloma 22). The aim of JM education remains the same as visualised by Claudine. It was and is "to produce women of faith in God, faith in themselves and faith in others; women capable of being good wives and mothers and of creating happy homes; women capable of earning a living by their honesty and hard work and thus contribute towards nation building" (Chiasson 58). For Claudine character matters.

She taught her nuns and the young students to self examine what they can give to others. She knew that if one has to give, one must be rich from within. And for her richness means, the power to love, love God, love his creation, love fellow beings and love oneself. She instilled in them the importance of belief in themselves and in others. Ultimately, that would help them to form good habits and good character. She belived that it would bring them closer to God and fellow human beings. In the modern times, we have our great Indian leaders like Swami Vivekananda and Mahatma Gandhi who repeatedly preached the same things to the people of India.

This vision of Claudine aims to impart Christian education to young girls in tune with their social position. Towards this end, JM Sisters run boarding schools in which they bring up the young by carefully instructing them the values of religion, culture, literature, and their social and domestic duties. This has been the founding mission of the JM educational institutions. In her mind, Claudine visualized the formation of young generation so that they should become good social beings with a sense of duty towards the society they in. The Congregation desires of its Sisters and all members of the educative community, namely, teachers, pupils, parents, domestic staff, benefactors, and all stakeholders that they become living witnesses in their own sphere of life and active social agents in building the nation.

When, in general, educationists neglect the significance of character formation, we become a nation without character. The very people of a nation should form and build their own character, and then it becomes the life of a nation. For a nation to live in continual progress, it is important that its people be well educated. Mahatma Gandhi believed that to have formal instruction without character-formation is a crime. Through value education and good example, we impart knowledge other than what is just given in the textbooks. It brings about an all-round development in the individual and forms men of character.

Awareness of oneself, knowledge of one's strengths and limitations, respect for other human beings, their race, colour, creed, culture and awareness of living things in the environment along with sensitivity to the feelings of others, an altruistic attitude, honesty and humility are the basic qualities of a person formed through a quality education. This is what Claudine dreamed of, and for which she opened her educational institutions. These educational institutions aim to instruct young girls and to lead them into the path of eternal truth and the Christian values that often find its expression in love of God and respect for the others. She went out in love and service to the poor in the society and demanded that her Sisters in the Congregation should continue to do the same till the very end through Christian education.

Founding Vision of JM Education

Claudine considered that education is the only potential means to attain the ultimate purpose in lives. Imbued with the Spirit of Christ, she hoped that the students would act as Leaven and Salt [2] (Matt5:13) in their own social milieu. This is quite evident that those who have studied in JM institutions learnt to cater to the socio-economic needs of the family and society, as responsible citizens by setting themselves as examples in various walks of life. If this were to be done effectively, students would need a strong intellectual, moral and emotional formation. She chose the best elements from the educational systems of her time and added her own ideas to it, adopted them and organized them into a whole, so as to achieve inclusive and transformative education for the empowerment of young women.

Her system of education had a scientifically tempered Christian outlook. To act as an influence in the social structure and in such a milieu, the students were required to be proficient in their skills. In her educational vision Claudine combined two ideals, namely, good life based on Christian values and the means to earn a decent livelihood. She offered subjects that helped them to become good citizens, leaders, mothers, wives, and teachers, within their families, society, and nation at large. Hence her liberal and innovative ideas already foreseen at that time were duly converted into vocational studies and preparations. One can see how Claudine's vision foresaw Gandhiji's own Wardha Scheme in which the same system was later put into practice. In fact, there were more similarities than differences between these two educational systems. Gandhiji proposed to teach India's children how to use their minds by teaching them how to use their hands; so "work schools" instead of "book schools." Chief subjects in the curriculum included spinning, weaving, agriculture, sugar-making; chief instrument of education the *takli*, a small spindle on which the student can spin yarn as one walks, talks, or prays. As they learn these trades, they would also learn history, geography, reading, writing and arithmetic (Kumar 169).

Similarly, Claudine's ideology of education centered largely on craft and skill-oriented creative curriculums. It was intended largely to create consciousness of self-reliance and self-esteem. The JM schools made every effort to make sure that the skill based creative work of each student is valued, honored, and promoted without compromising on the quality of their products. In fact, Claudine believed that the way in which a student attains the skill is not crucial, but the process of acquiring the skill itself is educative at large. The fact of the matter is that the money which was earned by the students out of their skill-oriented creative endeavours including spinning, weaving, lace making, and needle works, was judiciously spent for the exclusive use of the students, their higher education and married life.

Education, for Claudine, also had a social dimension. She insisted that its benefits were to be for all, even to the poorest. Hence, her schools would produce outstanding women leaders, and perhaps they even follow her footsteps in this great educational adventure. Like the earlier humanists, she wanted the whole person to be re-created through the integration of mind, body and soul crowned and guided by the philosophy of love of God and neighbour. She believed that it would provide the reason for a good moral living. Simultaneously, she also encouraged excellence in studies and intellectual pursuits.

It is widely believed that education must guarantee a decent livelihood, as it is definitely required for a just human survival, and to lead a life with due human dignity expected of every human person, no matter who he or she may be. This driving force, the respect for the dignity of every human being, was one of the chief marks of Claudine's pedagogy for the underprivileged. Much the same could be said of Mother Teresa of Calcutta as well. When she opened her doors to the destitutes and the outcastes, she claimed that by their very humanity they were equally worthy of a state of dignified human living and a dignified death as well.

With this vision, Claudine built the very foundation of the formation of a human person and a good decent human life. It is only such an education can inculcate these eternal values to enrich any society that believes in the universal brotherhood of humanity. People with such awareness will have a deep sense of mission in life. For them, education means service to society, without any compromise with the materialistic values of the world. Swami Vivekananda has drawn our attention to the tremendous moral qualities in every human being. For him, the goal of education was 'man in the making'. It is the gradual making of the whole human being. Another well-known leader and social scientist Vinoba Bhave stirred people to uplift village. Mother Teresa identified herself with the poor through a total dedication to the cause of the poor and marginalized.

Similarly, Martin Luther King Jr, who continued to be an apostle of non-violence till his last breath, also became a martyr to the cause of human rights. In the case of India, educationists of modern India such as Kuriakose Chavara, Dayanand Saraswati, Pundita Ramabai, Savitribai Phule, Jyotirao Phule, Rabindranath Tagore, D.R. Karve, B.G. Tilak, Mahatma Gandhi, Annie Besant, B.R. Ambedkar, Maulana Abul Kalam Azad, to name a few, continue to disseminate ideas of national education. On seeing the proliferation of social evils, their basic sense of values and humane qualities were stirred into action. Their real education began when they left the portals of their own educational institutions after having imbibed these eternal values. All these influential people were driven by their lofty and humane values, learnt to dedicate themselves to the betterment of human life through their powerful and profound experiences.

In the same way, Claudine too, in seeing the terror and degradation of the society of her times after the French Revolution, was profoundly moved to act towards the transformation of the ills of her own people. It had been and is still a life-long struggle continued by those who cherish her ideals and values. They aim to work for the welfare of all those socially excluded and outcaste children by rooting out the very idea of injustice, inequality, and discrimination. It is this distinct aspect of education that has been given prominence in JM education, beginning with the inspiration and impetus given by Claudine, and reaching right down to our present age.

Perspectives of Education

The society around us is riddled with hatred, strife, corruption, discrimination, and many other social evils. An emerging India needs citizens of character and fine moral fiber to withstand and to overcome the debilitating social evils. The need of the hour is a generation with a sound mind and a deep commitment to values. Indian society needs a generation of good morally upright and law-abiding citizens whose concern for humanity and whose profession is to be at the service of all in the society, especially of the needy and the downtrodden. This necessitates a value-based education system, which prepares the student not only for a future profession ahead but also prepares in him/her good moral values and human qualities for nation-building. In a fast-developing country like India, students have to be educated not only to earn a decent living, but also to be deeply involved in the concern and care for the deprived strata of the society. This is in tune with the Church's vision of education expressed in the Documents of Vatican II on Christian Education:

> True education aims at the formation of the human person in pursuit of his ultimate goal, and simultaneously with respect to the good of these societies of which, as a man, he is a member and, in whose obligations, as an adult, he must share (Flannery 606).

In the same manner, the JM education aims at enabling the pupils entrusted to their care to form a harmonious and integrated personality with a spiritual, intellectual, moral, social, and cultural bent of mind. The Vatican II document clearly upholds the role of Christian education in the modern world acknowledging the intrinsic worth of the child and the need to prepare him/her for the contribution he/she has to make to society. Fully conscious of the needs of a rapidly changing world rooted in the past, JM educational institutions are open to new ideas and weighing them well before implementing them in the institutions (Flannery 606).

Students in the JM institutions are made increasingly aware of their gift of faith and therefore, have the need to strengthen it in the teaching-learning atmosphere. These institutions introduce them into the mystery of salvation[3] and lead them into an awareness of the uniqueness of one's own religion. They are motivated by zeal and apostolic activity according to the spirit of all true moral values. The end result is that each one realizes that he/she is created by God according to His "image and likeness"(Gen. 1:26) personally known and loved by Him, and destined to eternal bliss in union with God from whom he/she derives his/her being.

The child gradually acquires a mature sense of responsibility in striving after values basic to all religions, namely, truth and goodness. So, JM Sisters try to develop in their pupils the ability to think, judge and act constantly and consistently in an atmosphere illumined by divine faith. This implies that the child is helped to develop a correct sense of values, capable to embrace them by personal choice and stand by them with an upright conscience. These educational institutions develop healthy attitudes in their students that will enable them to adapt themselves to the ever-changing times and circumstances without compromising the basic principles. Similarly, these institutions will enable the students to enrich their life as well as the lives of their companions. Social awareness and consciousness achieved through social service helps them to put their scholarship to practical use.

The purpose of true education is certainly to promote the quality of life of human beings and in consequence, the quality of life of the whole society itself. The *Readers Digest Great Encyclopedic Dictionary* defines education as a "systematic instruction or training in preparation for life" (Funk and Wagnalls 842). While speaking about 'the importance of Christian education', His Holiness Pope Pius XI said: "Education consists essentially in preparing man for what he must be and for what he must do here on earth in order to attain the sublime end for which he is created" (Gibbons 37). Therefore, to educate means to bring up, so as to form habits, manners, intellectual aptitudes, discipline, taste, and positive disposition in life. So, educating a person means refining him/her in character and behaviour. That is why it is said that the true teacher is not the one who merely imparts knowledge, but the one who corrects the deformities in character and personality of one's disciples. With good reason, therefore, did John Chrysostom say, "What greater work is there than training the mind and forming the habits of the young?" (Gibbons 39). It is the content of one's character and personality that determines ultimately one's success or failure in life and his contribution to the society to which he/she belongs.

As women constitute the most significant part of society everywhere in the world, Claudine was very well aware of the life and dignity of young girls of her time, particularly during and after the French Revolution. Like various other well-known reformers and missionaries like Raja Rammohan Roy and William Carey, Claudine also initiated several measures to improve the position of women. Special emphasis was placed on facilities like education of girls, better health, and provision of opportunities for taking up respectable jobs in order to make them economically independent. As one goes through the annals of JM history in India it is clear that from 1842 onwards, they were able to influence the society to improve the status and role of women through their formal and informal education.

Education for Holistic Development

Education and personality are mutually complementary and remain closely intertwined. One's personality is the identity which marks him/her different from the rest. In everyday parlance we often judge one's personality or identity by using certain common adjectives. We usually compliment someone by saying, 'he/she has a pleasing personality' and some other by describing him/her as dignified, elegant, or mature. Still further we may say, in not such a complementary tone, that someone is arrogant, proud, mean, narrow-minded and so on. These are no doubt external expressions of one's internal disposition.

The main purpose of education is to modify the behaviour of the child or any person. So that he/she may be able to adjust to the environment and to change it in accordance with his/her needs. Thus, an educated person can modify his/her environment to suit the needs of others. He/she can transform himself/herself and the society in which he/she lives, into an ideal one according to the vision he/she has. Human reason and experiences of man have shown that true education is the basis of the greatness of any nation. Impelled and inspired by this consciousness, JM Sisters in India have all along endeavored to establish educational institutions and impart knowledge and be part of nation building wherever they were invited.

It is an undeniable fact that St Claudine was an educationist par excellence. She communicated her zeal and enthusiasm to her first companions who very ardently participated in the charism which she had received and handed over to them. In the minutes recorded on the Canonical institution of the Congregation, Father Andre Coindre wrote: "Their special God-given talents have enabled them to educate young girls in the practice of virtues and to give them the necessary knowledge to become good religious minded people, exemplary mothers and excellent teachers"(Antonio and Paloma 13). Even today the Sisters of JM live the same charism of merciful love towards the least favoured with the same zeal and dedication of their Founder.

Claudine deeply appreciated the exigencies of education and considered it as a spiritual ministry. She made a special effort to instill into the hearts of her children a love of goodness and a vision to see God as their loving Father. She taught them that their duties in life consisted in being prayerful, kind, and helpful to others. She thought of opening the charitable institutions called 'Providence' where the poor, the abandoned or orphaned children were taken in and educated to be spiritually and morally good, and be given the necessary training which would enable them to earn their own livelihood.

The orphans were treated with great tenderness and respect that even the more favoured children might have envied. The older girls were given professional training together with a sound moral formation. There were lessons in sewing, lace making and accounts. This programme was carried out with a two-fold aim: to prepare the orphans to be self-supporting on leaving the Providence, and to assure a small steady income for the new establishments. Besides practical training, the children were given instruction in the fundamentals of reading, writing and arithmetic. Most important of them was that all were taught the truths of their faith. These girls whom suffering had already touched, soon experienced self-confidence and the happiness of knowing the goodness of God, and His personal love for each one of them, through the example of Claudine and her companions (Maria 103). Claudine's philosophy of education was not to be rich in material wealth but to be happy and to be humane. Then as they grew up, they would know the value of things, not the price. She was very particular in teaching them that there is a big difference between a human being and being human. Claudine understood this and she was sure that only true education could bring this difference in their life and the society in which they live.

It can be argued that the pressures of casteism, communalism, poverty and other exploitative structures in India make it imperative to equip their students not only with intellectual skills, but also to equip them with a set of good strong attitudes imbued with spiritual, moral and social values. As Religious Sisters and educators, JM Sisters are committed to this kind of education in order to serve the young girls, and the poorest and the least favoured. The education they imparted also aims to sensitize them of the existing social evils and exploitation in our materialistic and consumerist society.

The problems encountered by the JMs in the field of female education were still more serious. The 'purdah' system, the system of child marriage and the general indifference of parents to the education of their daughters became a hindrance to the progress of female education. A girl child was believed to be much different from that of a boy child as far as her education was concerned. Girls were not required to be independent of their established customs and domestic duties. Her general appearance was the main criteria in being selected as a bride. The desire to get their boys educated was openly expressed, whereas girls were good if they stayed at home. There was a rigid seclusion of women and it prevented the girls from having even the fundamental rights to elementary education

In such a given situation, the JMs invited their collaborators, students, parents, and benefactors to work as a team for the realization of the challenging vision of a new India. At the time of the French Revolution, Claudine set up schools through which she and her religious Sisters cared for homeless orphans giving them a trade by which they could earn a living. Following her footsteps, even today, the JM educational institutions continue to be a beacon at the testing times of India's struggle for peace and economic equality.

'The Kothari Education Commission Report (1964-66)' stresses the need for education to be related to the life and needs of the people. This is not a new idea for JM institutions. Claudine was well aware of this dire need in her time, long before the Education Commission was appointed. More than a century ago, she believed in training the girls under her care to be well prepared citizens for the future. They were trained in skills which would make them self-supporting, independent, and honest human beings.

It is true that the destiny of a nation is shaped in the classroom. The classrooms of our schools have girl children mostly of the age from four onwards till the university level in some cases. Claudine, like any other self-respecting educationist of today, was very sure of this fact. She even seemed to have foreseen the UNESCO's dictum even before its origin: "If we educate a boy, we educate a man, and if we educate a girl, we educate a family, and in consequence, a nation (Pal, "Women's Education"7). Education is one of the powerful instruments of change and development. We should see that the girls and the rural masses should get that education.

As women are responsible for fostering well-being at homes, education for women is essential to increase global prosperity and integration. In the 12th century AD, the renowned Arab philosopher Ibn Rushd declared, "A society which enslaves its women, is a society doomed to decay" (quoted. in Annan, "Best Defence"23). Almost eight hundred years later, Claudine proved this statement true that a society which empowers its women is a society sure to succeed. In classrooms we have children at the most formative stage of their lives. It is there that we either make or mar the future citizens of a country like India. We have the children's soft and yielding hearts in our hands, and the imprints we leave on them will never be effaced. Therefore, it is indispensable that we educators draw the best out of each child and lay the foundations of the uniqueness of each individual created in God's own likeness and image. Similarly, even great leaders like Napoleon emphasised the significance of women's education. He asserted: "Give me an educated mother, I shall promise you the birth of civilized society and educated nation" (qtd. in Mali 26).

Emphasis on women's education was made first by Catholic visionaries in British India. In North India, education for women began in the first half of the nineteenth century. In the postcolonial India, the idea of women's education had become explicit in government reports. In 1964 the Kothari Commission recommended a national system of education which would be a powerful instrument for the creation of a democratic, secular, and egalitarian society. This educational system would be a catalyst to eliminate the evils of poverty, ignorance, and ill-health through the use of scientific and technical knowledge. And it would bring out total development of the whole personality of each citizen. Jesus and Mary Educational institutions consider the holistic development of the individual. It covers all matters that concern the body, mind, and soul of the learner. In order to be authentic, the education must be complete and integral.

The Kothari Commission is our special guide in the field of economic self-sufficiency. Training in manual work, technical skills and home science help our girls to be self-supporting in the India of today. In JM institutions here in India, there are provisions to safeguard the interest of the intelligent among the poor, offering them an adequate number of scholarships and grants to facilitate their studies and to ensure principles of social justice and equality. Claudine's work is being continued in the same spirit up to this present moment. In fact, the institutions have a huge task of preparing pupils to adjust themselves to the great challenges and new patterns in a constantly changing world. They have been taught to respect authority at all levels, to accept failure and defeat with serenity and courage, to be well balanced even in the absence of parental love and companionship. It equips them to withstand infidelity within their family circles, to face their various disadvantages with a staunch determination. This will help them to avoid committing the same errors in their own lives, and to be good women and wives and builders of a happy tomorrow. It brings into focus the same points stressed by Claudine in her objective regarding education.

The Jesus and Mary Congregation has understood the fact that intellectual training alone will not produce an integral human being. They teach their wards in their institutions to move from self-orientation to service orientation. His Holiness Pope Pius XI wrote: "The supreme importance of Christian education, not merely for each individual but for families and for the whole human society, whose perfection comes from the perfection of elements that composed it" (quoted. in Gibbon 39).

The JM Schools and colleges are fertile grounds to create men and women for others. Accordingly, the JM educational policy moved from the elite to the option for the poor. The prophetic nature of the JM educational apostolate blossoms for them in the preferential option for the poor and the marginalized. In their institutions JM Sisters give twenty percent admissions for the marginalized section of the society.

In fact, the whole tone of JM schools is directed towards making pupils' true sons and daughters of the Republic of India. They should be loyal, worthy citizens of our motherland. Every effort is made to equip these young people, spiritually, morally, culturally, physically, and intellectually competent, so that they may take their place as future citizens of this country in the process of ongoing progress. India being rich with its various cultures and religions, we are religious and open-minded people. It is sad to see that we seem to be becoming poorer in the spiritual realms while the economic fields are advancing so rapidly. It is because we have somewhere lost sight of our high spiritual heritage and the lofty values that had made India so great.

The students in JM educational institutions, with the true spirit of this valiant Founder, are encouraged and given every opportunity to develop fully according to their own spiritual values and culture. They are taught to rise over the mediocrity and to raise the benchmark in their chosen fields. The fact remains that the knowledge of both Indian and foreign cultures, vital in acquiring the spirit of universal brotherhood and international peace and co-operation, is given equal importance in the JM institutions. Claudine and her companions believed that among the various means for the promotion of education, the school and home excel all others. It is in their own homes that the children learn the first lessons of their future education. So, the homes are the most natural and most fertile soil for education of our kids. Numerous and manifold are the things which exercise influence on children in a good home. The love and warmth of the parental care, discipline and nurturing of good habits are some of them.

A good and Christian education the students receive in their early childhood at the JM schools will prove their greatest safeguard in all respects. From a moral and educational point of view, all that is required for the training of the mind and heart is an early education based on a sound value system. As first fruit of a good school training, a daughter ought to return to her home as a help to her mother. A girl whose high-minded principles are her protection in the world, and it earns for her that respect which is highest homage rendered to womanhood.

JM Sisters believed that the school develops, unifies, and enriches the personality of the young by an education which is attentive to the formation of each individual, open to the world through the gospel of love. The direct source of all education is God, the supreme educator of the world. The JM Sisters draw inspiration and wisdom through St Claudine who drank deeply from this Eternal Fountain. Our work as Christians and religious educators will be only fruitful to that degree in which we are true followers of Christ. It is a pedagogical principle that one cannot give what one does not have.

The moral care of the people of other faiths or no faith at all under our tutelage is our primary concern too. The knowledge of the comparative religions in India and in the world will help our students to respect and understand one another, and thus attain that unity in diversity, for which our country has always striven right from the beginning. The spirit of charity, justice, truth, equality, and universal brotherhood that prevails in our schools is a visible sign that apt care is taken in moulding the characters of our students towards inter-religious harmony. In their moral education classes, they impart the value of respect for every individual and the lesson that one has the right to follow his own conscience. In this way, keeping in tune with the pedagogy of Claudine Thevenet, they prepare their students for harmonious living in a pluralistic society like India.

Claudine's Vision for Inclusive Education

According to the congregational documents, the aspirations, maxims, and the example of the Founder resulted in the creation of a unique spirit and an ideal educational system. This ideal embodies the following: a true family spirit, a deep spirit of faith, an intuitive understanding of the actual needs of students and a formation based on the whole integrated person. It is this heritage the JM Sisters have inherited from Claudine.

In their philosophy of education, as Claudine realized, JM Sisters believe that the education of a child is basically an education of love expressed in loving relationships in a peaceful harmonious family atmosphere. In practice, this meant that teachers and students are related to each other in a warm and caring way. The past pupils of our schools share the stories of Sisters' caring for the general welfare of each student as well as for their academic progress. The quality of relationship in a school community is a significant factor in determining the quality of the education in that school.

Education in faith, a top priority cherished by Claudine, was integrated into the harmonious development of the young girls. She understood and duly noted that the young grow with a sense of personal worth and feel themselves loved when living together in a harmonious social group. She insisted their development to be surrounded by a family spirit of love and security. She realized the need to prepare them thoroughly for the world of work, so as to enable them to face the future realities with faith, hope and confidence.

They should respond to a methodology which is characterized by love and patience. Teachers who guide them individually and progressively should consider their particular gifts, talents, and circumstances. The support and guidance, if given at the opportune time, can help forestall and prevent mistakes. Claudine's pedagogy was one of love and prevention. The work of education in preventive love still remains the best form we can offer. Her method of imparting education was simple: "Prevent faults," Claudine would say, "and direct them away from faults by vigilance, so that you will not have to punish them. The best leader is not the one who punishes, but the one who knows how to prevent the greatest number of mistakes" (Antonio and Paloma 42).

Claudine recommended teachers to refrain from all partiality, and only allow preferences to be shown to those who most needed their help. Claudine's maxim was that teachers should be real mothers to the children, who highlighted the family spirit of the school where students felt really secure and cared for by their teachers. The religious development of the students was the first priority in the school. In every lecture or course, the moral and spiritual values are given to children. The education of the young in spiritual values was a ministry that had priority in all the works of Claudine Thevenet. This philosophy still continues in the JM system of education. In order to foster a mature growth in spiritual values the young students are expected to be helped to relate personally to God through moments of prayer and reflection on their daily lives. They should express concern and compassion for the marginalized and the poor. They should be able to develop a critical sense based on true spiritual and moral values in order to grow with a sense of social responsibility, and to make decisions based on true moral values. They also should be trained to discern a course of action for the improvement of their spiritual well-being.

The JM educational vision and philosophy also demand the active and trusting participation of the young in their own development with a sense of responsibility. Claudine preferred to prevent mistakes by offering guidance and support at the appropriate moment beforehand. Yet she understood that mistakes were inevitable and believed they could be used as the basis for a new start, if teachers combined firmness with love and forgiveness. She believed that in a school, a conducive climate for learning supported by good organization promotes security and respect for others. Teachers, pupils, and parents became active promoters of a disciplined way of life as they co-operate in implementing the agreed code of discipline. In their own way, pupils become leaders and educators of the future.

From all teachers, both religious and secular, Claudine demanded foresight and thoroughness in carrying out their duties in the education of children. She wanted a uniform method of teaching, and an active supervision which would not, however, be burdensome. "It was", Claudine said, "the surest and most advantageous way of maintaining order, doing good, and making the children happy and well disciplined" (Barrel and Carlos 629-630). Since the social milieu of young people has greatly changed, there is certainly room for reflecting on the need for a preventive pedagogy adapted to our times.

The history of the Congregation emphasizes the attention given to each child. According to the testimony of the old Sisters, "the good mother Claudine always kept for herself the privilege of attending to a new arrival's urgent needs" (Barrel and Carlos 574). She visited each workshop giving goodies to the well-behaved, encouraging the workers, and gently reprimanding them when necessary. She never left without having received from them the promise and assurance that they would make greater efforts to be obedient and well-behaved.

Interestingly, the organization of the workshop at the Providence taught and permitted the children to put aside a certain sum of money earned from their own work, thus forming a helping-hand for their future. It helped them to develop the capacities of each one. At the same time, not even a few left the organization without the supply of a trousseau prepared by their own hands. This continued, even after the pupils left. Claudine wrote, "When the children of the providence finished their apprenticeship and if their continued presence was not a burden, they could be kept on definitively in the house. The departure of the pupils was always arranged as to ensure them a place where they would be spiritually and physically secure" (*Minutes of the RJM General Council,* 1823).

St Claudine insisted that there should be certain amount of collaboration of Sisters in their own formation and that of children. They should be given training in supporting the institution. It should help them to build understanding and trust among themselves (*Community*

Report 31, July 1820). Right from the foundation of the Congregation of JM, they had the desire to form women capable of running a house well. They gave importance to manual work without neglecting the intellectual formation that a young girl needed at the precise moment in history and in those concrete circumstances.

Education, Discipline and Order

The education and the training they imparted consists in doing what one has to do at the right time and in the right place, to foresee everything, put everything in the right place. This helped them to concern oneself only with one's own employment, to arrange everything so well that no one would ever be left without anything to do (*History of the Congregation* 92). And this order will work as an element contributing to peace, as a source of efficiency in work.

Claudine spoke about the simplicity in relationship of the staff with the children. She insisted that nothing sophisticated, nothing which could create a distant attitude between the children and their teachers should happen in their dealings. Little family celebrations, relationships full of cordiality and true charity, contributed to the creation of an atmosphere in which each one felt herself loved and appreciated (*History of the Congregation* 82).

Claudine knew how to stimulate the children. She aroused their enthusiasm for domestic work by means of the extra work, and the result of which became the property of the worker. She instilled in them a spirit of collaboration rather than of competition, thus inviting each one to give her best. This same spirit is found still in the Congregation and its institutions. Thus, in India, the pioneering visionaries adapted the method that they had learnt from Claudine. Providentially, the plan proposed by Mgr. Borghi corresponded exactly with that foreseen by the Foundress for her work:

> Children will be received at the age of about five or six; they will be taught not only the truths of religion, but also to work in order to accustom them to an active life that will enable them to earn their living honestly from the fruit of their labour. They may, in this way, earn some money

> during the period of their education which will be kept for them, and given them when they leave the establishment. Thus, it provides them for their first weeks and forestalls the temptation to return to their superstitions in the event of their finding themselves in a state of misery (Barrel and Carlos 649-650).

It is not necessary to emphasize very much to demonstrate the preference of Claudine for the poor, as instances of this kind are found throughout the history written by her contemporaries. It is evident that their preference was real but was not exclusive, and that her wishes on this matter are precisely set down in Article 3 of the Constitutions. She wrote, “The aim of this Congregation is to give a Christian education to young girls, according to the social position of each one” (Barrel and Carlos 378). The respect and love that she had for each child of God is clearly reflected in this Article. Nevertheless, it is necessary to keep this preference in mind if we wish to understand her thought and live in the spirit of Claudine. This preference is the consequence of her personal experience of the goodness of God, and the attention she gave to the needs of the people around her. It was a question of alleviating every type of poverty by Christian education, but very specially the spiritual poverty of those who did not know God. Work for the poor involved activities to improve the condition of the person in every sphere –spiritual, human, social and intellectual.

A hierarchy of values was well established in the thought of Claudine. It is a hierarchy that we find in the organization of all her educational works. Claudine adapted an educational methodology which helped her in recognizing, identifying, and fostering the unique capabilities of each child. Following the same methodology, the JM institutions train their teachers as well as parents to promote each child’s holistic development in both academic and non-academic activities. So that each and every one of the learners has the ability to select their future learning and further choose their own paths in life according to their varied skills and talents. She gave emphasis on ethics and human values like empathy, love, respect, patience, spirit of service, courtesy, responsibility, scientific temper etc., she also gave importance to creativity and critical thinking to encourage logical decision making and innovation in them. It was part of her educational plan to equip the little ones for life skills such as communication, cooperation, teamwork, and resilience. Today, when we look at our education system we see whatever was envisioned and practiced by Claudine about two centuries back in her educational system is brought as new practices in order to strengthen our education system.

Pedagogy of JM Education

It was from the love for the poor that Claudine decided to put her plan into practice; the one which she had conceived long before in 1821. Accordingly, she had the plan to open a boarding school for the daughters of more wealthy families. She realized that the income from this boarding school would contribute towards maintenance of the orphanage. Every section of children was equally dear to her and she would have willingly sacrificed herself for one, as for the other. She attached great importance to the education of the better class, but it was quite evident to all that her preference was for the weakest and most abandoned (Barrel and Carlos 574). The predilection of all the religious should be "for the poorest, the most miserable, for those who had most faults and the fewest good qualities" (Barrel and Carlos 628). Devotedness towards the intellectually poorest was a duty of each class teacher. Claudine wrote, "The mistress of class or workshops will not neglect the children who, on account of their incapacity or for other reasons, do not respond to their care" (*Rule Book 1843,* 86).

All these show that Claudine had a particular pedagogy of love and it was the most fruitful of the pedagogies. The simplicity of the pedagogical methods of Claudine can be discerned directly to the simplicity of her 'motherly heart'. Her pedagogy, therefore, was preventive because there was a greater delicacy of love in removing the obstacle which could cause a fall, than only to heal the wounds which are caused. Her preventive system consists in making known the rules and regulations of an institute, and then supervising in such a way that the students are always under the vigilant eye of the sisters and the teachers, who like loving mothers will converse with them, act as guides in every event, counsel them and lovingly correct them, which is as much as to say, will put the students into a situation where they cannot do wrong. The practice of this system is all based on the words of St. Paul, "Love is patient, love is kind it bears all things ... hopes all things, endures all things" (1 Cor. 13:4). Love is kind, and patient; it puts up with all things, but hopes all things and endures any disturbance. For this reason, only a Christian can successfully apply the preventive system.

Her pedagogy included attention to each individual. It was a pedagogy of participation and collaboration because only love and sharing of true communication can make a united school-community. It was a pedagogy concerned with practical formation because love is not satisfied with only seeing the necessity. But it wishes to furnish the means to bring a definitive remedy. It was a pedagogy based on simplicity and family spirit. Claudine wrote, "The teachers should be mothers to children, real mothers as much as to their souls as to their bodies" (Barrel and Carlos 628). She highlighted the family spirit of the school where students felt really secure and cared for, by their teachers. It is, however, a question of supernatural love. This love is thus described by Jesus in His command to one of the Jesus and Mary Sisters, Mother St Cecile-de-Rome: "Let the religious and teachers who are employed with the children be real spiritual mothers to them… The teachers should apply themselves to love the souls of their students…" ("A Family Treasure" 19). The moral development of the students was the first priority in the school. Therefore, lectures or courses on moral and spiritual values were given to the children every year.

An essential fruit of a good education is the happiness of the child. Let the children find in their teacher a mother's love, a father's strength. Let them find in their teachers a faithful friend, companion, and a true guide to whom they can go in time of joy and in time of sorrow, to who they are willing to show even their wounds. The gentler sex gifted with those natural talents and qualifications in an eminent degree which make women such excellent educators. There are many great and good men who have ascribed their brilliant actions or their success in life to the good aspects instilled into them on their mother's knee. Therefore, the old saying proves to be right: "Of ten great men, nine owe to their mother what they are" (Elise 205). A good mother is a priceless treasure. Happy is the child on whom God has bestowed such blessing. The mother is everything to the future man and woman. Let her continue to be the best friend to whom the child confides everything of whom the child can ask advice in every difficulty (Elise 206). At the end of her study the student will have the greatest respect for the teacher and will go on recalling with pleasure the orientation she was given, always considering her teachers and the other religious sisters as mothers and friends. Wherever they go, these students are generally the solace of their families, useful citizens, and blessings to their society. Regarding the ends of education, Claudine would have agreed with Jacques Maritain (1882-1973) who held that the end of education is the 'shaping' of 'dignified man', the fulfillment of his personality and individuality. Claudine would also agree with Maritain's view of education as a 'human awakening', a liberation of man through knowledge, wisdom, good will, and love.

Commitment to a Noble Mission

The educational community which integrates teaching and non-teaching staff, parents, and pupils, is the unifying force that brings all educational achievements to life. Consequently, the educative community undertakes to live out within itself the values it seeks to transmit, so that its work and its presence become credible to society. It expects the Sisters of JM to maintain the spiritual identity of the school within the charism of St Claudine Thevenet. Claudine belonged to a generation of people who actively struggled for the realization of the hope they entertained, namely the improvement of their society. The harrowing experience of the French Revolution did not deter her from doing good to people around her. When the storm of the revolution had subsided, Claudine and her companions dedicated their lives to the service of humanity and to the religious ideals formulated by Christ.

They chose the education of the young as the most efficacious means to achieve this end. The exigencies of their life situation lent itself to such a venture. Education for the masses was not prevalent, least of all for women in their time. The circumstances of that time demanded a shared enlightenment among the people and the universalization of education for the benefit of all. Claudine assured that only the educated could battle against superstition, social evils, and blind attachment to the past. She looked up on each man, woman, and child separately as a person invested with dignity.

Claudine believed that knowledge was important and necessary to enhance the fate of humanity. It will alleviate their suffering in so many ways. She knew for certain that education is quite simply an investment that yields a higher profit than any other form of investment. It is what makes possible the development of entire communities, countries, continents, peoples, and civilizations. It is the most effective form of preparing one for life's realities. Naturally, one might ask the reason for the denial of opportunity for self-improvement to so many millions of girls in different parts of the world. In 2000 AD, the UN Secretary General Kofi Annan, while speaking about women, children and human rights, said: "In many societies women are systematically marginalized, and yet when catastrophe strikes - whether it is in the form of illness, conflict or hardship - they bear the biggest burden of all" ("Best Defence" 23). Nothing illustrates this more amply than the impact of HIV/AIDS. Girls are most likely the ones to care for the sick in the family and to help to manage the household. Prevented from going to school, they are denied of the right to protect themselves against the virus. Deprived of proper education, they risk being forced into early sexual relationships with older men or earning a living as a prostitute, and thereby becoming infected. They pay the deadly price many times over, when denied a precious fundamental human right (Annan, "Best Defence" 23).

Claudine's vision was for all ages. She and her followers knew well that educating girls is not anymore, an option, but a sheer necessity.

For her, no other policy is likely to raise economic productivity, lower infant, and maternal mortality, improve nation and promote health. It increases the chances of education for the next generation. So, she was of the conviction that we have to invest in women and the girl child. What Claudine proved right almost two centuries ago, is now studied and experimented by many modern universities and research scholars. For example, one of the studies at Yale University a few years ago showed that the height and weight of newborn children of women with a basic education were consistently higher than those of babies born to uneducated women. A UNESCO project demonstrated that giving women just a primary school education decreases the child mortality rate (Kofi Annan, "Two-word Mantra" 52).

Claudine and her Sisters considered it worthwhile to dedicate their whole lives towards this noble cause. The Sisters knew that it required great sacrifice to realize this ideal. Claudine was ready to be the grain of wheat that had to die to produce a rich harvest, for she believed what Christ said so emphatically: "Truly, truly I say to you, unless a grain of wheat falls into the earth and dies, it remains alone but if it dies, it bears much fruit"(John 12:24). In their vision and philosophy of education, the JM Sisters were very particular that the love of Christ and the fellow being should imply that they should be educators with joy and hope. They are entrusted with the task to build a responsible community of staff, students, and parents. They should be guided by love, compassion and forgiveness as lived out in the life of Claudine who followed the model of Jesus, as her teacher.

Claudine and her Sisters realized that women, especially young girls, could be helped to obtain employment only through education. To prevent these young ladies from being exploited, she educated them, equipping them well with academic knowledge of reading, writing, and arithmetic. With these and the other skills, they would be able to cope with the hard times ahead prevailing in their society. A burning zealous charity placed Claudine at the service of the young girls. She showed great respect and affection for all her girls. She realized that education is not just the communication of academic knowledge from teacher to student, but the development of a whole person. Claudine wrote: 'We should assist girls in the discovery of their identity. Work with all possible means towards their authentic development and make them aware of the importance of the mission of woman, unique and irreplaceable, in the building up of a family, society and the nation at large '(Barrel and Carlos 248).

So, the Sisters of the JM carry on the work of their Foundress in preparing the young to face the challenges of today's world, and also making them strong and confident to face the future. Accordingly, they made sure that their education system should make an individual better suited to the needs of the ever-changing dynamic world. The changes in the educational system should also reduce the social gaps by enabling proper recognition to whatever extent one is able to pursue or acquire a skill. This demands a sound academic, moral, physical, and religious formation, and it is the greatest legacy that Claudine had left behind for generations to come.

Today, even in the 21st century, women in general are marginalized and looked down upon. They are denied of their basic rights. So, in this rapidly changing world, the daughters of Claudine have a greater responsibility and a higher vocation to shape a new world in and through their classrooms of JM educational institutions. According to the United Nations Population Report, at least a woman in every three has been beaten, coerced into sex relationships or abused during her lifetime. Increasingly gender-based violence is being recognized as a violation of human rights and a major world-wide public health concern (Dharchaudhuri 1).

The World Bank Report says that violence against girls and women throughout the world causes more death and disabilities among women than cancer, malaria, traffic accidents and even war or any other cause (Dharchaudhuri, "A Fair Career"1). Continuing the same vein of thought one of the UN articles highlights: "The simple most important thing that can be done to improve the world in general is this: educate its girls. It really is that simple. There is no other action proven that can do more for the human race than the education of the girl child" (Kofi Annan, "Two-word Mantra"4). This will certainly have its repercussions on humanity as a whole. However, in order to develop and raise their level of aspiration, adequate educational opportunities are to be provided so that they get motivated to participate, support and also ultimately learn to initiate their own programmes of development.

Scholarly studies and research projects have established what common sense indicates. If you educate a man, you educate an individual, but if you educate a woman, you educate a family and a nation. The evidence is striking. Increasing the provision for schooling of mothers has an immeasurable impact on the health of their children and on the child's adult productivity later on. The children of educated mothers consistently out-perform children with educated fathers and illiterate mothers. It is so clear and meaningful in the famous saying of the social reformer, Mahatma Phule: "If education is given to man, only an individual is educated. If it is given to a woman, the entire family is educated (Mali 44)." A girl who has had more than six years of education is better equipped to seek and use medical and health care advice, to immunize her children, to be aware of sanitary practices from boiling water, to the importance of washing hands and so on. A World Bank Project in Africa recently established that the children of women with just five years of school had a 40% better survival rate than the children of women who had less than five years in class (Pal, "Women's Education" 8).

The society that we build through our education must be a just and humane one, based on mutual understanding and co-operation rather than competition, where people are enlightened and strive for communal harmony. We try to form integral human persons, which mean forming them in their personal, intellectual, religious, and social development. As a result, they are ready to adapt to persons, places, and situations and begin anew again and again according to the changes constantly occurring in their society. Thus, social consciousness is awakened in the staff, students, and parents of our institutions. They are motivated to be responsible wives, mothers, and teachers, animating and effecting changes in society.

JM schools and colleges provide equal opportunities for quality education to all the beneficiaries, especially the poor and the marginalized girl children in their institutes. Being a minority group, our primary concern is not exclusively for the education of the Christians, but our schools are open to all students of all religions and people in every walk of life. The JM education visualizes the formation of mature people who have integrated themselves with God, humanity and nature.

The JM Sisters wish to form women of faith in God, themselves, and others who would live their lives in the light of faith. From the beginning of the Congregation, the study of religion and spiritual values took priority in every establishment. In the programme of education drawn up for the young girls, Claudine wanted religious and moral instruction to have the first place (Barrel and Carlos 578). They also work for women who are capable of acting from motives of faith and hope in the future. The children were given motivation and hope in their study and work. For example, during the time of recreation, the children of the Providence joined the Sisters in the construction of the chapel, realizing that they were helping to build the Lord's house. It gave them more strength for hard work (Barrel and Carlos 471).

They also dedicate their lives for religious and secular women who are faithful to their duties. The same spirit and teaching are found in all along the Congregation. Since the aim of the JM education is to form good human beings, they inspire their pupils as far as possible, with the love of solid virtues. The study of spiritual and moral values has the first place in all their establishments (*Rule Book of 1843,* 119). For instance, in her mystical experience, Dina Belanger, a member of JM Congregation from Canada, claims that Jesus had spoken to her confirming the spiritual and moral values of education, disseminated by Claudine. She said that she heard the voice of Jesus speaking to her in person as follows:

> I want faith and simplicity to be at the base of the education of your pupils. Give them an education which draws them to the Eternal God. Elevate their souls, form them, and make them seek God –that is your mission. Let the study of spiritual values always be given the place of honour. Teach in order to open their souls to light and truth. Work hard, to give them solid convictions. Teach souls to have an ideal. Lead them to God through a truly spiritual education (De Rome 56).

The JM Sisters are committed to make women capable of earning their living by work which enhances their human dignity. Claudine had insisted that the children should have an employment while pursuing education, not in the modern use of the term 'child labour'. For example, she taught them silk weaving with a view to mould their extra-curricular activities and to build their self-esteem. In her establishment's large rooms were chosen for the workshops. Here we see the importance given to hard work as an ennobling factor. At the same time, she gave priority to women who are capable of making happy homes. It emphasizes the actual role of education. In developing countries like India, students have to be educated not only to earn a decent living but also to show concern and care for the deprived strata of the society.

With this vision in mind, the JM Sisters started establishing day schools and residential schools in which they taught and brought up the young, carefully instructing them in religious ethics, moral values, in literature, skill development, and in their social and domestic duties. An elaborate account of different establishments and their function is discussed in a subsequent section. It explores historically the vision of Claudine's inclusive and egalitarian-oriented Christian education to enable them to be competent to face the challenges of contemporary world socially, economically, spiritually, emotionally, and intellectually.

Endnotes

[1] A specific and unique gift she has been to the Church.

[2] The Christian to be the teacher of the world, its leaven, its salt, its light.

[3] The faith in the life, death, and resurrection of Jesus, essential for Christian salvation.

Chapter 4

School Education in North India and Jesus and Mary Institutions

The predominant objective of the JM school education is to revamp the social plight of the children so that they may be able to adapt themselves to live in accordance with different social environments, and societal needs. They can transform themselves and the society in which they live, into an ideal place according to their goals. The human experiences all over the world have shown that true education is the basis of the greatness of any nation. Impelled and inspired by this consciousness, the JM Sisters endeavored all along to establish educational institutions, especially for girls wherever they were invited. They made thoughtful, ruminative, and significant efforts to raise the standards of both secular and religious education by imparting formal training and instruction to develop personality, character, leadership, and professional competence among all their students. The above-mentioned strategy inspired the students to live a meaningful life. This was a historic vision of Claudine Thevenet under whom the JM Congregation began to function efficiently.

The vision of the founder led young people to come closer to God whatever faith they belonged, and to experience joy and satisfaction in their lives. The reflection of Claudine's ideal of education could be seen in the lives of their numerous past and present generations of pupils, teachers, parents, and all people with whom they had personal contact. Therefore, it considers the establishment of the number of educational institutions from their inception to the present, which have become the icons of excellence in terms of the dynamic vision of its Founder. As it focuses on each institution with regard to its origin and struggles in the course of its establishment and progression of its growth, it also highlights the impact of these institutions on women education. It also traces the ordeals faced in the pioneering work of the founding members of each institution as epiphanic moments in the realization of the dream and vision of JM ideals of women education.

The Agra nuns have a small house situated towards the North-East of the present convent property which was donated to the Congregation of JM by Bishop Borghi, O.F.M.[1] Capuchin Vicar Apostolate of the Vicariate of Hindustan-Tibet Mission. The available historical literature tells us that the land on which this bungalow and the other JM institutions on the church compound was once part of an extensive tract of land owned by Akbar, the Great of Mughal Emperor, who was generous to the Jesuits. When Bishop Borghi invited the Sisters of the Congregation of JM to Agra, there was no formal or planned education for women. In fact, it was completely ignored by the members of the then educational department of colonial government. The women, especially the girl children, especially in North India, were oppressed, subjected and repressed a lot usually at the clemency of their fathers, brothers and their husbands. In fact, they were not allowed to express themselves anything on their own including management of their household affairs. For example, when the British arrived in India, the socio-economic life was at its lowest ebb because of the widespread social practices such as child marriage, sati, purdah, gender inequality and so on. Arguably, the women literacy in Indian society was regarded as a source of 'moral danger' since dancing girls only could normally read and write (Kumbhare 98).

It is in this context the arrival of the JM Sisters was a significant event in the history of women's education in North India. At that point of time, no one had heard of or even seen a religious Sister in North India. The Sisters of JM arrived in Agra in 1842, and for sixty years till 1901 no other religious Congregation of women had ventured into this mission of education in this area, till the Franciscan sisters came to Agra in 1901. When the JM Sisters reached Agra, they were welcomed in a royal manner. The whole day the guns boomed at the salute in honour of the nuns. Agra was their first endeavour in the field of education in India. Towards the end of the year 1842 St Mary's Convent School, their first school for the education of young girls, was opened at Agra by Bishop J.A. Borghi, who entrusted it to the care of the Religious Ladies of JM. The house of General Cartwright had been an airy and commodious building and it is the one where the present convent of JM and St. Patrick's School, Agra stands (Vannini 94).

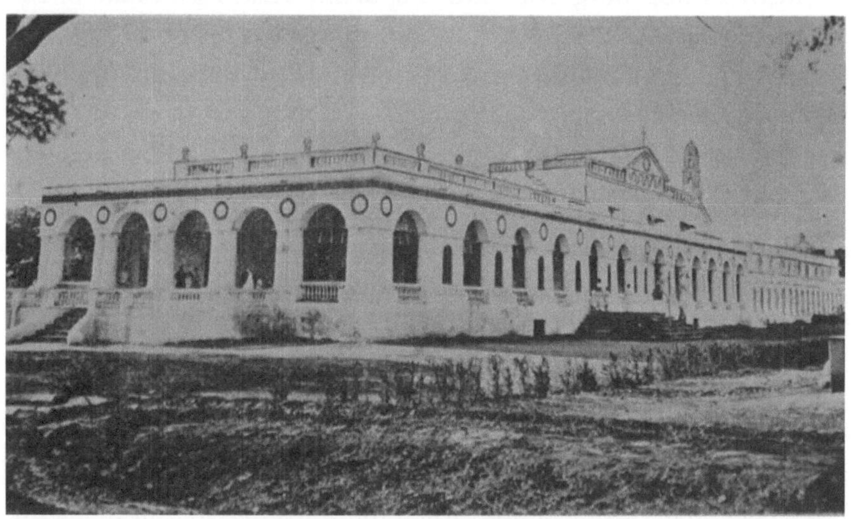

The First JM Convent at Agra 1842

The JM Sisters' educational work at Agra continued to cater to the needs of girls from all sections of the society. Following the establishment of the first ever Convent School, a large number of schools came into being one after another like St. Mary's School, Agra (presently known as St. Patrick's Junior College Agra) in 1842, St. Joseph's School, Agra(1843), St. Anthony School at Numillah (1845), (named later as St. Anthony's

School, Agra in 1902), CJM, Waverly, Mussorie (1845), St. Joseph's School, Sardhana (1848), CJM School, Sialkot (1856), CJM School, Chelsea, Shimla (1864), CJM School, Murree (1876), CJM School, Lahore (1876), CJM School, Dehradoon (1880), CJM School, Ambala (1894), CJM School, Dalhousie (1897), St. Bede's College, Shimla (1904), CJM School, Delhi (1919), CJM School, Hampton Court, Mussoorie (1922), Jesus and Mary College, New Delhi (1968)

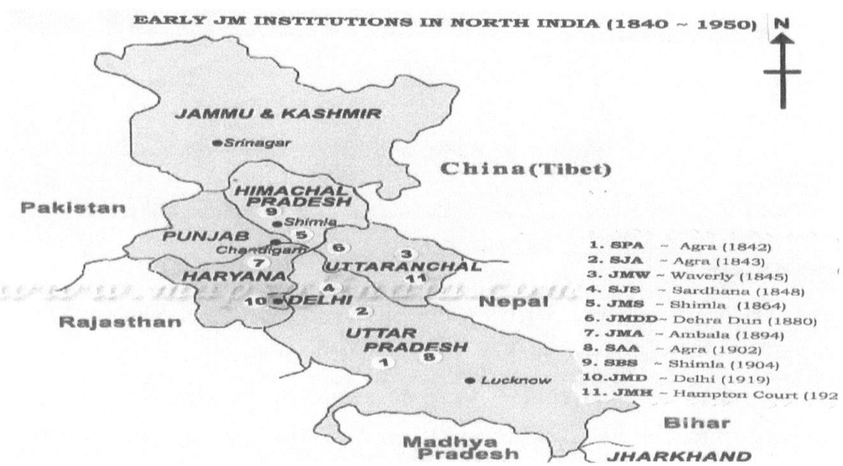

Early JM Institutions in North India

Agra was the first Convent of the Congregation of Jesus and Mary outside of France. The education of girls was the primary concern of the Bishop Borghi and Mother Theresa. In fact, the bishop made the request for educating the young ladies of English and Irish origin 'to form them in virtue, impart knowledge and instruct them in politeness and manners.' Notices had already been sent to the weekly Catholic Newspaper from Calcutta *The Bengal Catholic Herald* [previously known as The Bengal Catholic Expositor] in 1842 informing the general public that a boarding school for girls was to be opened on 1st December, 1842.

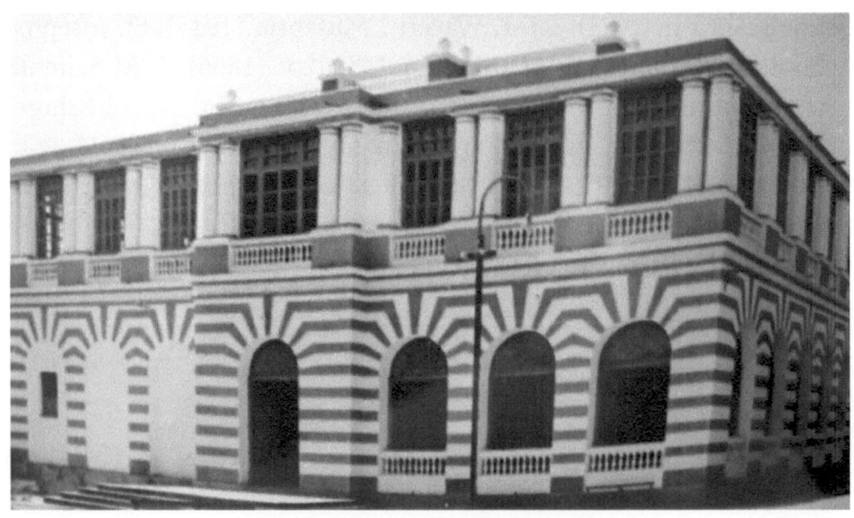

St. Patrick's School, Agra (1842)

At the beginning, the boarding school was known as St Mary's School under which name the Bishop had sent the notices of its opening to the *Bengal Catholic Herald.* And as announced, the school began with twelve pupils. The first Registers of the school, though they were partially destroyed by termites, provide the information that the names of the pupils were the following: Mary Gloriac, two Murphy Sisters, three Eyres Sisters and Maria Rehelani whose father designed the Cathedral of Sardhana (Mitra 9). The instruction in the school was entrusted to Mother Vincent de Paul. Mother Theresa acknowledged the fact that without this Sister the boarding school could not have been opened. The classes consisted of one primary and other three classes where English and French literature and Arithmetic were taught. Music and Drawing were the extra subjects. Parents were quick to realize the benefits the children received, thus the numbers increased. The Sisters who worked in St Mary's School were the first of many devoted, cultured, and enlightened religious who were to follow their vocation to India in the years to come.

In an article entitled "Missionary Institutions in the Agra Mission in the Nineteenth Century" taken from the *Agra Weekly Register*, 3rd

May 1862, in the Archives of Bishop's House Lucknow, reference was made to the nuns of JM and their work in Agra as follows:

> "These were the first of many devoted cultured religious who were to follow their vocation to India in the years to come. Under their care the Boarding school formed young ladies, the European school and orphanage formed soldier's children, St Joseph's School & orphanage formed Indian girls. Literature, music, art, good manners and above all the salutary influence of Catholic education and solid virtue bore fruit among girls of all classes from every part of India. No trial could daunt these valiant women; no work, however repulsive, could come amiss to these devoted souls". (Borghi 4)

Such were the experiences of the first groups of European Jesus and Mary nuns, and the idea of educating Indian women attracted these sisters. The difficulties of a strange and trying climate, diversity of languages, the turmoils of the Revolt of 1857, and the ravages of disease created a series of challenges for these sisters. Large scale troop movements from Bengal to northern India during the revolt was considered to have facilitated the spread of the deadly epidemic cholera in the whole of North India. In the aftermath of the Mutiny, cholera posed a serious threat to the wellbeing of European soldiers on whom the colonial rulers were heavily dependent. Cholera became the preoccupying consideration of the new sanitary commissioners in the1860s.The deadly epidemic gave the nuns an occasion to nurse their pupils, both European and Indian, at the risk of their own lives. In 1861, the great epidemic of cholera, spread all over North India, snatched away many lives. It did not spare the lives of nuns and the orphans as well. The Directors of the boarding school and St Patrick's orphanage died of cholera which ravaged everywhere. Others were struck down by consumption and exposure to excessive heat.

In the second phase of glorious fecundity stretching from 1859-1875 and beyond, the following nuns were its greatest exponents: Mother Xavier, the Provincial, Mother Bruno, Superior of Agra Convent and Mother Perpetua Directress of St Patrick's, Mother Epiphanies Lamure and MechtildeHickie and Mother Lucie associated with St. Patrick's

School, Agra and Assistant Provincial till 1881. As Provincial, Mother Lucie evinced the qualities of a wise and enterprising educationalist till her death, ruling with ability ten convents and schools in Northern India as well as those in Pune and Bombay. The following excerpt taken from the church archives in the possession of the Bishop of Lucknow shows the growth of the mission:

> The work at Agra went on and the schools began to flourish. The convent schools were started in Mussoorie, Sardhana, Shimla, Lahore, Sialkot, Murree, Dehradun, Ambala, Delhi, Hampton Court and elsewhere. The number of European nuns were augmented by local recruits. The traditions handed down by the French nuns are still held in veneration (*Chronicles of Lucknow Cathedral* 12).

The third epoch, from approximately 1875-1927, was marked by certain growth in some educational institutions but also by a gradual decline - the type of education imparted to the pupils in the Agra Convent School. *The Catholic Calendar and Directory for the Archdiocese of Agra* for 1907 lists some of the nuns then engaged in different departments of the establishment. The educational set-up in those years had obvious shortcomings. The frequent and thorough visits of inspectors of schools revealed that there were some traditional methods of teaching with an over emphasis on learning by habitual repetition. Similarly, there was inadequate attention given by the teachers, both religious and secular, to develop in the pupils the habit of independent thinking. The textbooks used were unsuitable, for they were compiled for students in western environments. A few of the school buildings also left much to be repaired, and noisy classes were sometimes a hindrance to serious study and progress.

Only a few pupils qualified for the leaving certificate examination. St Aloysius School report of 1901 shows that at the examination held in 1898 one pupil won a scholarship in the high standard. In 1899, three pupils appeared for the middle school examination and two of those were successful. The following year, the two who appeared for high school were successful. The majority of the students passed out of school with primary education. Nevertheless, these shortcomings were counterbalanced by much that was commendable and, in all departments, especially in music and other artistic achievements in both the boarding school and orphanage.

In fact, due to the natural calamities that occurred in different parts of India necessitated the establishment of orphanages. Due to the severity of droughts, and famines even some of the sisters died of terrible illnesses. A stroll in the compound of St Patrick's JM cemetery gives ample testimony to this fact. The cemetery at Agra in St Patrick's compound was silent but it was an eloquent testimony to these wonderful, dedicated women. Many of them bear the fateful words: "The labourers are dead but their works live even after them" (*The Funeral Records*, Agra 3). No record of their deeds is available except a few in the old archives of Agra Diocese, and St Patrick's archive relates a short story of their good deeds. The rest of them are written in the Book of Life (*The Funeral Records*, Agra 3).

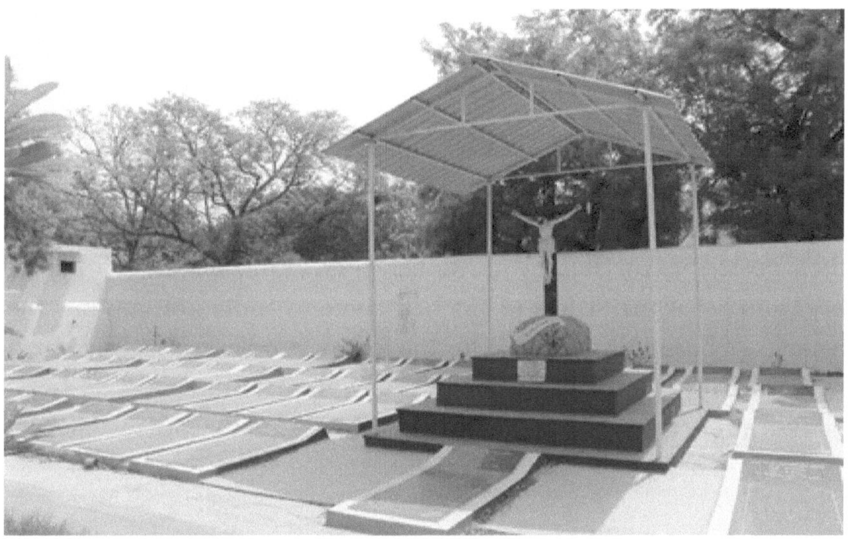

JM cemetry at St. Patrick's, Agra (1842)

The great famine of 1877 allowed a chosen number of people under the aegis of the Relief Committee to extend their devotedness to hundreds of stricken women and children in every stage of starvation. It should be noted that the post-famine period in South India, especially in Madras Presidency in 1870s, further accelerated the numerical strength of converts as the colonial missionaries were able to influence the famine-ridden masses by distributing one measure or two of rice and a coconut(Christhu Doss 23). The Black Plague slew thousands of people and struck terror into the very heart of all, especially the native population of Bombay. The British government sought help of the nuns of JM till nurses could be brought from Europe. The JM Sisters left their teaching and gladly helped the sick and the dying physically and economically (*Gazateers* 1877).

JM institutions in Agra, which were supported partly by subscriptions and partly by the subsistence allowance paid by the government to the soldier's children, have been left without any means since May 1857. Rations too were withdrawn after the first week. To feed the starving children and to pay the servants, they had been obliged to borrow Rs. 5000 from the government. On 21st December 1857, another letter from Bishop Persico was dispatched from the Agra Fort. He was appealing to the government for the relief of pressing wants.

St Joseph's School at Agra was founded on 1st January, 1843 with twenty-four Indian orphan girls. This school catered to the needs of the children of indigent parents who were incapable of supporting their posterities on their own. Mother Theresa made it clear from the beginning that the Sisters of JM had come to India not only for the benefits of Europeans, but also for the Indian people, especially women whose children needed education. At any moment there was no sense of discrimination between the British children and the Indian children.

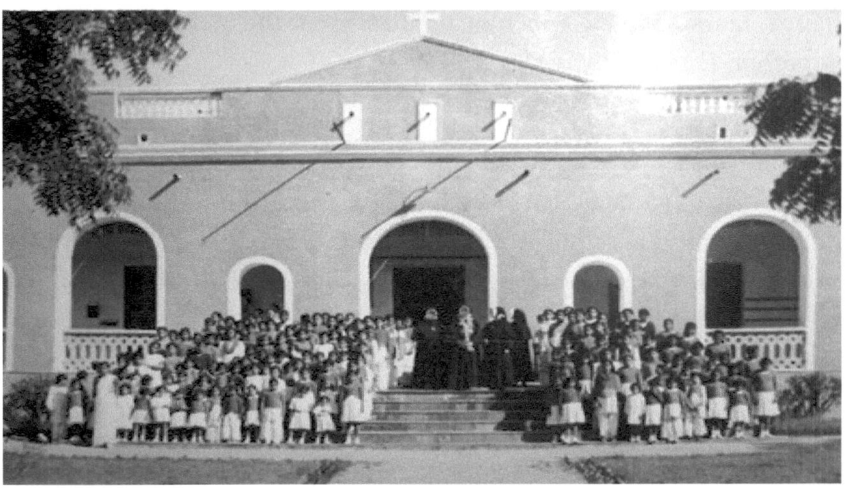

St Joseph's School, Agra

Over a period of time, the number of orphans both Indians and Europeans at St Joseph's orphanage increased considerably. It started as a vernacular cum industrial school. The orphans learnt weaving, spinning, basket making and carpet making. They also learnt to make paper flowers, dusters, tapes, and various garments. This was a good source of income for the students during this period. The school received the greatest encouragement and help from the industrial authorities. St Joseph's was the only school which was allowed to run industrial school parallel to the academic school. The aim of this school is to impart academic, moral, and physical education to the children. Along with that they are meant to train them in social virtues, especially respect and reverence to the elders, parents, and authorities in all circumstances, and to inculcate in them godliness and a sense of justice, truth and love.

The pioneer up-hill works of the Directresses and Sisters for over a hundred years are shrouded in the mist of obscurity because of the Mutiny of 1857. However, there are records that show the details of their work. The report of S.P. Singh's and the Municipal Inspector's visit to St Joseph's School says: "The early history of the school was almost buried in the obscurity but the year 1922, when Revd Mother Bertille took charge, marked a new epoch in the history of the orphanage" (*School Inspection Report*, SJA, 1922).

Mother Theresa noticed the poor people around her, thus decided taking in as many young girls as she could accommodate. Her generous heart was touched at the thought of all these little ones who were victims of all kinds of evils. She entrusted these little girls to Mother St Augustine who really loved them. She was totally dedicated to that work and she supervised both their curriculum and their personal health (Motte, "Correspondence of Mother Theresa" 1843).

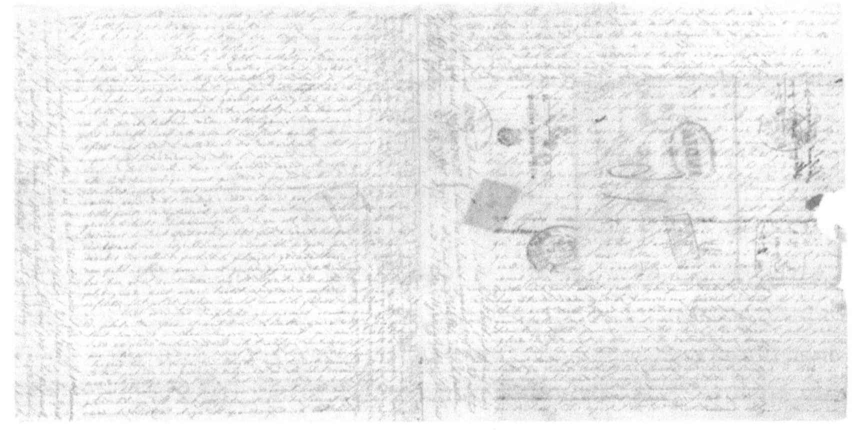

Letter of M.Theresa from India to M.Andrew in France 1843 (File No. II S/2b, Archives CJM Generalite, Rome)

Bishop Borghi already had twenty-two small orphan girls looked after by a kind woman. These were from different parts of North India and were brought to Agra. In November 1842, two little Muslim girls were added to them by Mother Theresa. While St Joseph's building was getting ready, the children were lodged in 'Padre Tola'[2] (Mitra 10). Since the house meant for the orphans was ready by 1st January 1843, they were brought from 'Padre Tola'and housed in the new building of St Joseph's School. These children were given basic education in Urdu, their mother tongue. The script also was in Persian-Arabic script. The spoken language was Hindustani. Apart from learning of skills, most of the time the children were occupied in learning a trade or a profession such as flower-making, home-science, lacemaking, embroideries etc. Mother St Ambrose taught the children the art of flower making. Flower making flourished for a period of time and St Joseph's school earned a name for itself for their beautiful corsages, wedding wreaths and bridal bouquets. The money generated from these skill-based extra-curricular activities was spent meticulously and judiciously for the growth and development of the students as well as the infrastructural development of JM institutions.

From 1843, St Joseph's was a lower primary school having only a few children and a couple of teachers. The routine of school life included an elementary study of the vernacular, arithmetic, and a few other subjects, such as hygiene of which the children could make practical use. A good part of their time was allocated to needle work, plain and fancy flower making and other handicrafts. The sale of which gave a certain steady income to the orphanage. The clouds of discontent and strife resulting from the Mutiny of 1857 appeared over Agra's horizon. From this point of history, the orphaned Indian and the European girls under the care of the JM nuns at St Joseph's orphanage often shared similar harrowing experience. Even from early childhood, they were victims of various famines like Rajputana famine of 1869, Bihar famine of 1873–74, Great Famine of 1876–1878, Indian famine of 1899–1900 and Bengal famine of 1943. After these catastrophes, sometimes the nuns as well as the children were ravaged by different kinds of diseases and death.

In the height of summer 1857, the little ones of St Joseph's orphanage formed one of the groups that slipped out quietly from the convent on a moonlit night, accompanied by Mother Sebastian, the Directress and a nun or two, to join the main party of Catholics fleeing to the security of Akbar's Fort. There they shared the hardships and fears of the bishop, priests, and nuns and of their European companions. When they returned five months later to resume their life on the mission compound, a kind priest built an upper storey to the St Joseph's orphanage building. A large dormitory surrounded by a spacious terrace then afforded roomy accommodation. This was the real joy and relief to Revd Mother

St Bruno, the Superior and to the nuns who were affiliated with the orphanage. This came as a huge relief to this particular orphanage at a time when it had sustained heavy losses due to the depredations during the Indian war of independence. The material losses were calculated and estimated to be Rs. 3320/- for which Bishop Persico and Mother Bruno demanded monetary compensation from the then government officials.

On 4th June 1843, Lord Ellenborough, Governor General of the British possessions in India, came to visit the new JM establishments in Agra. After the visit, His Excellency was impressed with the quality education provided by the JM educational institutions and applauded that he had never expected to witness such an institution of academic excellence in this province of India. He admired the elegance, order and cleanliness that reigned everywhere (Logbook, St Patrick School, 1843). The admission to these institutions increased as a result of the visit of Governor General. And later on, it was reiterated in the Governor General's comments on the work of the first French pioneer Sisters, who were known for their goodness and motherly treatment of the girls. This attracted a great deal of attention of parents who were not willing to send their daughters for education for some reason or the other, now willing to send them to the JM educational institutions.

With the success of these two schools, the authorities approached the Archbishop and the Sisters to begin another school in Numillah, both for boys and girls, as there was no boy's school nearby. It was here that the 30th Irish Regiment was stationed. Numillah, in 1840s, was home to the Irish Catholic soldiers, their wives and children. The girls' morality was in danger, and this became a source of great pastoral anxiety to their parents and to Bishop Borghi. He had evidently confided this concern to Mother Theresa who already thought of a plan to solve the problem. She suggested the opening of a day-school in Numillah where a large number of girls could be taken.

Accepting the invitation, on 1st March 1845 the JM sisters from St Patrick's school started their apostolate among the Irish girls and boys in Numillah along with another school later on known as St Anthony's

School. It was in the house of the military chaplain in the Cantonment area that the school made its humble beginnings. The school with 15 children on its rolls at Numillah, five kilometers away from the first foundation in civil lanes Agra, was the military camp from the time of the British occupation of Agra (Motte, "Correspondence of Mother Theresa" 1845).

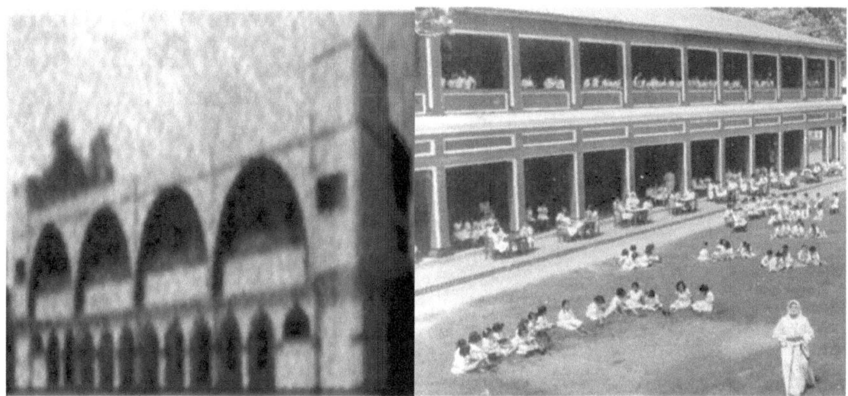

St Anthony's School, Agra

The bishop saw that it was necessary to acquire the property adjacent to the Women's Hospital, not far from the barracks for the school. This property containing a bungalow with large spacious rooms belonged to Mr Upothecard Pool who transferred it to Bishop Borghi on 15th October 1845. Mother Paul went daily to Numillah with a Sister and a postulant. By December 1845, the entire English army moved on towards Lahore. Not much was recorded about the school in Numillah till it re-opened in January 1846 with seventeen pupils. During this time, the work of the Sisters was not restricted to children. It appeared that their mothers too needed spiritual instruction. Mother Paul devoted herself with tireless zeal to her little mission. The children were becoming quite angelic and were a great consolation to her. In 1902, the school shifted its premises to what had been the Alliance Bank (the present Pre-Primary Block), a building on the Mall Road which was more suitable in every way. After a brief period of time its re-opening, it was renamed as St Anthony's Day School.

Seeing that the first Sisters suffering from the unbearable heat in Agra, and as a result being threatened by sickness, namely, cholera and typhoid in the 1800s and so on, the bishop was looking for a property in the Mussoorie hills for his educational associates to avoid practical commutation difficulties. It helped them to continue the educational work in full health and vigour. The convent at Mussoorie was founded in 1845, three years after the arrival of the Religious of JM in India. When the Bishop purchased the fine property, the Waverly Estate, he wished the nuns to have a place where they could recuperate, when necessary, from the heat of Agra. Gradually the two houses on the estate became boarding schools. Also, a school in the hills was evidently a part of the Bishop's plan. In 1844, he had already approached Mother St Andrew, Superior General of the Congregation of JM to send more religious for another foundation for the British families who went up to the Himalayan hills in April and remained there till October.

The climate was ideal and cool all through the year, except intermittent cold and snow in mid winter. Mussoorie, with the adjacent station of Landour, is situated on a series of hills forming the Mussoorie range part of the Himalayas. In this range where a number of 'Goths' or small plateaus were used by the villagers who kept their herds of cattle. Besides having good grass, the animals could be sheltered there during winter and the rainy season. These flat lands attracted a great deal of attention of a good number of enterprising European gentlemen and their families. By 1828, a good number of private houses had sprung up on the Mussoorie slopes. Anxious for the health of his nuns, Bishop Borghi commenced looking around for a property suitable to be adapted as a school, which would have at least two sections and two boarding schools.

His vision began to take shape when he again decided to visit Europe to seek the assistance of the Jesus and Mary Sisters. His presence, his sermons and interesting details of India fanned the flame that was already burning in the hearts of the daughters of Claudine Thevenet. Each one hoped fervently that she should have the happiness of being chosen to share in the mission of the Sisters in India. They prayed earnestly that God would give them the opportunity to offer themselves in the selfless service of humanity in general and quality education in particular.

Eventually, after having deliberations with Bishop Borghi, Mother St Andrew, the General, named those who had been chosen to be sent to India as missionaries. Thus, the sixteen-member team led by Mother St Gonzaga and Mother St Leo got ready for their great educational mission at Agra, India (*Chronicles of CJM Mother House, Rome* 1845). The available records reveal that it was an emotional day and there were mixed feelings all around. The hearts of the Sisters were filled with joy and gratitude. With the fervour of the spirit of St Claudine to inspire them, on 4th October 1845 they boarded the steamship 'Alexander,' leaving their homeland forever for a distant destination (Gonzaga, Letters from Mother Gonzaga, 1845). The co-passengers who accompanied these young missionaries expressed aloud their feelings of admiration and pity. These co-passengers were also sentimental in their expression as these young women who were departing their country were so young and beautiful. They even expressed their discontent saying, "How can they be sacrificed in this way?" (D'Rozario "Missionary Journey" 5). It was Claudine's legacy and zeal for educational mission and their total commitment to Jesus the supreme teacher which gave her admirers the much-needed strength and dedication to fulfill her historic vision. They believed that self was nothing, and God was all in all. They were filled with love for Him, and sacrifice was sought as a special privilege.

The pioneering educational visionaries took eleven months to arrive at Agra, whereas the journey of the second group from France to Agra lasted only three and a half months, from 4th October 1844 to 17th January, 1845. Two months later Mother St Theresa set out with eight religious, to establish a boarding school in Mussoorie, where Bishop Borghi had bought the large estate of Waverly from Baron P. Solaroli, an Italian Count. The Sisters made a difficult journey from Agra to Dehradun in bullock-carts and from Dehradun they had another uncomfortable trip along steep mountain tracks in palanquins. In those days that was the only mode of travel (*The Chronicles of St. Patrick's, Agra* 1845).

Thus 'Waverly' came into existence in 1845, and its formal opening was on 18th September 1845 (*Chronicles CJM, Waverly* 1845). It was the first of the Convent boarding schools on the hills of the North Indian Province. Bishop Borghi had already announced his plans to the newspapers, on his arrival from Europe with these resolute and zealous nuns. *The Bengal Catholic Herald* of 15th February 1845 bears the letter of the Agra correspondent informing the safe arrival of the group. He also spoke about the nuns, and the glowing hope with which they looked forward to the labour that awaited them in the field of education. The Bishop had sent out the prospectus for the new convent and the school, which *The Bengal Catholic Herald* proceeded to publish in its issue of Saturday 22nd March 1845.

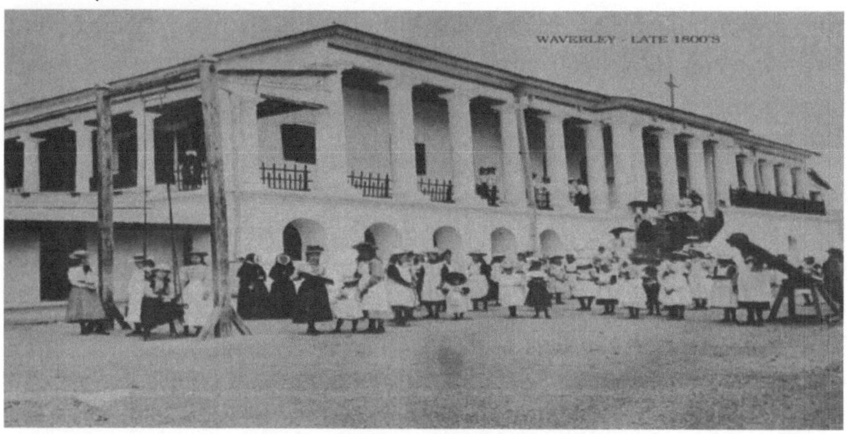

Jesus and Mary School, Waverly

Instructions in reading, writing, arithmetic, English grammar, geography, ancient and modern history, elements of natural philosophy and geometry were given to the pupils. Embroidery and every other kind of needlework were also taught with a fee of Rs. 36 per month. The above charge includes the money used for bed sheets, mattresses, other furniture, medical attendance, washing, use of books and stationery. The application for the admission of pupils was to be made to the Lady

Superior of the establishment or to Rt. Rev. Dr. Borghi, Bishop of Agra (Chronicles CJM, Waverly 1845).

There were three houses on the Waverly estate: Waverley, Belmont, and Thistle Bank. Waverley, the largest became a first-class boarding school chiefly for the daughters of officers; Belmont was run as a second-class boarding school for a short while and then became the junior school. Thistle Bank was, and still, is the Chaplain's residence. Fr Jean Marie de Brione, a man of great merit who had been in India for many years, was the chaplain. The first Superior and Principal was Mother Gonzaga. By June there were seven pupils on the roll, and some day-scholars also came to take drawing and music lessons.

Eight religious, all young, all used to the good things of life, arrived in that house which now is so splendid, but which then was nothing but a simple little middle-class house in 1845 (*Chronicles of CJM, Waverly* 1845). They came to a beautiful sight in the mountains, but as to a house there was literally nothing. It was absolutely empty. There was not even a chair or a bed or even a vessel to prepare their food. They tried to sleep like true missionaries of the Lord in a large carpet which had been lent to them. At least for two years they had very few pupils. They had barely any resources even to live on. The endurance, the passion, a strong spirit of poverty and dedication kept these religious lively and supported them during this dire testing period. They worked hard and waited for the blessed hour when God would provide for their needs. Bishop Michael Angelo Jacopi with genuine concern wrote to his fellow priests, "Send something to our Sisters because they are hungry" ("Correspondence Bishop Michael Angelo" 1846).

The Bishop, himself being poor, could not come to their aid but the good Mother Theresa worked all day, encouraging the young community that passed this time of trial very joyfully. The venerable Mother did not leave them until she had seen the end of these adversities and sufferings. This is how the work of God always began (Cuthbert, *Echoes of a Century* 52). The Sisters with their zeal and dedication made 'Waverly' a great institution, where the students acquired not only academic excellence but sound moral values. It really made the 'Waverlites' as they are called, stand out among the crowds as balanced personalities. The dream of the pioneers to impart a sound education based on the ideals of Mother Foundress continues to be fulfilled by succeeding generations of devoted Sisters, committed staff and dedicated students.

In 1848, Bishop Carli, who had succeeded Bishop Borghi, was filled with pity for the widows of the soldiers and the destitute after the death of their husbands. The Indian society then rejected the plight of the widows completely and remained unconcerned about their needs. Once widowed in India; twice scorned. To be a Hindu widow in the 1800s, at least a poor one, according to Uma Chakravarty, a sociologist at Delhi University, is still to suffer "social death." Appealing to the Press Bishop Carli expressed:

> She, the widow, must either marry again, or go forth into a cold and heartless world; there is no honest or honourable calling, which she could follow to learn a decent livelihood.... Therefore, in order to secure for these poor widows an asylum, where they will be sheltered from the machinations of the wicked...I would propose to open an asylum at Sardhana (which belonged to the Archdiocese of Agra) under the direction of a few of the nuns from the Agra Convent (Carli, "Women in the Society" 6).

He then appealed to the charity of the public in his letter to *The Examiner*, the Catholic weekly published in Bombay, in order to carry out his project.

Sardhana is the third Convent in India by the Sisters of JM. The Sisters were called here to look after the orphans and the children who were introduced to reading, writing and arithmetic, along with needle work, embroidery, flower making and tailoring. The little town of Sardhana lies 23 kms from the city of Meerut, amid green and golden fields, presenting a landscape of peace and serenity. Walter Reinhardt, an adventurer from Treves, Luxenbourg, came to India as a soldier in the army of the French East India Company. After the fall of Chandennagore, he was employed by the Nawab of Bengal Mir Kazim, whose army he trained in warfare and fought against the British in the Battle of Plassey in 1757. As the East India Company sought his life, Reinhardt fled to the North West, where he formed and disciplined his own army, hiring it out to the neighbouring princes as mercenaries.

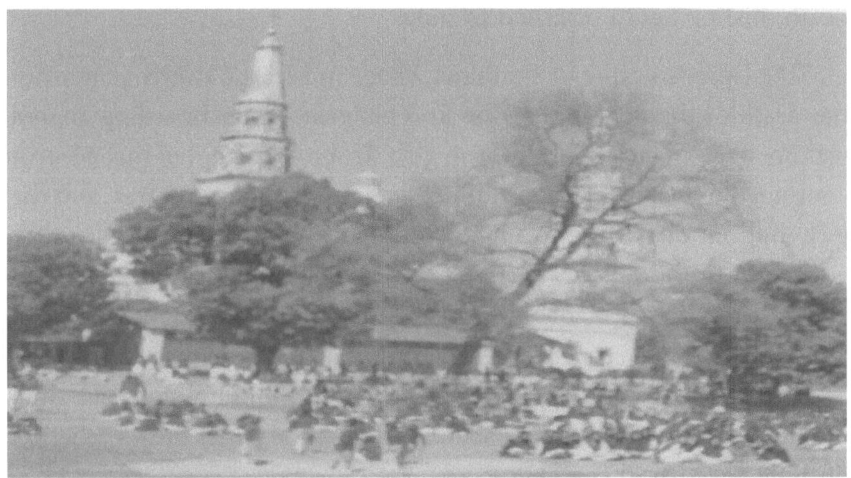

St Joseph's Inter-College Sardhana, Meerut

Shah Alam II, the Mughal Emperor of Delhi, took him into his service and as a reward for his invaluable services assigned him the 'Jagir'of Sardhana. This was the origin of present day Sardhana which is famous and well-known as a center of Christianity in North India. He married a Muslim girl named Farzana according to the Muslim rite, and she was known as Begum Sumru. Three years after her husband's death on 17th May 1781, Fr Gregory of the Presentation, the last Carmelite priest, baptized her in Agra in the historical Church built by Akbar (Keegan 73). She took the name of Joanna and she was a fervent Catholic in the rest of her life. Her later years were spent in using her God-given administrative talents to the administration of her own lands, the uplift of her people, and building worthy temples to Christian worship.

She ordered the building of the church in Sardhana in 1809, which was opened for divine worship in 1822.When the Cathedral was opened, she had written to Rome to have a Bishop, since Sardhana did not then belong to the Agra mission (Keegan 16).The Begum's long reign finally came to an end in 1836. Before her death she received the last rites of the Church from Julius Scotti, the Bishop of Sardhana. After the Begum's death, Bishop Scotti returned to Italy.

The JM nuns came to Sardhana village in Meerut, twelve years after the death of the Begum. For the first ten years, their Boarding School was opened only for the European girls. It should be noted that Meerut continued to be one of the prominent colonial military centres, and the girl children of the European soldiers had the exclusive privilege for education in the school. The work in the field of education increased and it demanded more qualified people to come and continue the work started by the six French nuns in Agra. So, at the request of Mother Theresa and Revd Carli, the Bishop of Agra, more missionaries were sent to India. Ecclesiastically, Sardhana then came under the jurisdiction of the Agra Mission.

Mother General St Pothin in Lyons, being informed of the Indian situation, Bishop Carli's appeal to Mother Theresa did not receive a deaf ear. Being alive to the signs of the times, ready to alleviate pain and suffering, she gave three nuns to the Sardhana Mission. These were Mother St Gonzaga, Mother St Chrysostom, and Mother St Macaire. From the information, one may presume that the presence of the JM Sisters in Sardhana coincided with the setting up of a Widow's Home in 1848. The JM Generalate archives in Rome appear to confirm this fact. However, the foundation that Mother Theresa planned in 1850 was a boarding school for European girls in Sardhana. It was not meant for Meerut, since Meerut, a well-populated cantonment station, was not far off from the military base (Motte, "Theresa's Letter to Mother House in France" 1850).

Mother Theresa' Letter, dated 24 September, 1850
(File No. II S/2b, Archives CJM Generalite, Rome)

During her lifetime, the Begum had rooms built at the back of the Cathedral as a residence for the chaplain. Bishop Julius Scotti, the first and the last Bishop of Sardhana, had lived there. After her death in 1836, all her land and property came under the jurisdiction of the Agra Archdiocese. They were converted into a Convent when the first religious Sisters of JM arrived from Agra. Fr Michael Angelo Jacopi, the Chaplain, made several additions to this building in order to function it as dormitories, classrooms, refectory and so on for the students and nuns. These are the rooms, which, despite many vicissitudes, the JM nuns still occupy today.

Begum had left funds for the Catholic Mission and the school for boys and girls. Since the value of the money had come down, the Congregation was responsible for the upkeep of the establishment. The houses of the Indian Province contributed according to their means, and with the assistance of a small government grant they could develop and improve the school considerably. The rooms at the back of the

Church, once the residence of the Chaplain and the Bishop Julius Scotti, were converted into a JM Convent school and widow's home in1848. Gradually, the nuns, their students and the widows started living permanently in those rooms.

In the new foundation of the building in 1850 they attached an orphanage for European and Eurasian girls. Mother St Louis Gonzaga, who pioneered this foundation, wrote to Lyons in 1851 saying that though there were only twenty pupils, they had two divisions for each class. It is certain that there was an orphanage. (Gonzaga, "Mother Gonzaga's letter to Mother General in France" 1851). Mother Gonzaga, the Foundress of Sardhana Convent, was one of the members in the second group of self-sacrificing nuns who crossed the deep seas to work in India for the cause of women education. The same spirit lives on in Sardhana even today. The history shows that a large number of missionaries who left Europe to serve India in the early 1840s included sixteen Jesus and Mary nuns for the Agra Diocese mission. They arrived in India in November 1844 and were shown every attention by the Governor of Bombay on their arrival there, and provided with camp equipage for their nearly 2000 miles overland journey to Agra. The boarding school was still in its infancy when another request came to the nuns of Jesus and Mary at Agra from Mgr. Carli who opened an orphanage at Sardhana. Keegan, in his *Sardhana and its Begum,* notes that the nuns of Jesus and Mary established an orphanage in Sardhana especially for Hindus in 1850-1851, for there were a few Christians. The Education Department of the British Government had offered to raise it to a High School proper, a status much coveted by the other Middle Schools in the district. According to an Inspection Report of 8th February 1886, the school had about 100 girls. There were three departments (*School Inspection Report, St. Joseph's School Sardhana* 1886).

The first Catholic School in the Punjab was the Convent of Jesus and Mary, Sialkot, which was opened at the request of the Archbishop of Agra, Mgr. Michael Angelo Jacopi. Observing the need for a good educational establishment for young girls, he informed the Provincial

Superior of the Convent at Agra of his desires, and invited her to open a foundation in Sialkot and extend the good works of the Congregation of JM already established in the United Province of Oudh and Agra (Vannini, Hindustan Tibet Mission 43). At that time, Pakistan did not exist, it was a part of great Hindusthan - Tibet Mission. So, the Sisters at the urgent request of the new Bishop of Agra Mgr. Angelo Jacopi, opened their next foundation at Sialkot, where an empowerment-oriented school for young girls was felt a desperate necessity.

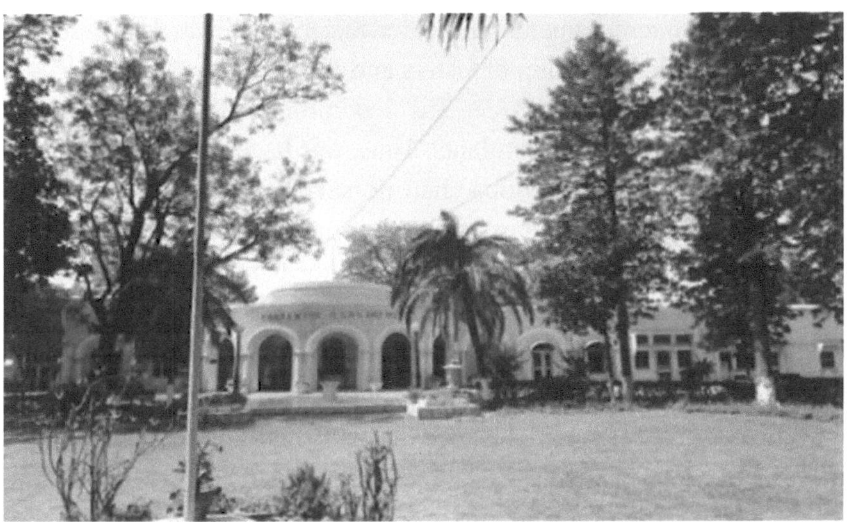

Convent of Jesus and Mary School, Sialkot, Punjab

In December 1855, five Sisters left Sardhana for Sialkot, via Lahore, accompanied by the good Archbishop himself. Mother Gonzaga Bergonhoux was named the Superior. Accompanying her were Mother Chrysostom Gubbins, Mother Macaire Derviex, Mary St Patrick O'Sullivan and Mary St Veronica Reghilini. It was a long, wearisome and dangerous journey from Sardhana to Sialkot in those days, but the zeal of the tiny group of nuns who were charged with the desire of educating young girls was not to be daunted by dusty roads and difficult journeys. The bullock-cart had rough wooden wheels and no springs, and it broke down frequently on the bad roads, a route of about three hundred and twenty-nine miles. They travelled at night since the midday sun was too hot. Meals were taken at small villages on the way, with rice and milk being the daily food. Eggs were a treat on certain occasions.

What must have been most dreaded were the long stretches of road at night, where forests came to the edge of some roads, and these were infested by wild beasts and even by bandits. But hardships and perils did not affect the valiant group at all. Reaching Lahore from Meerut was a tough and challenging task. It demonstrates how these young women with an indomitable spirit for quality education were able to overcome inter-cultural, intercontinental, and inter-racial differences despite severe climatic changes. The group of Sisters and Bishop Jacopi finally arrived at Sialkot on 15th February 1856. The first community consisted of five nuns and three possible postulants. Thus, was begun the first Convent of JM in the Punjab. The house had no surplus furniture. There was a total absence of anything extra, which might mean ease or comfort. They were really poor. This austerity did not dampen their zeal. But nothing could stop them from their determination and destination. History would always bring them back to our memories for what they did for our country and for the noble cause of education to the daughters of our great land.Describing the beginnings of the apostolic works, Bishop Jacopi writes:

> With Mother Gonzaga at the helm, work was begun to ready the place for boarders and day-scholars…. Parents were informed of the importance of sending their daughters to school. Visits were made to the homes. It took time for many to grow accustomed to the idea that girls should attend school. Finally, the day arrived for the opening of school and the nuns thought of the work so dear to the heart of their Foundress, 'to train souls for heaven by imparting a truly good education' ("Correspondence of Bishop Jacopi" 1855).

The work progressed well. The children came slowly, but they did come, and soon the house was full. With joy all looked forward to a new year when the work would progress even further, but there were growing signs that all was not well. Shadows of an uprising were spreading all over. The first shots were fired on 9th July, 1857 and the Sisters went on to suffer the terrors of the 'Great Indian Mutiny'or the 'First War of Indian Independence'. At the urgent and repeated supplications of the people of Shimla for a school from 1852 onwards, the Sisters of JM finally decided to grant their pleas.

Shimla in the Himalayas was one of the prizes won after the Anglo-Gurkha War of 1814-1816. Situated at the height of 8500 ft above sea-level, with its beautifully cool, dry climate and the majesty of the Himalayan snowcap mountains, Shimla provided a pleasant summer residence for the Viceroy and Commander-in-Chief, as well as for the Delhi and Punjab Secretariats in the North. During this period in the history of northern India, the Gurkha Wars came to an end and the Cis-Sutlej states had been subjugated. Garrison stations had been opened in the hills and British troops were posted in all the cantonments in the North. Lord Auckland was the first Governor General to have a summer residence in Shimla. His sister Emily Edon, in her biography, wrote that it took the Governor General and his household two months to make the journey from Calcutta to Shimla.

By 1860, Bishop Angelus Bedenick, the successor of Bishop, Jacopi felt the need of a school for European and other children of this area, as no Catholic school existed there then especially for girls. He opened negotiations with the British Government at Fort William, Calcutta, for the establishment of a military orphanage at Shimla. It is necessary to note that at this period of British history, religious bigotry was rife, and those in power Protestant by denomination, looked on Catholic institutions with a different perspective as rivalries in faith. Though the Governor General in Council was in favour of the Archbishop's project, the permission was refused, since there was already a Protestant military orphanage established at Sanawar. Fort William, the Calcutta Head Office, was not in favour of making further monetary grants to the Archbishop of Agra. But none of these made the Archbishop to give up his demands for a social cause. His holy perseverance did bring some result by 22nd July1862, which was positive and encouraging.

Finally, after some years of official correspondence, and the successive endeavours of Earl Canning, permission was granted for the foundation of such an orphanage. It was to be known as the 'Roman Catholic Military Asylum' and was to cater for both boys and girls. There were certain conditions attached to the permission as the following extract from a Government notification shows:

With reference to your letter, dated 26th June 1862, I am directed to acquaint you the information of the Hony The Lieut Governor that His Excellency the Governor General in Council, approves of the arrangement therein proposed, for the inspection and visitation of the Roman Catholic Orphanage, which is to be established at Shimla, in modification of that authorized in the 3rd paragraph of the letter to the address of the Bishop and Vicar Apostolic of Hindustan, a copy of which was forwarded to you with the letter from this department, No.50, dated 22nd July 1862 (*The Gazetteer*, National Archives, New Delhi).

The Governor General in Council, at the same time, directed that the institution should be subjected to the inspection of the Director of Public Instruction and the Inspector of schools, Ambala Circle, instead of the Superintendent of Army Schools.

The Convent of Jesus and Mary School, Shimla, popularly known as Chelsea School, was established in 1864. Mother Lewis Gonzaga was the first director of the institution. Begun as a small school it grew profoundly within a short span of time. For example, in 1866, there were one hundred and thirty-seven students belonging to different age groups, particularly four to sixteen years of age. They were under the able guidance of a lady superior and a Principal. This school also had seven educational missionaries-cum-teachers. They occupied a spacious two storied building; the lower portion of which was used for meals and classrooms, the upper portion was used as the dormitory. The kitchen was in a building adjoining the main building and connected with a covered way. It was of ample dimensions and kept clean.

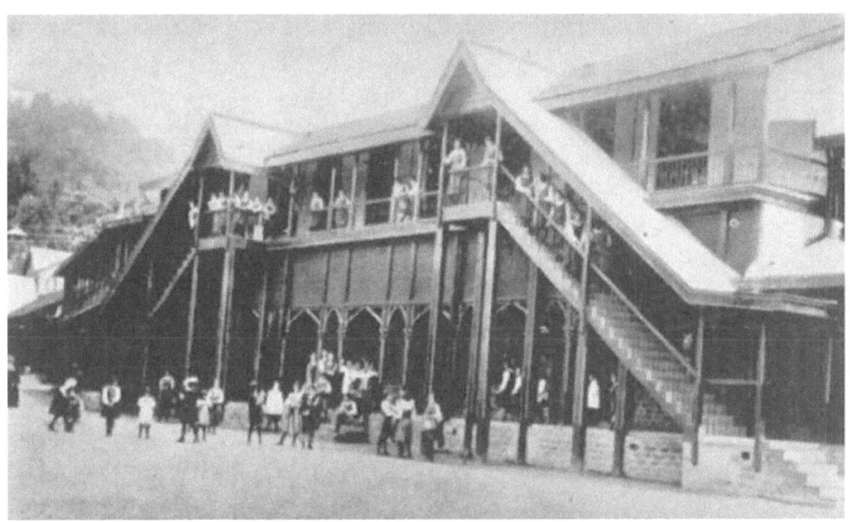

CJM School Chelsea, Shimla

In 1869, once the new school building was completed and named as St Francis School, the number of children began to increase on its rolls. The orphanage then had about 155 children on its rolls of whom fifteen were boarders and the rest were children of soldiers. The ages of the girls ranged from three to eighteen years. The report states that there was accommodation for a larger number of children. The toilets, in the form of round tower with central shaft, were on the edge of a precipice, and they were open for both the floors. The form of flushing used at that time was unique and sufficient in the wet season, but it was recommended that a supply of disinfectants be kept on the premises and that the authorities were permitted to purchase it.

The JM Sisters, pursuing their Founder's vision to make formal education available to as many young girls as possible, decided to open a foundation further north in the Himalayas at Murree. In 1876, the Convent of Jesus and Mary at Murree, an important hill station in the Himalayas on the road to Kashmir, was founded. A boarding school was opened in an existing house, and a military orphanage was erected on the same property. A few months after the foundation, the community soon lost one of its most capable subjects who died of cholera raging at that time.

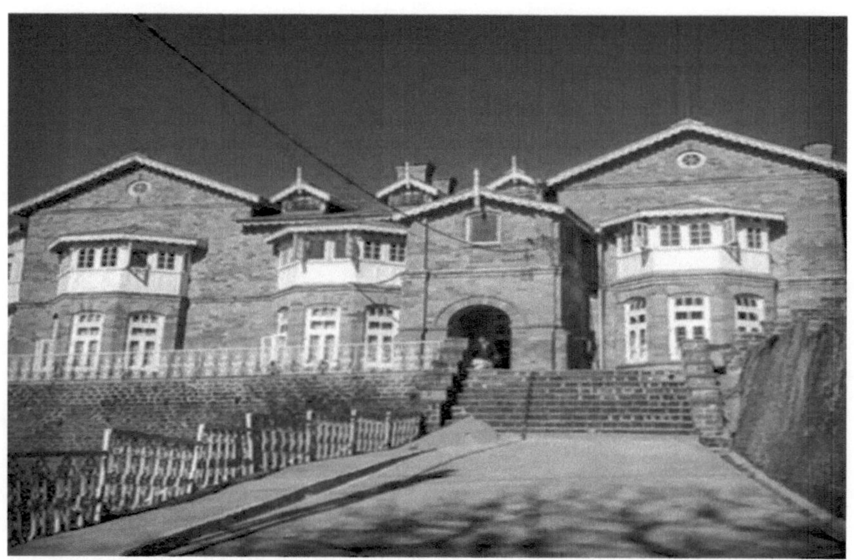

Jeus and Mary School, Murree

After the formation of Pakistan, Murree suffered from its proximity to Kashmir, but as the only hill station in Pakistan it had good prospects for the future. The Convent consistently held an extremely high place among schools in the Punjab for its scholastic successes. Some time at the end of the same year 1876, the same Bishop at the plea of the British Government, requested the Sisters to open a day-school in Lahore for the poor young girls.

The Convent of Jesus and Mary started serving the cause of women's education in the city of Lahore on 17th November 1876, in the Anarkali district, south of the city wall. They opened a day-school, and a little later a boarding school. It was not long before the school was placed under Government, and the Grant-in-Aid proved a great help (*Chronicles of CJM, Lahore* 1876). A small day-school for Indian girls was opened, and as the Superior was particularly attached to these children, she kept them under her personal supervision and taught them with the aid of a Sister who had learned Hindustani well.

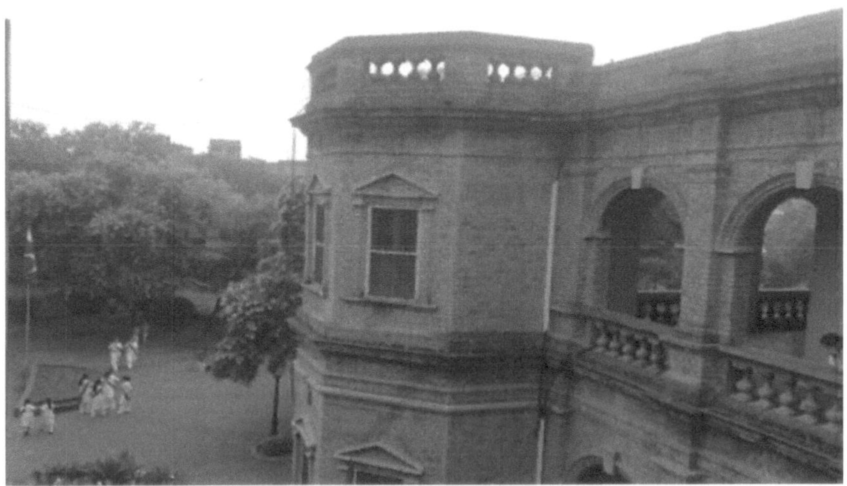

Jesus and Mary School, Lahore

The Lahore Convent had fluctuating fortunes, and had always worked under difficulties, some of these arising from the climate, but it always enjoyed the special blessing of God on account of the number of poor Catholic and many other children educated free or at very low cost. Inspectors' reports always recognized the good work done and the happy atmosphere existing there always. It became very necessary to open yet another Convent as a result of existing circumstances and the JM nuns opened a day-school at Dehradoon.

The nuns of the Waverly Convent were obliged to descend from the Convent during the long winter holidays on account of the intense cold, the snow, the wild animals which prowled around at night, and the difficulty of obtaining food supplies in the winter. The origins of the Convent of Jesus and Mary School, Dehradun could be traced back to 1880. Then, a half-yearly school, for European children returning to the hills, was opened with the approach of summer. This kind of educational work went on for a few years. And when the residents of Dehradun appealed to the JM sisters to stay on, they decided to open a full-fledged school officially on 1st February 1901, with fifteen pupils on the first roll (*Chronicles of CJM Dehradoon* 1901).

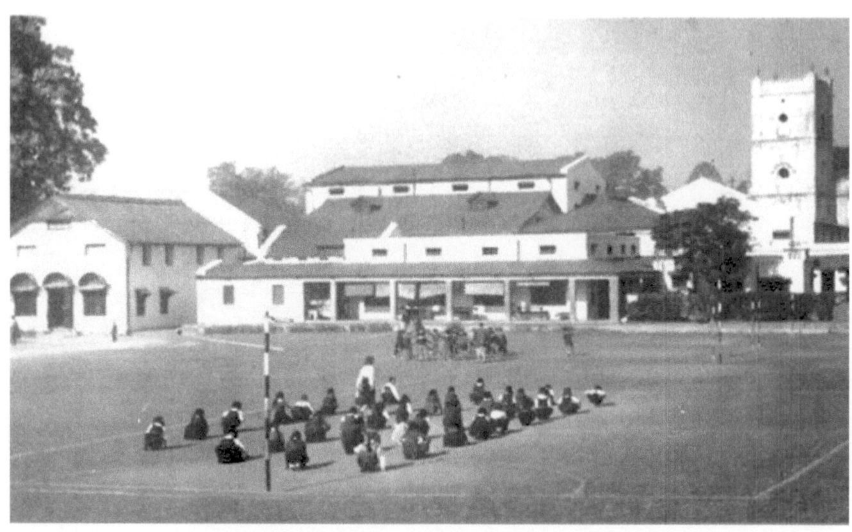

Jesus and Mary School, Dehra Doon

The school was later named St Joseph's day-school, and Mother St Isabel was its first Principal. It was not plain sailing for the Sisters in those early days. They were troubled by minor epidemics of measles and whooping cough that swept through the valley, and with having to live in tin-roofed buildings, but the nuns bravely persevered. On 4th April 1905, a devastating earthquake had its epicenter in the Kangra valley rocking the whole of Northern India. The building of St Joseph's day-school suffered damages. Mother St Isabel and Mother St Joachim were praying in the chapel at that time. In a display of supreme faith, they did not move. They were confident that it would come to no harm, and considered the chapel as the best place to die in. They were fortunate and no one was injured in the earthquake.

As the nuns at Shimla were unable to cope with the rigours of Himalayan winters, a house with a school was opened specifically for the health of the Sisters in 1894 in Ambala, Haryana, and subsequently, the growing need for the education of young girls in this part of India where not much had been done in this regard. It may be interesting to note that the famous poet Rudyard Kipling lived in a house just opposite to the present Convent.

The new foundation was first meant to be a little Kindergarten School for the children of families residing in the Cantonment area. At the same time, it was also intended to be a winter-home for the old and sick nuns from the hills who could not bear the winter weather of Shimla. The pioneers were Mother St Gabriel Hayes, Mother St Agatha Dundon and Mother Immaculata Dwyer. But somehow the plans failed. This little Convent was temporarily closed because of war and political troubles in 1901.

It was reopened during Mother St Aloisia's second visit to 'Umbala' (Ambala was spelt in those days as Umbala). The state of affairs continued until 1933 when RevdMother Borgia, Superior General visited India and decided to close the Convent altogether and dispose the property, but there were many who loved the little school and wanted it to continue. One of these was Archbishop Kenealy who was convinced that the JM nuns should remain and try to do good work in Ambala. Revd Mother Dominic Cahill, who had been appointed as Provincial, also longed to make a success of this school, and many parents begged for it to be kept open.

Later in 1905- 06, the Congregation was asked to open a day-school in Ambala by Fr Julius, the Vicar General. The need of a Catholic school was essential in that area. If Jesus and Mary Congregation could not accept, another Congregation would have to be invited. A house quite near the Church was on sale or could be rented. Mother General sent instructions from Rome that the Congregation should accept the apostolate of education and purchase the property. The 121, Staff Road, Ambala Cantonment property consisting of a cottage with outhouses, stables and a fine garden was purchased in 1908. This was done through Fr Julius acting with a power of attorney from Mother Lucie. By 20th November 1909, the community consisted of three religious, namely St Colette Cournane, St Clothilde Daly and St Margaret Christie arrived, and on 2nd December 1909 school was started. It is important to mention that Convent of Jesus Mary School was opened at the request of Fr Julius, Vicar General of the Archdiocese of Agra. Archdiocese of Agra was under Most Rev Gentili then. According to the school attendance register the first pupil was Albert Mortimer, son of Mr Connaught Ranger, a leading Catholic.

Agra again became the focus of the JM Sisters' attention when once again, the institution at Numillah having closed, the inhabitants asked for a school in the Agra Cantonment area No.44 A. The mall having been purchased by Mother Lucie, a school was opened in 1902, and a young newly professed Sister Vergine Simon was sent out to teach. The Agra Cantonment Records mentions this school as 'Mother St Loucie's 'School', holding 2.30 acres (*Military Records*, 1902). Clementine Murphy, one of the first orphan pupils of St Patrick School, Agra, who later became a Religious of JM observed the following:

> "When the second colony of nuns arrived in Agra early in 1845, the day-school for soldiers' children was opened at the house of the military Chaplain in Agra, three or four miles from the Convent. Mother St. Paul, one of the pioneers, went into the day-school daily, accompanied by other Sisters."She also observed that some girls in the Patrick School showed an inclination for the cause of selfless service to the needy. ("Correspondence of Mother St Clementine Murphy" 1845).

This school was closed with the opening of St Patrick's Orphanage Agra in 1846 as the girls were admitted in the orphanage. The day-school in Cantonments, founded by the first nuns of JM in India, was relinquished when St Patrick's Military Orphanage was built. This Orphanage was opened for the girl children of European Protestant and Catholic soldiers. They were instructed in reading, writing, English Grammar, Arithmetic, History, plain and fancy knitting, needle work, artificial flower making, and house-keeping.[3] Nevertheless, over a period of time, it was re-opened as St. Anthony's day-school in 1902 and has carried on with great success ever since (*JM Annals* 1949).

The Mother General Revd Mother Clare Bray, having seen the establishments on her visit all over India and being much impressed by the work of her nuns, decided that it was time to complete what had begun in Chelsea Shimla, by an institution of higher education and a much needed training college for teachers. It was not only for the teaching formation of her religious Sisters but also for secular women students as well. She was dedicated to the idea of developing Northern Indian women to be pioneers in the educational field.

In 1902, Mother St Clare visited all the Convents of JM in India that were in existence at that time. As she traveled around, her mind absorbed details and impressions which fired her zeal. She realized that though much good work was being done, what was needed most was a training college where the students could study and qualify under highly professional teachers. The idea of establishing St Bede's College gradually took shape in her mind but nothing could be done without the permission of the Government. Though her distinguished appearance and manners were irresistible, and she won all hearts, she met with strong opposition as soon as the question of a Teachers' Training College was mentioned. Gradually she won over the Director of Education, but not so the Governor of Punjab who had the final word. Then Mother Clare invited him to visit the Convent in Shimla.

The Governor accepted the invitation and came with his officials and outriders. He was courteous but stiff. He was received with simplicity and respect by Mother Clare, the students and nuns at Chelsea school and given a wonderful reception. Mother Clare took him over to the existing boarding school Chelsea and explained to him her ambition to establish St Bede's Training College for women, and how it could be done. Finally, she took him to the chapel where there were some sisters praying silently and showed him to the Lord. When he came out to his carriage, he agreed to look at the plans, and he took them along with him.

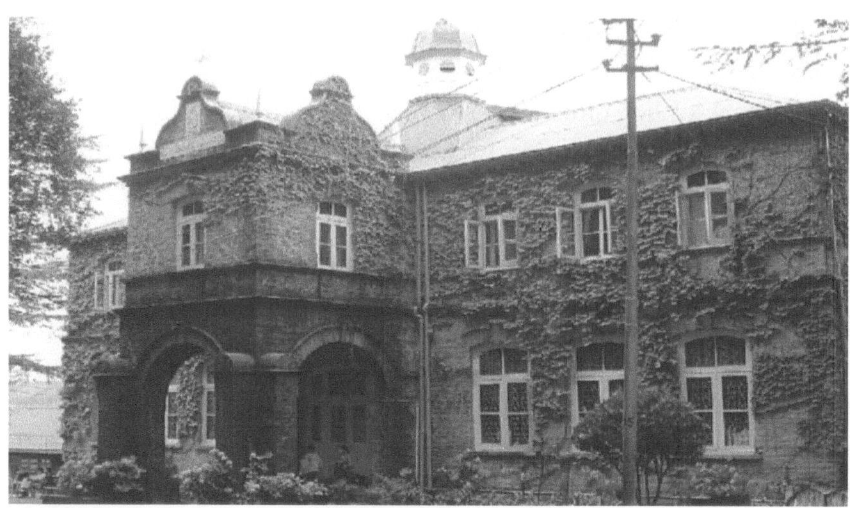

St Bede's College, Shimla

Next day Mother Clare received good news. The building work of the college could go ahead. The deeds were signed on the feast of St Bede on 25th May 1902. St Bede, the patron saint of scholars and historians, was an 8th century English historian, scholar, and Doctor of the Church. He is also known as 'the father of English history.' Mother Clare began the work immediately. The foundations were dug. Stones had to be carried up hill on the back of coolies. It was a very tiring work. The workmen were not accustomed doing things quickly, but Mother Clare encouraged them, and got the work done.

The building was almost finished when she had to return to Europe for the General Chapter in 1903 which was being held, with special permission, in 'Villa dei Mille', the temporary Procure[4] in Rome. She was unanimously elected Superior General on 24th October 1903, on the anniversary of her profession. Immediately after the Chapter, Mother Clare lost no time in completing the work to be done before returning to India. Two months later, she completed the founding of St Bede's Training College as she had planned the details not only of the building but also the furnishing and interior decoration. She even drew up a provisional schedule for the students' timetable. She chose qualified lecturers to teach and appointed Mother St Gregory Canty to be the first Principal of the College. She made provisions for a few young Sisters to study along with secular students. Only when she was sure that everything was right, and as good as could be provided, she returned to Europe.

The history of CJM, New Delhi dates back to British times, when in the year 1919 King George V in England proclaimed Delhi as the imperial capital. Archbishop Bernacchioni commissioned Fr Luke OFM Cap, longtime Missionary to India, to plan for a church and a school. Fr Luke expressed his hope to Provincial Superior M. Dorothy Tarleton for the JMs to be the pioneers of education in New Delhi, then known as Raisina. The same year 1919, Mother St Clare Bray, then Superior General of the Congregation of JM, decided to open a school in Delhi. So, like a mustard seed CJM School in New Delhi started as a co-educational school in a rented room on Alipore Road, Old Delhi, on 1st October 1919. They had scarcely moved in when the Chamber of Indian Princes came for their prescheduled one month long Annual Meeting. The sisters moved out to tents pitched as residence and school rooms in St Mary's Church compound. Sometime later, Hon'ble Chief Commissioner, Barron foreseeing the future educational needs of this imperial city, was keen to see the promising little school shifted to New Delhi. Mother St Collet Cournane and the other pioneering Sisters of this institution M. Aloysius O'Dwyer, M. Rose Smith, Sr Francis and Sr Zoe obliged. On 25th January, 1923 they shifted the day-school to a little cottage 'Maria Bhavan', near the Sacred Heart Cathedral in New Delhi. They themselves found no place to reside near the new location and had to commute daily by bus from Alipore Road. They endured joyfully the hardships and perils especially of a hot climate. The little school, which was housed temporarily at 'Maria Bhavan', was gaining in reputation, and there was a great demand for admission to the school.

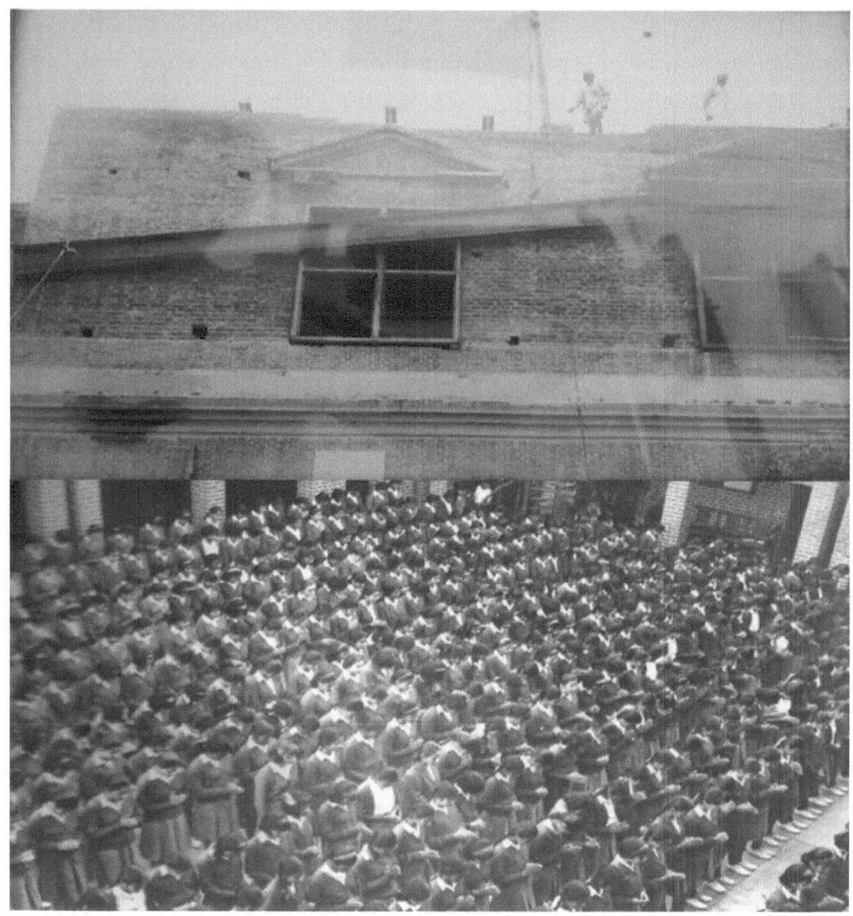

CJM School, New Delhi

The school was growing, and now a new a large building was needed. The prayers of the nuns, staff, students as well as their well-wishers played a vital role in tiding over difficulties of securing land and the sanction for the school building. The Chief Commissioner of Delhi, the Superintendent of Education, and the Engineer in Chief, all were in favour of establishing the School. The State Officer lent the Sisters some tents to be pitched in the Cantonment which they vacated in winter to occupy the 'Old Club' nearby. The sisters were happy, therefore, to receive the sanction for land and a building grant of Rs.10,000 from the Director of Public Instruction. In March 1926, Major Hubens laid the foundation stone of the new school, not too far from 'Maria Bhavan'. Seven years of trials and hardship did not deter the courageous enthusiasm of the Sisters in the uphill task of promoting education for the growing number of girls. In spite of adverse economic conditions as an aftermath of the World War I during 28th July 1914 - 11th Nov 1918, the sisters continued giving the children the best of everything in education.

It was not until the summer of 1921 that the Religious of JM seriously considered opening a school for small boys in Mussoorie. For many years, the parents of the Waverly girls had begged the nuns to admit their little sons because they did not want them to go to the Preparatory Departments of the large Boy's School. They wanted them to have the motherly care of the nuns. Waverly had no room for such a department, and the suggestions were always set aside. Then in the spring of 1921, Mother St Clare, Superior General of the Congregation, made her visitation to the Indian Province, and circumstances proved favourable to the often-repeated request. The Hampton Court, which for many years had been a select school for European girls, was up for sale. The Principal Miss Holland was aged, and she could no longer maintain the high standards of her greatly respected institution, and reluctantly she closed the establishment and sold the property.

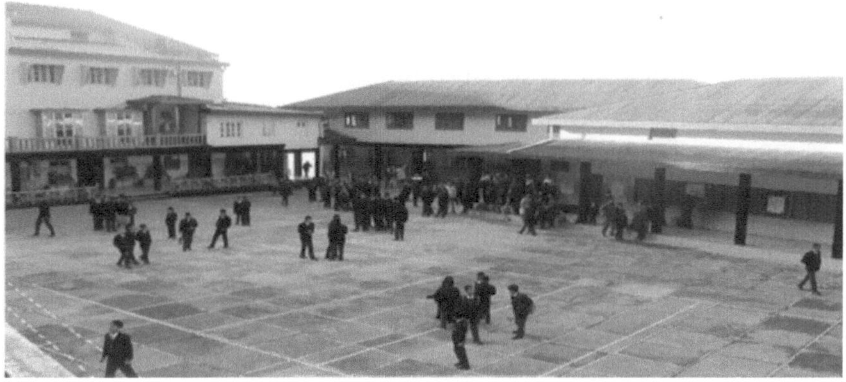

CJM School, Hampton Court

Hampton Court Preparatory Boarding School for boys began its life as an integral part of the educational work of the nuns of JM in 1922. But alas, it was no easy venture. To begin with, the nuns were short of qualified personnel for such a responsible and arduous work. Little boys needed great care and constant attention, and the only nuns available for such responsible work were those of the New Delhi day-school, which had opened a year or two previously. It was, therefore, decided that they would staff Hampton Court during the summer months with the help of qualified teachers. During the winter of 1921, a group of nuns were sent to clean and repair and furnish the cottages. They found them in a state of truly distressing despair. The nuns had to face a lot of practical difficulties, not only for the first few months, but for long years afterwards. Gradually the problems became less and life in Hampton Court began. The nuns were able to secure the co-operation of good, experienced, and professionally qualified teachers. When the other young nuns joined the institution, they worked with untiring energy towards the growth and development of the institution.

Having followed the JM pioneer Sisters on their trail in the educational field for promotion of women, now it turned to observe the advances made in each of their institution already established for the promotion of their educational work. With the inception of JM educational institutions in different parts of India, particularly in North India in 1842, the history of women's education began to spread profoundly cutting across social stratifications. It should be noted that Bishop Borghi of Agra and his successors, along with the JM nuns played a significant role in establishing educational institutions at different places in North India. These educational institutions continued to cater to the needs of both European and Indian children. The mission and vision of St Claudine Thevenet propelled her followers to teach, train and enlighten the young Indian minds. This facilitated the young children to be good citizens. These enlightened and empowered young Indian women, in turn, strived to instill in the ideas of liberty, equality and fraternity through various ways as bureaucrats, politicians, entrepreneurs, social activists, academics, artists, scientists, doctors and other professionals.

Endnotes

[1] *The Order of Friars Minor is a Catholic religious order*, founded in 1209 by Francis of Assisi.

[2] *A Christian colony around the Cathedral church*, Agra.

[3] *Bengal Catholic Herald*, p. 14.

[4] *The official residence and administrative centre of a religious Congregation.*

Chapter 5

Growth and Development of JM School Education

The growth and development of JM educational institutions in the colonial India, along with accounts of the historical happenings of that time, the founding members' positive response to the challenges are significant in the development of school education system in North India. They have striven to bring their work up to the demands of modern world. This can be seen explicitly in the growth and expansion, and most particularly in their all-out energy put into these institutions giving quality education. The Jesus and Mary missionaries played a pioneer role in promoting female education in North India. They were the initiators in this pioneering work as the East India Company was not happy to take up such issues. They were busy in fighting wars and consolidating its hold over newly acquired territories. Though they were familiar with the Indian culture and traditions, they were reluctant to take up the issues of women's education. They thought it might create hostilities among the Indian people and would amount to interference in social and religious activities which they never wanted to do. The Indian intelligentsia who had received western education on the other hand, had no clear perception of female education and it had not drawn out any plan of action.

The JM visionaries not only entered the scene at this stage, but they did so with a motivation to take up the dangerous and sensitive issue of female education in North India guided purely by their humanitarian and evangelical zeal. It was the general thinking amongst the missionaries, both Catholics and Protestants, that the female education alone could help in developing the personality of women in India. The JMs also thought that female education will enlighten the women and prevent them from submitting to irrational customs like sati, child marriage, enforced widowhood etc. Like their founder Claudine, the JMs believed that education could promote essential qualities in women such as natural tenderness, love, domestic and social virtues, and above all ability to mould the character of the future generations. Like the Indian liberals, the JM missionaries too, notwithstanding their religious undertones, attempted to educate the women and ameliorate the pain and suffering of the Indian woman. Having lived through the aftermath of the French revolution, the JM visionaries knew very well that for men to rise in society, accompanied by an educated wife and also for the purpose of rearing children and providing a conducive atmosphere at home, women's education was essential.

After its historic establishment in Agra, the present Uttar Pradesh, the Congregation of Jesus and Mary started spreading rapidly northwards to the heights of the Himalayas, southwards to Maharashtra and westward to Gujarat. The colonial government had always shown great appreciation towards the Congregation largely due to the reason that it rendered valuable education, social and other services to society and the nation. The same spirit and aim continued to guide the Congregation wherever it spread: "To give a Christian education to young girls suitable to the social position of each" (Horny 58). To that end, the Congregation established boarding schools and day-schools, where the pupils receive a thorough education in the field of three 'R's, literature, society, religion and family life.

Claudine Thevenet's remarkable sayings and precepts to her Congregation permeated through the whole organisation. In fact, her vision continues to inspire and encourage the widespread and ever-growing Congregation even today. "God will provide" was a maxim that inspired her daughters to venture out to distant lands (Barrel and Carlos 258). Today, JM institutions are rendering valuable educational services in different parts of the world and in India. In modern India it is spread to different states like Himachal Pradesh, Haryana, Delhi, Uttar Pradesh, Uttrakhand, West Bengal, Chattisgarh, Nagaland, Assam, Rajasthan, Gujarat, Maharashtra, Goa, Karnataka, and Kerala. Here the five states of North India, namely, Delhi, Uttar Pradesh, Uttarakhand, Himachal Pradesh, and Haryana are on focus. In these northern states, JM Sisters are actively involved in educational works, sustained by a pedagogy in which love is of upper most importance. "To go out to others with the heart of a mother that can love in truth" (*Evangeli Nuntiandi* 22), is explicitly in synthesis with Claudine's pedagogy which demands the active and trusting participation of people. This has been done as a part of the realization of God's plan for them.The congregation has an unshakable conviction that it is God who gives motherly hearts to those who educate, in other words, He replaces our hearts with His own. Being a Teaching Order, all the members of the Congregation spend their lives in the education of girls, and in the varied offices connected with teaching and running of large boarding and non-boarding establishments.

As stated earlier, the Congregation of JM came to Agra in India for the first time in 1842 and then moved to other parts of the country. Following the footsteps of sisters Theresa, Paul, Ambrose, Augustine, Joachim and Vincent de Paul, therefollowed in succeeding years a great number of other valiant women of letters. An outline of the type of education to be imparted to young girls admitted to the JM schools at Agra, was clearly mentioned in one of the letters exchanged between Bishop Borghi Mgr. Rossat, later published in *Echoes of a Century in India*. Referring to the number of children on the register, Mother Theresa wrote: "Our pupils like being with us, and we should have a greater number in our schools if the English Government had not transferred its headquarters to Delhi, which obliged the officials to take up residence in that town"(Cuthbert, *Echoes of a Century* 92).

A letter sent five months later by Mgr. Borghi to Mgr. Rossat informs us of an enrollment of thirty-two boarders and more applicants for the hostel. Mother Theresa also had expressed her displeasure with Bishop Borghi saying that "very soon we should have a week passing without bringing new ones to the school" (Cuthbert, *Echoes of a Century* 95). In view of this expectation, Mgr. Borghi started building another large dormitory when his friend Mgr. Rossat made a generous contribution of 8000 francs.

In a letter to Mother St Andrew, General of the Congregation, dated 28th June 1843, Mgr. Borghi wrote:

> Seeing our establishments in Agra getting on so well, I put aside a certain sum of money which was given to me by the 'Society of the Propagation of Faith.[1] at Lyons, and with this I am building a new dormitory capable of containing fifty beds. I also intend having a small chapel built near the Convent and an orphanage for the young Irish girls (Borghi, "Correspondence of Bishop Borghi" 1843).

There is further evidence in *Echoes of a Century in India* of the pleasure evinced by his Excellency Lord Ellen Borough, Governor General of India, when he visited the Convent and boarding school, on 4th June 1843. He was received by Bishop Borghi, his co-adjuror[2] Mgr. Carli and the nuns with their twenty-two boarders robed in white. He visited the Boarding School, St Patrick's School and St. Joseph's School and expressed his deep appreciation of the work done, and the great sacrifice made by the nuns in a completely different country and atmosphere of life. As a token of his high regard, a beautiful piece of English work was presented to the nuns. From the beginning both the institutions functioned as a single school for the purpose of teaching and for other activities. It is an assured fact that with the breadth of vision, clear objectives and aims of Mother Theresa and her religious assistants, Government recognition was soon sought and obtained.

Different Phases in the Growth and Development

The history of St Patrick's can be divided into certain stages of life. The earliest stage of the Agra Convent's history was fraught with the joys and pains, the triumphs, frustrations, holy ambitions and even death of the optimistic young French Sisters. They had the noblest ideals to realize their educational dream, and whose sole aim was to fulfill their worthy aspirations. In an article entitled "Our Catholic Schools" in *Franciscan Annals* published in May 1912, the writer provided the list of girls who passed the examination from St Aloysius and St Patrick's Convent Schools. The author also claimed that the JM schools in Agra secured 'good places' in comparison with other schools. In the same article he wrote: "These are grand and undoubtedly most brilliant results, which go far to prove that the education given in our Catholic schools in every respect is not only equal to, but in many instances, better than that is given in any other similar institutions"(28). No labour is considered too great to produce brilliant results.

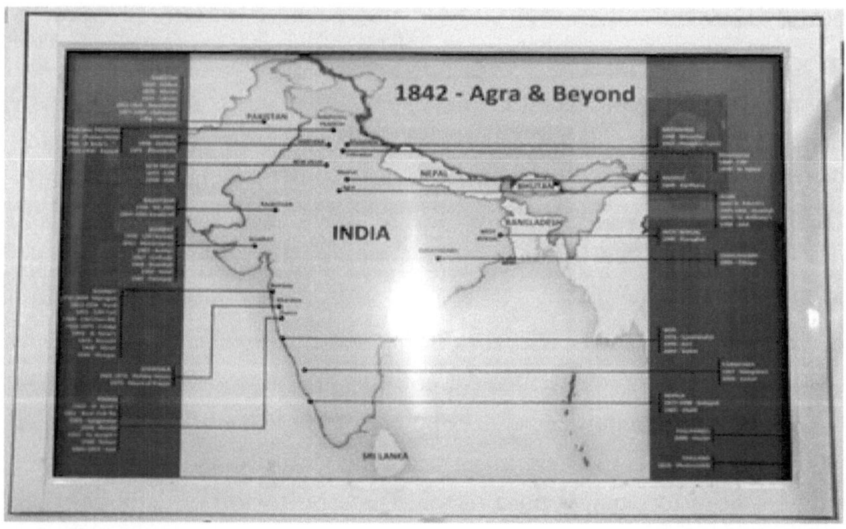

The Catholic Church has ever shown herself the patroness of sound learning. Her educational institutions stand foremost in the work done for religion and education in every branch, both intellectual and technical. They have turned out by hundreds, both boys and girls not only educated in the highest sense of the word but also truly religious. An article in the 1912 issue of *Franciscan Annals* highlighted the following:

> On Saturday June 22nd at 6.30 pm an entertainment programme was given by the young ladies of St Aloysius to celebrate the anniversary feast of their patron saint. The music presentation in the function presided over by Johnson and H. Woodward was a perfect treat. We fancied ourselves back in the land of music and art ("Our Catholic Schools" 22).

No pains were spared to make the evening a success, and the whole programme reflected the greatest credit on the nuns and their scholars.

Despite all these favorable situations which helped dissemination of knowledge through JM schools, there were challenges as well. The 19th and the first half of the twentieth century India witnessed a number of natural calamities, epidemics, and wars. The tragic events of the First War of Indian Independence left deep scars on the hearts of many people in Northern India, who lived through several months of fear and anxiety. The Catholic mission at Agra was no less affected by the traumatic experiences of the summer of 1857. An extract from a copy of a long letter written on 15th November, 1857 by Rt Revd Dr Ignatius Persico, addressed to the clergy and faithful, gives a picture of the tragedy that befell Christians in the North with the outbreak of the 1857 revolt. This worthy prelate wrote of a heart heavily laden and a spirit weighed down with affliction because those who rebelled, unfurled the standard of their religion against the rulers of the land. Holy Temples were plundered, sacred altars polluted, anointed ministers slain, defenseless citizens massacred, and matrons, damsels and weeping babes were barbarously butchered. After describing the atrocities committed in Delhi, Sardhana, Ferozepore and Lucknow, he mentioned related experiences of his own mission as well.

Many have been the sufferings during this period, but what weighed heavily upon the hearts of all were the inconveniences of every kind, to which the JM institutions were subjected to. But God gave them patience, courage, and cheerful resignation to face these trials with Christian fortitude. The churches and institutions which caused our predecessors so much anxiety, toil and labour for nearly half a century were demolished in a night. The Catholic bishop's house, convent, college, male and female orphanages, schools, chapel, and priest's house in the military cantonments were pillaged, shattered and fired. It was a heart-rending experience to look over the rampart at the ruin that was going on. Even strangers to Christian religion could not witness the spectacle with dry eye. Similarly, three nuns of the JM, the Rector of St Peter's College and a lay brother have been hurried to a premature grave by disease. General debility and sickness have prostrated our clergy, nuns, and children. A copy of the original letter of the same prelate in the Agra church archives, addressed to Cecil Beadon, the Secretary of Government Home Department, put forward his points for consideration before His Lordship the Governor General. In the letter dated 3rd November 1857, he wrote that his anxiety was grave, for he had under his care twenty nuns, three hundred children mostly orphans of European soldiers and many natives. When directed to take the nuns and children into the Fort, they were permitted to take only a small box or a bundle for every nun with five children. Consequently, all their property even wearing apparel was sacrificed.

An excerpt from July 1914 issues of *Franciscan Annals* marked an account of damages suffered by JM institutions in Agra:

> The Convent suffered the loss of Rs. 14082, St Patrick's Orphanage lost Rs. 5846 and St Joseph's School Rs. 3320 from the accounts given of the dreadful events which occurred from the outbreak of hostilities in May 1857 till the end of that year. It is not difficult to conjure up a mental image of the hardships and privations endured by the nuns and children of the Agra Convent and its schools (Persico, "*The Catholic Mission*" 26).

They were housed in neglected elephant sheds, the verandahs of which served as a chapel. In the early morning it functioned as a classroom, refectory, and a recreation room during the day, and as a dormitory at night. The brave nuns of Agra Convent faced a most unlikely happening at this critical phase of Indian history.

In *The Congregation of Jesus and Mary–Cameos from its History Sydney,* Smith reveled that though the British Government in India offered a free passage to all the European women to return to their respective countries after the 1857 Revolt, the nuns preferred to stay back in India. Even the warm welcome that would await them in Lyons could not change their decisions, for their hearts were very much in India for women's cause through transformative education. The way in which they displayed their social affirmative programmes suggested that they made India their home country by extending their loyalty towards India's struggle for independence. Consequently, they convinced themselves that God was undoubtedly on their side. The Convent and its schools sprang up and started flourishing once again. Little by little, life took on its normal aspect. Agra Cathedral Archives has a letter that records the forwarding of a total sum of Rs. 546 by the government for the maintenance of the orphanage at Agra and traveling expenses for some of the orphans migrating from Agra to Sardhana Orphanage. More orphans were brought from Hamirpur and Jhansi. 130 girls were admitted to the Convent and the government undertook to pay Rs. 2 per month for the support of each child until she attained the age of 18, unless she should soon die, be married or be self-supporting.

It should be admitted here that the number of rescued children taken into St Patrick's and St Joseph's Orphanages run by the JM nuns during these critical periods is unknown. No information to this effect was found either in the Convent or church archives in Agra. The only thing that we know by word of mouth is that the orphanages were full with its optimum number. However, the letters written by the Apostolic Administrators[2] to the priests in charge of the mission with instructions to receive destitute little ones give the general impression that the latter were always warmly welcomed and cared for by the JM nuns. If one is to judge by numbers both these JM orphanages seemed to be extremely popular.

Royal Patronage and Historical Milestones

Life in the Agra convent and schools with its daily round of duties could perhaps be drab at times, but there were also thrilling moments that must have left their impression on nuns and children alike. It was clear when they came in close contact with great personalities who evinced interest in one and all. There were rare occasions too when patriotic or religious sentiments were in the foreground. The colonial officials also paid visit to the educational institutions and orphanages. For instance, Lord Canning, Viceroy of India during 1856-62, paid a few visits to the Agra Convent and encouraged nuns and the staff for their valuable service to humanity. He also boosted the children for their hard work and their study. There were also visits by Prince of Wales Edward VII. He was quite astonished to see the good education imparted by the catholic visionaries in this part of the world. These are recorded in Franciscan Annals of June 1910, as great honour to the Agra Schools. On the occasion of his visit to the JM schools Fr Hyacinth wrote, "Lord Canning granted Rs. 500 per month for the support of the orphan children in the two establishments which the Agra mission proposed to build in Shimla. One of these was run by the JM Sisters at Ellisium Hill in May 1863" ("History of Agra Mission"6). Bishop Bedenik also opened St Francis School, a girls' military orphanage in Shimla, and it was also managed by the same Order of nuns.

Much of the academic work in St Patrick's School from 1875 to about 1927 seemed to have been stereotyped and therefore, of not great educational value for the children. But there are records in the Agra convent Archives which inform us the annual visits paid by the government officials during 1920s. These inspections revealed some shortcomings, and a tremendous stimulus was consequently given to the Principal and her staff to cultivate a more liberal outlook geared to the pupil's needs. Consequently, the late twenties and thirties showed a marked all-round progress during Revd Mother de la Salette's tenure of office as Superior. According to one inspector these improvements were due to "the employment of qualified teachers, to the understanding and wise direction of Mother St Evangelist, a highly educated and well-prepared teacher and Headmistress. In 1929, the government grants totaling Rs. 2110 was welcomed by the school authority and the money was judiciously spent for the construction of a new kitchen, repairing of the school hall and levelling a large plot of ground for games. The following year there was ample scope for organized activities for the pupils, and a good-sized plot of land was given to the nuns and children.

In 1931, the brick building, mentioned in the government official report, situated towards the North-East of the property, housed St Patrick's, and St Anthony's School staff. The same year a pleasing report was made about the attractiveness of classroom apparatus and furniture, and some on the improved quality of the textbooks. So, the decade passed registering ever more progress. Under the able direction of Mother Mary of the Sacred Heart, the school made provision as before for all compulsory subjects to the departmental schedule of studies and for sound religious instructions but special attention was given to handicraft as an optional subject. Mother Sacred Heart herself taught and supervised the handwork and was highly qualified to undertake such work. It was a self-support for the institution and later on for the children themselves. Thus, in the 1930s, skill-oriented handwork was freely introduced and a good deal of it was exhibited in the school hall illustrating a variety of occupations. Many of the articles were later put up for sale to swell the school funds.

At that time, Mother St Joan Switzer was also on St Patrick's School staff and because of her efforts, the work in the infants' classes was of extremely high standard. The inspector W.E. Andrews wrote in the School Report that "Mother St Joan combines a love and understanding of small children with a thorough knowledge of modern kindergarten methods and a high opinion of the children's capabilities. Exceptional results were produced under her able guidance". In the same Report he adds, "I saw the little ones do folk-dances, and heard them singing party songs and performing in the percussion band conducted by the children of class I as part of their training in the appreciation of music and rhythm" (*School Inspection Report, St Patrick's School Agra 1930*). It was a revelation of achievements to which children can be led everyone who knew her, accepted the fact that she was a person of high dedication who drew the best of her staff and students. She also spoke with great fluency and correctness of Hindi language, and later on she was made in-charge of the Hindi medium school in Delhi. There was always something to learn from the Mother St Joan Switzer who proved to be a tremendously beneficial to students, teachers and all the staff members.

Later it was understood that the developments took place largely because of Mother Mary of the Sacred Heart who took charge of the school in 1930,with the able assistance of Mother Joan Switzer, who took charge of the kindergarten classes" (*School Inspection Report, St. Patrick's School, Agra* 1930). It should be stated that from the 1930s onwards the question of the amalgamation of St Aloysius Boarding School with St. Patrick's Orphanage for the European children were in the mind of the nuns. The sisters believed that there was no longer a need to take care of military orphans. The inspector's report showed that only twenty-six pupils paid full fees out of a total enrollment of two hundred resident children. St Patrick School received the government boarding grant for 174 boarders, 73 of whom ranging from KG to class X were entirely free. Besides this, right from the very beginning the pupils from both schools enjoyed most of their activities in common.

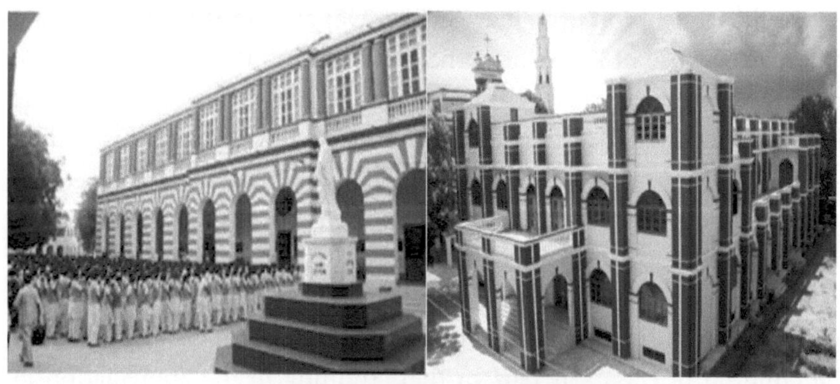

St. Patrick's Junior College, Agra

According to Mother Mechtilde, then Superior of the Agra Convent, the amalgamation of both institutions and the formation of the junior and senior school sections finally took place in 1942. The 1940s, when

Mother Bonaventure was at the helm of school affairs of St Patrick School at Agra, it marked a high standard of achievement. It was during her time the foundation stone of a beautiful large two-storeyed infirmary which was dedicated for the cause of education. One of the Sisters Mary St Paul who knew Mother Bonaventure wrote:

> As the Principal of St Patrick's Mother Bonaventure was a dynamic personality who did much for the school. Educationally and materially her efforts were fruitful in getting government to sanction substantial grants.... The money obtained for the latter purpose she wisely ear-marked for the education of the orphans. It was also due to her endeavours that the school was provided with good reference books and the kindergarten classes got individual apparatus (Paul, "Correspondence of Mary St. Paul" 1940).

The 'Well-bent Reading', 'Number scheme' and the 'Westminster Reading Scheme' were much appreciated by teachers, and up to date methods were introduced in the lower section of the school which raised the already high standard still higher.

St Joseph's orphanage was founded in 1843 for the Christian education of Indian orphaned girls and for the children of indigent parents incapable of supporting their offspring. When the JM Sisters came to India to educate the European children, they felt the supreme importance of educating the Indian girls as well. For this they needed the language and the personnel. Somehow, little by little, they learned the language of India, at that time it was Urdu, and without any hesitation started a vernacular school side by side. In the beginning, the Indians looked on this school with great suspicion. They refused to send their girls to school because learning for girls was not common in India, which they considered totally unnecessary and unprofitable.

In her book *Echoes of a Century in India*, Mother Cuthbert recalls that the children had the best spirit in the world; they were deeply grateful to the nuns for all they tried to do for them, and were eager to show their gratitude in so many ways (52). Mother St Ambrose and

Clementine assisted Mother Augustine in the school. They were the ones who started a flower-making industry, which for a long time was the chief source of revenue for the orphanage. Unlike the orphaned children of European soldiers maintained by a monthly government allowance received into St Patrick's institution, the Indian orphans depended entirely for their support from the charitable contributions and the proceeds from the sale of their hand work. The stream of life flowed smoothly enough in St Joseph's throughout the years.

There are hardly any written documents either in the orphanage or in the convent to support a continuous narrative of the institution and its management for the period from 1862 to the end of 1930s. There are, however, a few stray gleanings from the *Franciscan Annals of India*. These brief publications provide some idea of the school and provide brief pen portraits of some of the Sisters who worked there. The Catholic calendar and Directory for the Archdiocese of Agra tell us about Rev. Mother St Euphrasia, Directress of St Joseph's School, and orphanage in 1905, and all the work done under her.

In the 1920s, the orphanage at Agra had to undergo a severe financial struggle. When Mother Mary of Jesus was its Director , she induced influential people to organize fancy fairs. Her Sisters and the children were always engaged in handicrafts for sale. Her correspondence was considerable with Government Municipal and District Boards, with charitable institutions, and with charitably inclined people in all parts of the world. Observing the charitable nature of Mother Mary, the Director of Public Instruction once observed that she was the most accomplished beggar he had ever seen.

In December 1922, *Franciscan Annals of India* published a notice pertaining to St Joseph's School in Agra. It expressed that though the school had restricted itself to receiving only children of Christian parents; in the future, admissions of pupils of other creeds, as boarders and day-scholars would be considered as well. The advertisement further pointed out that the school taught according to the requirements of the Vernacular School Code, and the government sanction for raising it to an Anglo-Vernacular middle school was sought. Having referred also to the health promoting conditions under which the children worked, due recognition was given to the high standards attained in the industrial department, for which there were awards and the moral training imparted in the school was significant. The modest fees charged to the day-scholars gives some insight into the financial position of the school: Class I (A&B) Rs. 1 per month, Class II (A&B) Rs.1/8 per month, Class III (A&B) Rs. 2 per month and Class IV (A&B) Rs.2/8 per month.

Undoubtedly, it was Mother Mary of Jesus' dynamic spirit and breadth of vision which made an influential impact in opening the doors of St Joseph School to children of all classes and creeds. It was due to her dynamism, concern for the school's progress, and for the children's welfare and the policy of Mother Bertille, a kindred spirit, who became Director in 1922, that the raising of its standards in general, won it further government recognition and approval. The School Report read on 10th August 1928 stated: "The year 1922 when Mother St Bertille took charge, marked a new epoch in the history of the orphanage" (*School Inspection Report, St Joseph's School, Agra* 1928). Since then, as a result of the selfless service rendered by her to the orphans, the once Lower Primary School has now become an Upper Middle School, the first and the only one of its kind in the whole of Agra, with more than a hundred boarders and an efficient and highly qualified staff.

In fact, St Joseph's School was a vernacular one with classes up to the VI standard during the 1930s. It became a Junior High School in 1940. Mother Bertille's term of office was a period of progress in the history of St Joseph School. She was an educationist, and therefore realized that the children committed to her care must be well prepared as far as possible to counter the challenges of 20th century India. She respected the worth and innate goodness of every student and believed that their gifts and talents are to be nurtured to their full potential. She made sure that each student is encouraged to use her attributes for the creation of a just world and for the living of a personally fulfilling life through service to others. Her aim was the formation of resilient, confident young women, equipped to make wise choices with open minds and hearts. She insisted that her girls who love learning and who are imbued with the joyfulness of living should have compassion for others. She trained her students to develop a strong understanding of self and also a sense of being connected to others. These women of hope should be able to meet the inevitable difficulties of life with courage and faith. When the young women leave the institute, she wanted them to be discerning beings who understand the value and beauty of life, so that they could confidently transcend society's stereotypical expectations and demands.

Being a woman of vision, Mother Bertille wanted her students to be multi-talented. So, the ordinary daily routine was sometimes interspersed with profitable variety entertainments. These much-entailed practice played a part in helping the little ones to appreciate their religious and cultural heritage, and to attract other parents to bring their children to school. The children started to put up programmes in aid of the Indian orphans and disabled and for many other causes. For example, in 1937 the December issue of the *Annals* tells us of an enthusiastic audience enjoying the concert put up by the St Joseph's orphans for three consecutive days in aid of the Indian orphans and disabled. Appreciating the efficient and historic work done by Mother Bertille, *The Agra Citizen* expressed its wish that she might be spared to guide the destinies of St Joseph Orphanage and School. It also attributed the transformation of this school into a regular educational institution from a home sheltering orphans.

The fact of the matter from history is that St Joseph's orphans' routine duties in various apartments of the convent and school were occasionally punctuated by visits of the dignitaries of the Church and the State. In 1875, Edward VII, the Prince of Wales, visited India and the Agra Mission. The Agra Convent archives and Revd FrVannini's *Hindustan-Tibet Mission* provide some account of the visit: "There stood the venerable Mgr. M.A. Jacopi, surrounded by his priests, the nuns of JM, who crossed the sea for the cause of education of girls. One side counted by hundreds was the daughters of the British ruling class, on the other side the Indian orphans" (116).

In 1936, there was an enthusiastic reception accorded to Lady Haig, wife of the Governor of the U.P. by the Agra nuns and girls when she visited St Joseph's School in connection with its Girl Guides. It was then called 'The Fourth Agra Guide Company'. The following year, four teachers of the school were given the opportunity to take a course in 'Girl Guiding' in Nainital. The year 1940 saw the inception of 'Blue Bird' Guiding for junior school pupils. In 1940, St Joseph's became a Junior High School. This institution became a Hindi-medium School after India's independence.

The Convent of Jesus and Mary School, Waverly, started in 1845, was the first of the Convent Boarding Schools in the hills of the Northern Province, and its growth and development was very visible and fast moving. Waverly in Mussoorie, the present-day Uttarakhand, the second oldest of Jesus and Mary institutions in India, is beautifully situated at the top of a high Himalayan range. From its inception, the nuns, the staff, and the students together worked hard with great zeal and dedication. And they made 'Waverly' a great institution where the students acquired not only academic excellence, but sound moral values which make the 'Waverlites' stand out among the crowds as well as balanced personalities. The Waverly estate comprised of two large houses: one, the convent and the other, the boarding school. Even its early years Waverly has been one of the leading schools in the North.

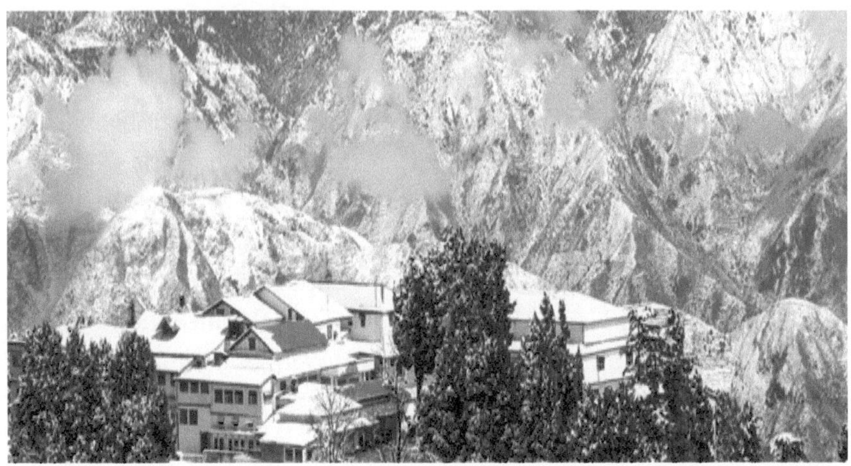

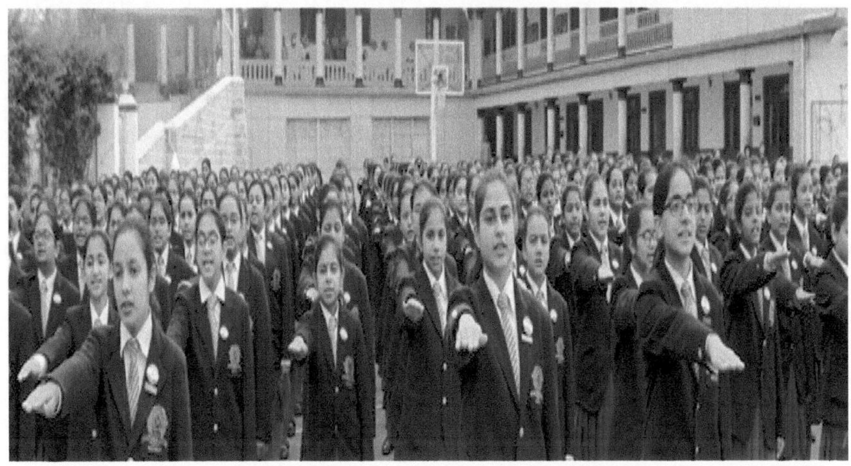

CJM School Waverly, Mussoorie

The dream of the pioneers to impart sound education, based on the ideals of Claudine Thevenet, has been realised and fulfilled by the succeeding generations of devoted Sisters. In the past more than 175 years, innumerable pupils have left the portals of Waverly as self-confident and disciplined young women, fully prepared to face the challenges of contemporary India. When Waverly celebrated its Centenary, Archbishop Vani spoke at the Mass celebrated in Waverly chapel. He spoke about the marvellous work done by the spiritual daughters of Claudine Thevenet: "What charms the visitor most at Waverly Convent and its boarding School is the friendly atmosphere of the place, the ready welcome one receives, and the spirit of camaraderie that exists among the inmates, Catholics and non-Catholics alike" (qtd. in *Souvenir of the Waverly School Centenary* 3). Since 1845 the institution built several buildings and made extensions, additions, and improvements on the constructions already in existence for the purpose of running an educational institution.

The Admission Register of 1890-1903 showed that among the admissions about 90% were Irish children and 10% were English, German, French, Scottish and Eurasian together. According to the register a few boys also were admitted in the School, perhaps as boarders. In 1913, the first Indian student was admitted. She was Rajendra Kaur from Khalsia district and in 1914 the second Indian girl who studied in this prestigious institution was Mary Agnes Rikh, the daughter of the Raja of Tajpore (*School Admission Register Waverly* 1913-1914). Since then, Indian daughters from royal families and Indian Christians also started enrolling themselves in the Waverly Convent School for education. In 1916, Lucy Rikh-Tajpoer living in Dehradun and seven-year-old Rani of Sherkot also took admission in the Boarding School (*School Admission Register Waverly* 1916, 176). In 1921, Amrit Kaur of Nabha [who later became the first Indian Health Minister in the Cabinet of Jawaharlal Nehru, India's first Prime Minister] and in 1922, Indira of Kapurthala and so on took admission. So, till 1940 more than fifty Indian girls studied in the Waverly Convent School. There were a good number of boarders and day-scholars, including the children of neighbouring Rajahs.

In 1913, as the number of children increased, Mother Borgia enlarged two rooms, one in Waverly and one in Belmont by throwing down the dividing walls, and she made two more classrooms as well. On 19th March 1914, there lashed a dreadful cyclone through which tremendous damage was caused to the school. The whole roof was torn apart and thrown away. As the number of students increased in the school, it was necessary to appoint more resident teachers also. So, in 1917, two new rooms were built for teachers at Belmont. In 1918, there were 118 boarders and 40 day-scholars studying in the boarding school. It again demanded for more dormitories and classrooms.

By 1922, the strength of the school went up to 120 girls. The increase in number was due to the fact that the Indian railway gave substantial aid to their officers towards the education of their children in good hill schools. The school needed a hall and a playground. So, the school authorities decided to raise some funds for it. In 1931, when the Health Inspector inspected the school, he certified the school as the best kept school in the station (*School Inspection Report CJM, Waverly* 1931). In 1932, when the school opened, 60 more children were admitted in the school. In 1933, another group of 90 more children joined the school. The school had always nine to ten nuns teaching on the staff besides its secular teachers.

In 1948, the school re-opened with a few . After Independence nearly all the Europeans and Anglo-Indians left the country and naturally, they took their children too with them. Now many of our Indian families began to bring their daughters to the school and enrolled them for their academic studies. From 1920 onwards, the school had its High school classes IX and X. Waverly was mainly a residential school, but it had a large proportion of day-scholars even from its earliest years. This continued almost till the 1950s. In its early years, the school had to face much financial distress. So, in the 1940s, the fee was raised from Rs. 50 to 60. His Grace Archbishop Vani in his sermon said:

Who can count the spiritual works that have been performed in this Convent since its beginning, the prayers that have arisen to heaven from this very chapel, the masses heard, the many acts of mortification, of penance and sorrow enacted in this place! Truly we can exclaim with Solomon, 'this place is holy and the gate of heaven!' (quoted in *Souvenir of the Waverly School Centenary 1845-1945,* 12).

Today when we look at the world, we see it is too engulfed, too deeply sunk in the mire of material pleasures, to appreciate and understand the spiritual ones. But no one understands the spiritual value of a good Christian education, of prayer and sacrifice. *The Statesman* reports, "We are grateful and heartily thank the Almighty for a Religious house and a School whose name is great and famous all over India, and which has earned and established an enviable position on account of its traditional, solid and sound education imparted to its children, and for its well-regulated discipline" ("A Hundred Years of Service"). Records of the first hundred years are scarce, the nuns have preferred like their Founder to write on spiritual topics, but tradition carries down to us the story of their virtues, their patience, charity and zeal. Many generations of girls have felt their salutary influence, and their memory has been an inspiration to all.

When Waverly celebrated its hundred years of existence as a women educational institution, His Grace Archbishop Evangelist Vani in his sermon said:

> Besides its geographical and material beauty and aspects what principally concerns us today is the fact that this Convent, started hundred years ago, has been a medium, has been the instrument for imparting good, sound, solid and Christian education to thousands and thousands of children, in forming their character and enabling them to occupy an honourable and even high position in social life. And today scattered as they are all over India and other countries, they … sacrifice to see to their temporal and spiritual welfare, and were to them more than tender and loving mothers (qtd. in Souvenir of the Waverly Centenary 12).

In the 1840s, the Congregation of Jesus and Mary, out of great zeal for the love of God and the service of humanity burning in their hearts, had two ends in view: the education of European girls and the education of Indian girls. The Sisters were invited to Sardhana, a village about 30 km away from the Meerut town, by Bishop Carli to open a home for the widows of the soldiers and destitute whose plight was pitiable. Their work grew daily from strength to strength and spread rapidly. As we have already seen in the previous chapter, the boarding school at Sardhana was at first opened for the education of the children of European army officers chiefly from Meerut, and the offspring of skilled craftsmen and other professionals who were in the service of the famous Begum Sumroo of Sardhana.

Ever since the school was set up in 1848, the JM sisters began the noble work of serving the poor children with few orphan children of the locality of Sardhana village. The sisters began to take classes for the needy and poor children of the locality. Many children, who could not afford to go to English medium schools for economic reasons, were able to attend this school, as it was a government-aided school. Over a period of time, sisters felt the need for expanding the school in all possible ways to cater to the needs of many.

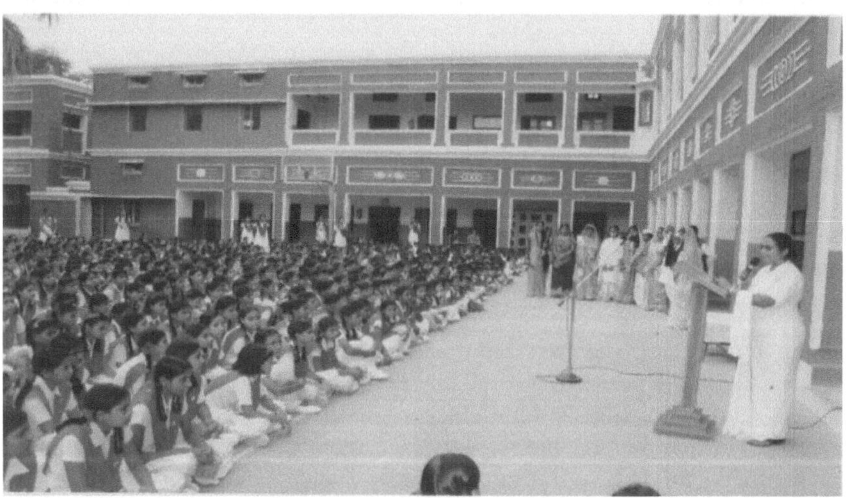

St Joseph's Inter College Sardhana, Meerut

The school had to undergo a series of difficult times and changes in its early years of its existence. Dr. A. Hartman, Bishop of Patna, who visited Sardhana on Christmas Day in 1853, attests that the nuns of JM had a most flourishing school for European girls in Sardhana (Vannini 119). He found five nuns in charge of the school. The mutiny of 1857 had a bad effect on the establishment. In the afternoon of the 14th May 1857, the nuns and boarders set out from Sardhana to the military quarters in Meerut. The survivors returned to Sardhana on 8th October 1857, nearly five months later (Chronicles of St. Joseph's School, Sardhana 1857, 153).

After the return of the nuns to Sardhana, the Europeans thought that the place was too far from their centres and was not sufficiently safe for their daughters. Hence, when in 1858 the nuns re-opened the school, they had to think out ways and means of carrying on the work of their mission. The government decided not to pay for the boarders but only for the orphans and extremely poor children (Albert 12). In 1858, the school re-opened as an orphanage and primary school for Indian girls; but educationally it made little progress.

In 1902, the nuns were ordered by the Bishop of Agra, Dr Charles Gentili to move to another of their houses, in order to make room for a number of Franciscan nuns whom he had brought from his native town in Italy, as he had no other house for them. The nuns of JM, of course, had other houses to go to. After five years the same Bishop appealed to them to resume their work at Sardhana. So, they returned and worked at Sardhana in 1907. From then on, they devoted themselves anew to this work, the one so dear to the Founder. In 1922, the nuns of JM at Sardhana were asked to shift again but to another location. This time, however, it was to be in Sardhana itself. They were offered a house nearby.

In 1936, the school was recognized as a Middle School. Over a period of time, there has been a real impetus in India towards the education of women, much neglected in former times, and so the school in Sardhana was recognized by the government as a Junior High School by 1950. At that time there were 115 resident children, for whom practically everything was supplied by the nuns. Some of the resident students were orphans; others were children of poor parents with large families or girls from the village around, where there was no Catholic school at all (Theodora, "Correspondence of Mother St. Theodora" 1958). They received good training to make them useful and capable women, good wives, and mothers. Most of them married at a noticeably young age, but some of the students, who were more intelligent, became nurses or teachers and their record was very competent and satisfactory. Besides 115 boarders, there were also 65 day-scholars who followed the same course.

In Sardhana for nearly 160 years, the Sisters of JM gave Catholic education in the vernacular to poor Indian girls. In addition to the usual course of studies for the middle school, the children were taught all domestic crafts also. The daily sweeping, washing, and cooking were done by the girls themselves. They also were taught to make their own clothes and learn embroidery, flower-making and knitting. This was an important part of their training for they were extremely poor and had to do this in their own homes afterwards. One of the Sisters said: "We are grateful to God that we can make their young lives happy and keep them from wrong-doings; their childhood is all too short and they have a life of hardship before them, owing to the conditions in which they are likely to live" (Franciscan Annals 1949). This was true of most Indian women.

Marriage was the usual career for most of the girls, but some had become teachers, and a few had joined the ranks of the devoted Associate Sisters in the Congregation of JM. Religious instruction was given to them daily. It was in 1940s St. Joseph's Sardhana won shield three times, competing with various vernacular schools. The children, apart from their academic pursuits, were also facilitated in harvesting and gathering of wheat and other crops in the convent grounds. They were also keen on games. Among the permanent residents there were some old women, crippled or blind, who had been here since infancy and brought to the convent in times of famine. In 1949, there were 142 students on the roll, among them 112 were boarders and 30 were day-scholars. The teaching staff consisted of 12 members and six of them were nuns.

It should be noted that in 1936, the school was recognised as a Middle School. In 1947, the medium of instruction was changed from Urdu to Hindi. The girls were taught religious instruction, sweeping, washing, and cooking. And by 1950, it was promoted as a Junior High School. When the school got the status of Inter College in 1965 a large number of students started joining the school. In fact, this school, popularly known as St Joseph's Girls Inter College was the first School in Sardhana.

During its early years of establishment, the CJM Chelsea, what was then called the Roman Catholic Military Asylum, had to go through a lot of ups and downs. Bishop Bedenik's grand schemes were sadly frustrated. He could not raise the necessary fund for the building of the school as the army headquarters at Calcutta openly opposed the founding of a Roman Catholic educational institution. The Chief Secretary announced disapproving of Canning's early generous gesture, though they were supposed to abide by it. The military authorities would render no other financial assistance. This attitude of sustained opposition continued for years. Religious antipathy played no small part in the frustration, for Roman Catholic institutions were viewed with disfavour. At that time Catholic involvement was in its early stages. The conflicting ideological orientations between the Protestant and Catholics did affect the social affirmative actions. Despite a series of oppositions and criticisms, the nuns persistently endeavoured to care for the poor and the neglected by building a comfortable home for the orphans and the needy.

By the end of December 1866, the Bishop decided that the boys' orphanages should be transferred to Mussoorie, and the girls were to migrate from Elysium Hill to the Chelsea estate. Certain operations had been commenced the previous September to extend the main building of the institution there, and the accommodation was far from satisfactory. But by selling the property of Elysium Hill, owned by the Diocese of Agra, it was made possible to build a larger new school at Chelsea. This was eventually to hold about 3000 children.

Mr Willmot, the Inspector of Schools at this time, verified and found that the state of the orphanage was very creditable to all engaged in the tuition of the girls. Every official report confirmed that from their looks the girls appeared to be remarkably healthy. The number of boarders by 1874 had risen to thirty. They were charged various fees the highest being Rs. 25. The number of children in the lower school had risen from 122 to 155, and the average maintenance of each child was Rs. 14 per month.

Mother Gonzaga, the Superior of the institution, wrote to the government to be kind enough to reconsider the order that limited the number of children to one hundred:

> This restriction would, if enforced, deprive a considerable portion of the community, especially women and non-commissioned officers, soldiers and pensioners of the advantage of removing their children from the influence of barrack life and from unhealthy localities, to a hill climate combined with a sound educational end so essential to their future prospects in life. The enforcement of the order would press with very great severity on orphan children ("Correspondence of Mother Gonzaga" 1864).

This appeal of the Superior makes us to believe that the order passed in the Council was not enforced, and the nuns were left free to admit as many poor children as the orphanage could possibly hold.

An interesting feature of life at this time was the preparation of the older girls for their future life. Practically all remained in the school until they were 16 or 18 years of age. European life in India at that time offered little scope for a professional or business career for girls. Therefore, the nuns kept them until they were ready to face the world. If they had relatives in England or Ireland who were willing to take full responsibility, the army sent them home. If there were no relatives, the nuns found a place for them in families of good repute, where they worked as children's nurses or companion helpers to elderly people. The more intelligent and capable pupils were sent to other convents as pupil-teachers. Similarly, quite a considerable number of them, if they so desired and decided, got married. The nuns, guided by the advice and help of good secular friends and the parish priests, met the families of the young men, and made all the marriage arrangements carefully. They, thus, selected suitable girls, with a trousseau, prepared them for their future life, and often had the marriages celebrated in the convent chapel or nearby parish church.

Many were the succeeding generations of Chelsea pupils who were the children, grandchildren, and great grandchildren of these alumni members. The available records suggest that these Chelseans, of whom a large number of them were Anglo-Indians, proved to be responsible and responsive individuals who continued to contribute to the Indian society at various levels. This is to suggest that serving India was one of their main objectives until the great exodus of European and Anglo-Indian families. Even after Indian independence, the nuns kept their contact with most of these families. The old nuns knew the parents and grandparents of the little girls in the schools, and Chelsea became an ever widening and increasing family. Even today by correspondence and by occasional re-unions in England and other parts of the world, they keep up these old ties and foster an old family spirit.

It bears mentioning that a chapel was built in 1872 - 73. It was planned as a little cruciform church to accommodate nuns, pupils, and Catholics from nearby bungalows. Intriguingly, the nuns and the children worked with the porters, carrying, and stacking stones or putting up logs of wood. Since the funding from missionary societies and the government was inadequate, the nuns themselves were able to execute the construction programme efficiently. The chapel came to be used for religious worship in July 1874. Meanwhile, a little plot of land at the foot of the Chelsea hillside was obtained to make a cemetery. It was and is a 'most beautiful and peaceful spot,' as Sir Edward J. Buck describes in his monumental work, *Simla-Past and Present.* He also depicted the cemetery as 'God's heaven' (23).

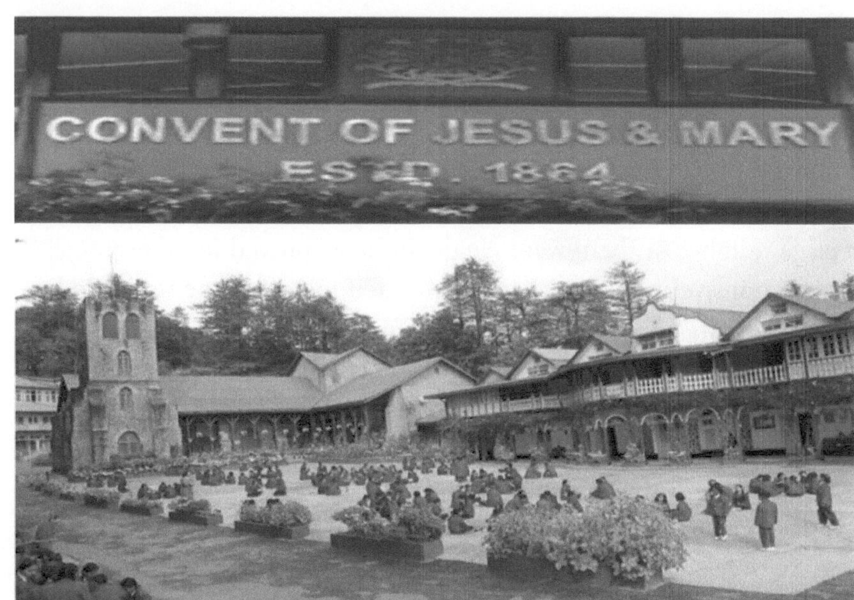

CJM School Chelsea, Shimla, 1864

For some time, there had been a request for a Boarding School for girls to be opened for the daughters of the economically and socially affluent families. As the military children were now well settled in new buildings, the bungalows were renovated and re-constructed to accommodate a good number of girls of varying ages. This necessitated additional classrooms, music cabins, a hall, a spacious dining room and some large well ventilated dormitories. Therefore, the last decades of the nineteenth century witnessed a tremendous growth and development infrastructure facilities to advance academic and co-curricular activities. Finally, the Education Department approved it and gladly gave some assistance through grants for these improvements.

In the 1890s, there was a change in the military regulations, and it brought about a series of changes in the orphanage too. Since regiments were no longer kept for such long periods in India, the number of orphans decreased, and St Francis School admitted pupils as boarders at a very small fee. Though a considerable number of parents wanted their children to be sent to the hills, they could not meet the ordinary boarding school charges. In this way there grew up in the Chelsea compound two schools – St Francis and St Aloysius. The plan worked well and greatly to the advantage of the orphans. As far as the middle school was concerned, promising pupils were inducted into the high school for the final examination.

The convent schools enjoyed many special advantages during this period. There were practically no day-scholars, so the children formed a little colony quite apart from the turmoil of life in the town or on the plains. They had mountain roads and beautiful wooded hillsides where they could feel free. There were plenty of facilities for games and healthy exercises, even though the age of strenuous physical training had not yet arrived. Discipline was easy and homely, and conduct was consistently good. Problem cases were few. Juvenile delinquency played no part in the lives of these pupils. The moral tone was sound and healthy, and the girls found unlimited interests in their routine work, daily occupations and in their games. The religious atmosphere with its succession of celebrations and feasts was a powerful influence leading to the good of the pupils. They also enjoyed many privileges socially. Although the military authorities had not wanted the orphanage and had opposed its foundation for a variety of reasons, the Punjab Education Department gave the schools their patronage during the first two decades of the 20th century.

Set out to ensure that European education in India should not lag behind that of the West, more frequent and searching inspections were carried on and the curriculum and syllabus for the classes were revised regularly. Courses in art and physical training were organized and the standard of the high school examination was raised considerably. World War I did not seriously affect educational life in the Punjab. In fact, in many ways it helped to widen and deepen the children's knowledge and experience and opened up activities which were beneficial to them. First aid courses were given in the schools. Girl Guiding found a place in their school life and the girls became interested in different topics which they studied to get their extra badges and stars.

A strenuous course of physical training was made compulsory for teachers and pupils, and Fire Drill had an important place in school life. The girls worked really hard for the Red Cross and they made a very considerable amount of hospital linen, while recreation hours were devoted to knitting for the soldiers. On the cultural side contacts of this institution got widened. The pupils met many people from the allied countries. Lectures were given, and with the growing use of bioscope and the cinema they saw pictures of various lands and many phases of war campaigns. Nevertheless, given the fact that they were far away from the centers of fighting and disaster, the Chelsea children were not called upon to suffer under any circumstances.

Once again, in spite of wars, life at the Chelsea Convent went on undisturbed considerably. When Burma was in danger, refugees flocked to India and a number of Burmese and Anglo-Burmese children came to the school. They were intelligent, ambitious, friendly little people and several of them were distinctly above average in attainment. Children of other nationalities also came, and the school became a little Commonwealth of Nations living under ideal conditions unspoiled by national conflicts and antipathies. Radio broad casts of news from all over the world, musical programmes and plays also helped to widen the children's interests and deepen their cultural world. Cinemas presented some fine films and the newsreels kept the children well-informed of developments throughout the world.

The pupils of the school and the students at St Bede's College annually produced first class performances which were widely patronized by both civil and military authorities. As the war years dragged on and events became more and more soul stirring in the East, the school children became fully aware of the possibility of even India being drawn into the conflict, but they were spared from that. However, no one ever could foresee what had awaited them when the war was over. The year 1945 brought the beginning of a new era in the school's history. As the regulations for Independence proceeded, British and Anglo-Indian civil and military men made plans to take their families to England or Australia. Some even decided to go to Canada.

The vacancies in the schools were filled immediately as many Indian parents were anxious for their daughters to be admitted. This was, however, a change lasting throughout the years from 1945 to 1950. But it was during those years that the school suffered two of the most tragic events. The first took place on the night of 26th April 1946, when three quarters of the building were destroyed by a devastating fire. The morning of 29th April was delightful. All was set for a year of happy successful work, but within twenty-four hours everything was burned into ashes. During the previous winter, the entire building had been repaired and redecorated. Practically all the furniture had been renewed and no effort had been spared to restore it to pre-war attractiveness.

The Archbishop of Delhi-Shimla lent his house 'Eagle Mount' for the Junior School for a year. Within a fortnight, arrangements were made to re-open the school. Tents were put up in the compound and classes continued in the compound for a couple of years in tents lent to the nuns by the military authorities. The novitiate house accommodated some of the girls. Every corner of the remaining portion of the building was made as comfortable as possible, and for the remainder of the year, classes and routine school life continued under sadly different conditions. But staff and pupils met the situations courageously. Meanwhile, ruined building was demolished, and plans were made to erect a new building. The disaster had brought a closer bond of union between the local people and the school. The old spirit and religious ideals produced fruit. The children and the general public loved the school still more truly and loyally in its hour of trial than ever before.

But the plans that had been made for a speedy restoration were razed to the ground, for the estimated loss had been over ten lakhs. The old building had been insured at an incredibly low valuation. When all the expenses of clearance were met, they decided to erect a small additional block to the novitiate house and to reconstruct a portion of the building which had been only partially destroyed. The Education Department, though deeply sympathetic, was in no position to help with a building grant, for partition had left Punjab in a most difficult financial and political situation. Only temporary restoration was possible. However, by early 1947 it was evident that the country had to face a terrible crisis. Still more European families left India, so the school numbers consequently decreased. A few new pupils were admitted, so the accommodation sufficed. There were, however, nearly two hundred children in the school that year. Muslims, Hindus, Sikhs, and the Europeans lived happily together almost unmindful of the tornado of violence which was about to break over Northern India.

By August 1947, the crises were upon the Punjab and a great dread began to enter into the hearts of the authorities of the school. Care was taken to ensure that the pupils were strictly and carefully supervised. Extra police were employed to guard the compound at night and every effort was made to ensure peaceful relations among the servants, for they too were Hindus, Christians, Muslims, and Sikhs. All went well until rioting began in Shimla. Then, far away across the valley at night came sounds of trouble from the distant townships and along the hill roads. The sound of distant firing on the mobs could be heard and servants and staff brought in stories about the atrocities. The neighbouring houses, owned by Muslims who had fled, were looted. It was impossible to hide all these from the children, but they were kept calm and happy. The hill men, most of them were Muslims, who carried provisions were forced to run away because of the growing threats. Consequently, a group of nuns, teachers, and some of the senior girls from the school formed a well co-ordinated group and marched out to the town to purchase tinned goods, groceries and other necessary items. They carried these in packages on their backs while the boys of Milsington, St Edward's School brought wheelbarrows and helped to push the heavier loads.

But a more painful menace hung over the establishment. It was known in the town that there were some Muslim pupils, daughters of well-known men in responsible positions, who were anxious to get back to Pakistan. Just when anxiety was at its climax a European officer appeared. A special secret convoy was being arranged by which the children from various schools were to be taken under military protection quietly at dawn. One morning the party left to the relief of all, but some days of anxiety had to be passed before news was received from Lahore.

When the school closed in 1947, the nuns had deep sighs of relief, and many prayers of gratitude were offered to God for all the anxious periods. In the school's history, this had been the worst period but here again trial had strengthened the bonds of union in the school and college. The pupils became even more sisterly, more loving, and careful of one another. Suffering made them one great family. March 1948 found the school somewhat depleted in numbers but that was not to last for long. Once life in the East Punjab settled down, numerous Sikh families who had settled there, applied for admission for their children as boarders and day-scholars. Hindu parents too applied in great numbers. The Europeans and Anglo-Indians, who had remained in India, still recognize Chelsea as their home school.

At a time, when the notion of charity faced a series of challenges largely due to financial constraints, the JM institutions did not stop in assisting the students generously by giving fee concessions. Even today JM educational institutions all over India offer quite a number of scholarships and fee concessions to the economically weaker sections, who pursue their education under multiple challenges and difficulties. It is this generous support that made Chelsea reach new heights. The more help it gave to the poor, the more it received from people who benefited from the missionary labour. They also used the resources carefully and meticulously although they had to set aside some of the construction programmes for the benefit of the underprivileged. Nevertheless, the standard of education was maintained and even raised. The examination results were outstanding, and much was done to enhance the general culture of the pupils. Indian dancing, Indian music and Hindi were encouraged, even in the church services one heard the children singing Hindi hymns and saying prayers in the vernacular.

During this period, the Chelsea school was advancing forward in the interest of Indian education. The institution had a certain degree of an international atmosphere. The members of the diplomatic and other services sent their daughters to the school. There were pupils from Africa, Thailand, and Indonesia, Singapore, also from Europe and America. Professionals and businessmen appreciated the school. The daughters of engineers in India's development-oriented projects formed quite a large percentage of its alumni then and now. All this increased the opportunity for general culture and international understanding.

Expansion into the New Horizons in the 20th Century

Nestling in the foothills of the Himalayas, the Convent of Jesus and Mary, Dehradun was born on 1st February 1901 with fifteen students on the roll. Revd Mother Isabel was the founder and the first Principal. The beginning of this establishment was so humble that hardly any tangible vestiges remain, but the school has grown and progressed greatly over the years beyond all expectations. The pioneers and their successors, by their love, selfless devotion, and dedication, made the service of education meaningful and relevant. It is this sensational spirit of those valiant women still guides and inspires the present management and staff. They continue to educate and train their students to meet the challenges of a highly technological and competitive society. Presently, the CJM, Dehradun imparts education to about three thousand girls from lower kindergarten to class XII, in all streams of study.

The CJM branch at Dehradun in Uttarakhand is one of the oldest educational institutions especially for girls. In fact, according to the Indian Census Report for the year 1901 the literacy rate in the field of women's education was nearly 2 per cent. To dare to start a school for girls in those days was a great step towards the upliftment of women. Dehradun, therefore, owes this institution a great deal of gratitude for what it has done in the field of women's education in the city and in the state. When we look back into the history of the school, it is astonishing to see that the seed that was sown a hundred and twenty years ago, with barely fifteen students on the rolls, has become a full-grown tree, giving shelter to almost three thousand students today. Meanwhile, thousands of cheerful and energetic young girls have passed through these portals of learning, fully equipped to face the new challenges of contemporary India. We are proud to note that all these students are successful in their life and most of them occupy laudable positions in the country and abroad, through which they serve their country and their fellow human beings. Thus, the institution has rendered yeoman's service not only to the city of Dehradun but also to the country at large.

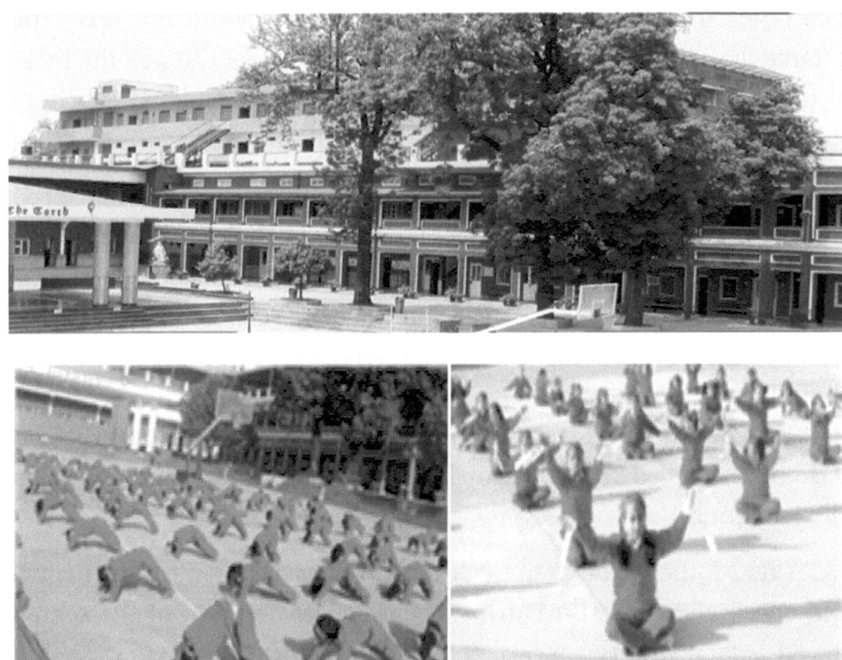

CJM School, Dehradun

Over the years of growth and development of CJM Dehradun, the credit goes to the management, Principal, and staff in the past and present, for their selfless wonderful dedication and meticulous planning. They provided quality education by making the students intellectually sound and physically fit. In the beginning the school was named St Joseph's Day School. It was not a plain sailing for the school in those early days because of the natural calamities like earth quake and minor epidemics like measles, whooping cough and cholera were sweeping through the villages of north India where people lived in tin-roofed buildings and poor conditions. On 4th April 1905, a devastating earthquake that had its epicenter in the Kangra valley rocked North India. The earthquake occurred in the Kangra Valley and the Kangra region of the Punjab Province (modern day Himachal Pradesh) in India. It measured 7.8 on the surface wave magnitude scale and killed more than 20,000 people. The repercussions of the devastating earthquake did not leave the Uttaranchal hills free. People of Uttaranchal also had to pay the price in different ways. As a result, the building of St. Joseph's Day School suffered a considerable damage and devastation.

In spite of these bizarre situations, 28th February 1906, was a red letter day in the history of the school. Her Royal Highness, the Princess of Wales, who would be Queen Mary of England, visited the school. She was very much impressed by the way the school was run by the JM nuns. Mother Isabel continued her tenure till 1910-1911. The sixth cholera outbreak began in India, subsequently spreading to the Middle East, North Africa, Eastern Europe, and Russia. According to WHO the outbreak killed 8,00,000 people. However, the nuns bravely survived all vicissitudes.

After Mother Isabel's tenure, Rev. Sr. Anastasia became the principal and continued till 1917. During her time the children of the school staged several charity concerts to raise funds for the war effort, and to keep up the morale of all. Meanwhile, the students did not neglect their studies. Gradually the numerical strength of students increased, and new classrooms were being built at this time. The School Log Book noted that the school was gaining ground in spite of a series of opposition (*Chronicles CJM School, Dehradoon* 1912).

In 1917, Sr Colette steered the school through the turbulent years of World War I, setting a brilliant example of fortitude and faith. Even though she could not make much progress in terms of buildings or increase in the strength of students, she preserved the existing ones. In

1920, Sr Clementine became the Principal of the school. Perhaps she was the most creative Principal to date. She gave the lead to perform entertainment programmes, while not neglecting the academic and moral development of the children. During her time in 1923, five little boys were taken in as boarders. The 'little fellows' were the first boys to study in this school. The school was visited annually by the Inspector of European Schools and reports indicate that the pupils did particularly well in Music, French and English. The Convent was now beginning to send their pupils for drives and picnics and to the occasional lantern slide show or magic show.

It is crucial to note that in 1935, the school had its first Indian nun Mother Maria Laetitia Lobo as a teacher. By now the nuns realized that there was a need to educate the Indian children as well. With this in mind, a separate school for the Indian children was started in 1938 with Mother Ursula Neary as its in-charge. This school was called the St Francis School. The Indian parents also realized the need to educate their daughters. Meanwhile, another World War had been brewing up in Europe. The nuns and staff of the school were very particular to give the children all the possible information about what was happening in the world outside their school. The students of St Joseph's and St Francis' schools spent an hour and a half every day listening to the news on the radio. Ever aware of the tumultuous World War outside, the nuns were alarmed. They taught the children how they had to be caring and sharing towards their brothers and sisters. Once again, the children began to host charity teas, luncheons, concerts and so on to raise funds for the war-victims.

A new building, part of the present Red Block, was opened in 1940. Now the school could accommodate more numbers. The house system was introduced for the first time in 1941. There were only two houses then – St Clare's and St. Hilda's. This was the first time the house captains were appointed from the students, and a best House Cup was introduced. In subsequent years, the house system was dissolved and modified several times. It was around this time that the District Sports

Competition, then called the Dehradun Olympic Games, was begun. The students of the Convent were encouraged and trained by the Sisters and the staff to participate in it. They participated with the utmost zeal and won many prizes, often setting district, even state records. The school Sports Day became an annual event.

During this period Burma was again attacked by Britain and the Burmese people were scattered. Many of them came to India as refugees. Several refugee children from Burma joined the school in 1942 onwards. They remained in the convent till they were repatriated at the end of World War II. In days overshadowed by reports of war, the school continued to set a consistently impressive record of achievements.

In 1947, with Indian Independence, the European soldiers went back to their own native places; naturally, their children also had to leave the school. Because of this great exodus in the same year, the boarding section had to be closed, much to the regret of the nuns, the children, and their parents. "It was the food question that made us close the boarding" (*Chronicles CJM School, Dehradoon* 1947). Soon after the Independence in 1947, St Joseph's day-school for European children and St Francis' school for Indian children were formally amalgamated and the whole unit was named as the 'Convent of Jesus and Mary School, Dehradun. Mother Ursula Warrington was appointed Principal. In the beginning, there were 390 students on the roll. The new Principal led the school through the difficult period of transition that followed the Independence of India. The school has always been responsive to the turmoil in the surrounding world. During the wars, the frequent natural calamities and occasions of civil unrest, the school has maintained the spirit of compassion for the suffering people of our nation who needed the support of the schools of JM Congregation. The children were constantly taught that they have to give back to society, nation, and the world selflessly what they have learned in the school.

Over the decades, the school building has been extended and refurnished many times. In introspect, it cannot be denied that the school has had a glorious run in the past century. The Principal Sr Janet

Kottamkombil and the staff remarked that the list of our illustrious alumni is long and impressive. The school has not only done well in the fields of Music, Sports, Academics, Debates, and Dramatics, but also had a distinguished record in terms of social service projects, exchange programmes and excursions. The institution has undergone many transitions in the past decades. The school is more than a brick and mortar façade on the edge of a dusty field. It is a veritable monument to the aspirations and accomplishments of the some very remarkable people. It is a legacy that continues to be fulfilled. So many young people have passed through these hallowed portals, and so many more shall follow. The school, management, principal, staff and students, past and present, with one voice assert that "one tie binds us all is the vision shared by each member of the CJM, Dehradoon family"(quoted in *Souvenir of CJM School, Dehradoon* 2001, 4).

It should be recorded that the dawn of 1845 saw the inception of St Anthony's school in Agra. It was in the house of the military chaplain in the Cantonment area that St Anthony's made its humble beginnings. It was the vision of St Claudine, Foundress of the JM congregation to train the minds of young girls, so that they could lead a life which was purposeful, positive and constructive, to be able to live fruitfully and happily in society with others.

The invitation came from the Archbishop of Agra to open a day-school in Agra Cantonment. It is written in the *JM Annals* that one could hardly take a journey in North India without meeting former pupils of the Agra Convent who are still devotedly attached to their old school. Most of them had been orphaned because of the Afghan and Sikh wars. Military officers and civilians also commenced to build their bungalows in this area. Most records being probably destroyed in 1857, there is no information regarding the civil population at that time. After 1857, the old area Numillah having been destroyed, had to be rebuilt. Similarly, the British military enlarged their occupation land towards the North-West. The development of the district brought a set of civilians, who served the cantonments in various ways. Unfortunately, however, the pre-mutiny records are not available otherwise it would have been apparent. Consequently, no further reference is made of this day-school either in its archives or in the Convent, Wazirpura Road until 1902.

From the Cantonment records it seems that there were repeated requests to SrLucie to open a JM institution there in the Cantonment. An old Agra Cantonment board register of land properties undated lists 44A, Taj Road as 'Mother St Lucie's School'. There is no mention again in any other records. Since Agra had only the JM nuns who had connections and friends in Agra Cantonment it may be inferred that perhaps this was the beginning of what is now famous as St Anthony's School. There was a school in the cantonment; it was clear to Mother Virginie Sunons who recalled that immediately after her profession on 23 November, 1901 she was sent to help out in this school, which already seems to have borne the name 'St Anthony's School'.

It should be noted here that the Numillah school was re-opened in January 1902 at 44-A, the Mall as St Anthony's School and in 1926 moved to the present address No.5, the Mall. On 26th December 1926, the school was recognized as a primary school by the Department of Public Instruction (DPI). At the time of its inception, it was a primary school with classes up to VI. Even though the institution made steady progress, the Government requested the closure of class V and VI to maintain its primary status. But as some parents who did not wish to send their children to a Boarding School requested to the government and to the nuns not to close down the classes. At the pressure of the parents the government allowed the Classes V and VI to be continued. But most of the records related to this were destroyed during the 1857 revolt.

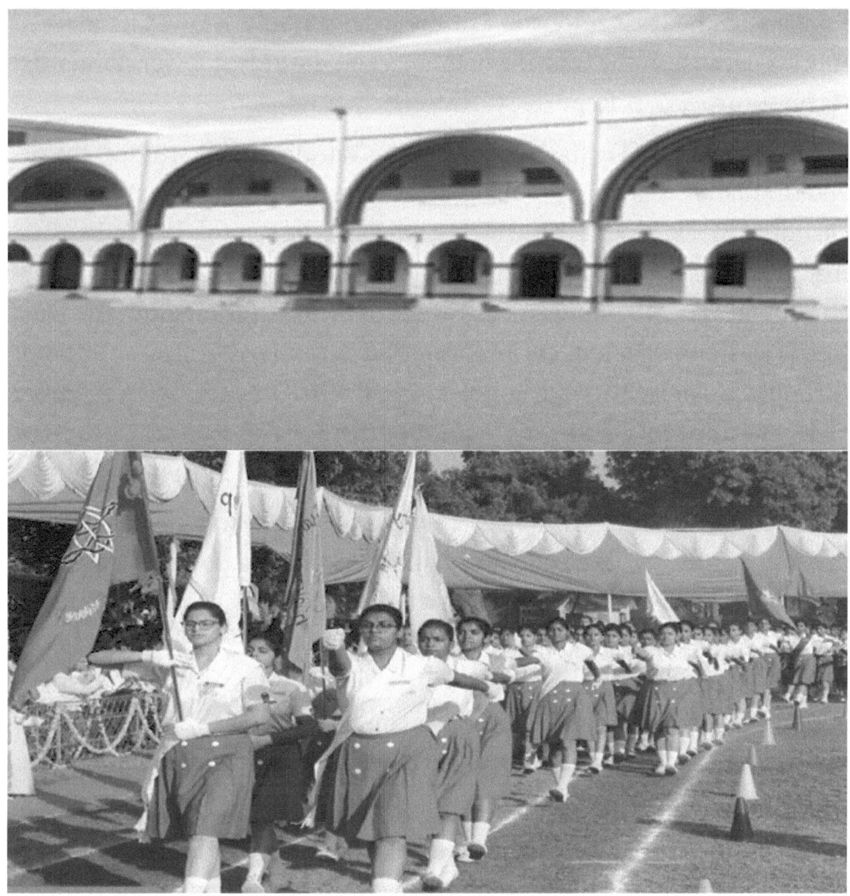

St Anthony's Junior College, Agra

Despite the fact that the school opened with fifteen pupils, its strength increased rapidly. In February 1910, the total number of students increased to 157. As the space became inadequate to accommodate these pupils, the school moved in 1926 to the house formerly occupied by the Alliance Bank in order to make the students more comfortable and convenient (Chronicles of Antony's School, Agra 1926). The work of the school is efficiently carried on by the staff, and the Inspector of European Schools appeared entirely satisfied. In his report, the Inspector of European Schools observed: "The school is the youngest of the schools in Agra and has risen rapidly. It is now by no means the smallest or the least important of the local schools. It owes its marked success because of the training of infants and the kids at lower standards" (School Inspection Report, St. Antony's School, Agra 1926).

By January 1927, the school had an enrolment in studies, music, and dramatics. Efforts were made to raise funds for the construction of Claudine Block, to suit the growing needs of the school. When in 1942, Agra became the headquarters of the Central Command, the school's enrolment was 240 pupils. As the needs of the institution grew, the Dina Block was constructed. As Indian culture received a strong impetus through music with traditional musical instruments, by November 1949 St Anthony's was fully equipped with a full Indian Orchestra. Since 1942, music has a place of prime importance in the curriculum.

Initially, when St Anthony's Day School, Agra was opened, it was predominantly for day-scholars. This is largely due to the fact that St Patrick's School was inconveniently distant for many of the residents in Agra. As a result, Mother St Lucie, the Provincial, purchased a house on the 44-A-Mall. The larger objective of her intent was to construct a school so that little girls and boys could attend the school regularly with-in an easy distance from their homes (*School Admission Register*, Antony's School Agra 1910).

Once the DPI had recognized the school as a separate institution of primary standard in January 1927, there was a notable fall in the number due to the suppression of standards V and VI, which were opened at the request of some parents who were unable to send their children to a boarding school or who objected to a boarding school. In March 1927, the Principal wrote that the Congregation was trying to secure the Alliance Bank Building for the school. In April they obtained their aim, and an imposing ceremony for the blessing of the building was done by Dr. E. Vani, the Archbishop of Agra. The school re-opened on the 20th April, 1927 children were delighted in their new quarters.

The school prepared the children for the music examination from the Trinity College of London. The school gained a name and fame, and numbers kept on increasing over a period of time. In 1931, the number of students rose from 159 to 175. In 1933, the school received Rs. 3000 from the colonial government as a building grant to construct the K.G. classroom. They continued to get grants from the government with great regularity. The military made arrangements for the conveyance of the children to the school. In 1948, for the first time an Indian Inspector Mr. S.S. Saxena came to inspect the school. Hindi was made the second language. Progress in admission kept on increasing. When the number increased still further, the boys were asked to go to a boys' school. St Anthony's Day School in the cantonment was opened as a Primary School, consisting of a Nursery, a large Kindergarten with all modern equipment, and four higher standards under Mother St Antonia and Mother St Francis. It won a fine reputation, which it continues to enjoy till today as being the best of its kind in the then united provinces.

Since the Declaration of Independence in 1947, Hindi has played an important part in the school curriculum. The school was highly appreciated by the Inspector, Pandit Shiveharanlal Chaturvedi when he visited the school in May 1948. He was highly pleased to see the classes, and surprised at the excellent tone of the school, especially at the standard of Hindi already attained in song and verse. He voiced his appreciation in a memorable speech to staff and pupils. The school used to stage a variety of entertainment programmes for the public, both in Hindi and in English. In 1949, the school had 286-day scholars on the roll, and there were 13 teachers, among them three were nuns. In the academic year 1980-'81 school had classes up to VIII grade, and there after each year the school started adding new classes. During the academic session of 1983-'84 class X was introduced. The 'No Objection Certificate' was granted to the school on 15th December 1983. Now the school is a Junior College with classes up to XII.

The school in Ambala began with sixteen to twenty-seven children from the Army families in 1909. The School was opened at the request of Fr Julius, Vicar General of the Archdiocese of Agra, then under Most Revd Gentili, to whom Archdiocese of Ambala then belonged. The first pupil was Albert Mortimer, son of Mr Connaught Ranger, a

Catholic. Mother St Colette Cournane was the first Principal of the school. Mother St Celestine Tarleton was the successor of Mother Colette. The number of students gradually increased, and in 1919 the military authorities requested the Sisters to transfer the school to Kasauli for the summer months. The political situation required that the children be evacuated to the Shimla hills. As the military moved between Ambala in the winter and Kasauli in the summer, the school also moved with the military regiments in order to accommodate itself to them. At that time, the school catered to the needs of the British children. The military officers who sent their children to the school resented the presence of the children of civilians of the poorer section of the society. A clause in the contract of the Ambala school posed a problem which was difficult to solve, relating to the pupils of the hill station Kasauli. They could only be admitted to the schools on the plains provided that they could reach the same standard of study and level of work as the children of the plains. This difficulty and other inconveniences obliged the Sisters to give up the school in Ambala in 1924, but without neglecting the Catholic pupils in Kasuali where the nuns helped the Chaplain by teaching catechism during the week and on Saturdays ("General Summaries" 1950).

The school had a precarious existence and was closed down more than once. However, in 1929-'30 at the request of Archbishop Kenealy of Shimla, it was re-opened and has functioned uninterruptedly since then (Cuthbert, *Echoes of a Century* 53). Mother St Dominic Cahill took over the school in these precarious times. She had a difficult time in accommodating the increasing number of children in the school. The nuns had no finance for a new building. For many years, the school was in a single-storeyed building. Nevertheless, when the school building was about to be expanded, the World War II broke out in 1939 and put a stop to it ("General Summaries" 1950).At first there had been only a primary school, but this rapidly advanced to middle and later a high school. The Cambridge Examinations were introduced which later gave way to the ISC Examinations. In 1940s, a new School building was planned with fine, large classrooms and wide shady verandas. After that still more children flocked to the school and so the senior section was opened. It was Mother Good Counsel Mascarenhas who was responsible for the first school building which still had only one storey, but it had spacious airy classrooms and wide shady verandas. After the reopening, the school has prospered, receiving a new span of life. By now the Indian parents felt the need and value of educating their daughters. As a result, a number of Indian girls had already been admitted into the classes.

The World War II brought a lot of physical and material loss to the school. The school was not in a position to continue. At last it was decided that the school should be given a chance, and the Provincial Mother Dominic Tightarwith and one young nun, spent the winter scrubbing, cleaning, and painting the dilapidated building. They did everything in their power to make the classrooms attractive, and on the opening day everyone was delighted. Mother Mecthilde Finnigan was given the charge of the school. It was indeed her true life's work. During the next thirty years she spent long periods as the Sister in charge, and it was she who was mainly responsible for the fine buildings which stand even today.

The main events that happened at that time needs to be critically studied and historically explored. First of all, Mother Mecthilde endeavoured to build up the school's reputation and make it popular. Parents were delighted with the progress their children made, and the happy, carefree atmosphere of the school and its surroundings. But the buildings were very old, and each monsoon season brought new problems: roofs leaked, servants' quarters fell down and the old school building constantly needed repair. Then the number increased so rapidly that a great part of the bungalow had to be used for classrooms and for the school library.

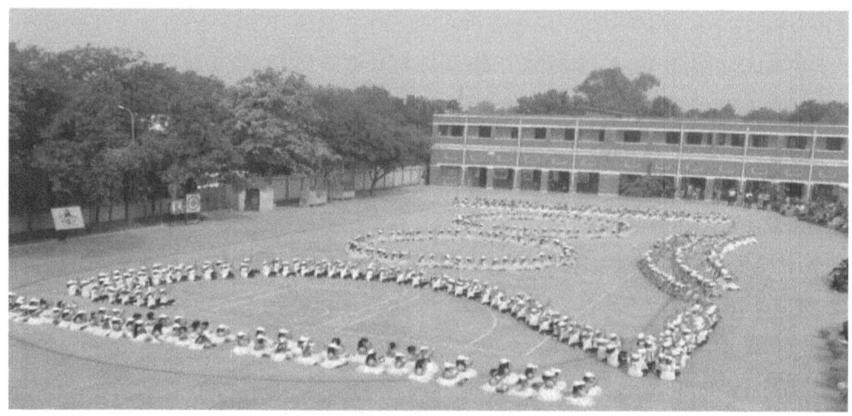

CJM School, Ambala, Haryana

Mother Mechtilde spent much time and energy in re-planning the compound. She laid out good playing fields surrounded by stone steps where the children could sit and watch the games and matches. There were beautiful flower beds, with such a profusion of brightly coloured blossoms that passersby in admiration stood to watch the children at play amid such attractive surroundings.

By now the new capital of the East Punjab Province was about to be constructed at Chandigarh, a few miles away on the Kalka Road, and this probably increased the importance of Ambala. In 1947, the capital of Punjab was shifted from Lahore to Shimla and subsequently then Prime Minister Jawaharlal Nehru declared Chandigarh as capital of Punjab in 1950. The Capital of Punjab (Development and Regulation) Act, 1952, defines Chandigarh as the capital of Punjab. The officers of the Indian regiments which took the place of the British troops after the passing of the Indian Independence Act of 1947 were very eager to have their children educated at the convent. There were well over four hundred day-scholars and many had to be disappointed as there was not sufficient accommodation for all the applications. The station is now an important training centre for the Indian Air Force, besides being the Headquarters of the Northern Command of the Indian Army.

In the 1940s, there were four nuns and eleven other teachers on the staff. The strength of the school was 300. Among them only 21 were Catholics. The aim now became the education of children from all walks of life, in order to fit them for the position in society they were later to fill. Up to this time the school had catered mainly to European and Anglo-Indian children, but the percentage of Indian children permitted by the government had to be adhered to. The dawn of independence changed all that, and after this great event, the school was thrown open to Indian children. The numbers now increased out of all proportion to the existing accommodation. So that almost the entire school building was taken up by the primary and junior classes. One of the old buildings was then remodeled, and although quite unsuited to the purpose, it served the purpose of the tiny High school as well as for the science laboratories, so that at that moment the school was in danger of dying out at the senior level for lack of scientific and suitable accommodation. While the Primary and Junior classes had increased phenomenally the numbers, the numbers in the high School remained static for lack of amenities.

Ambala had its own peculiar difficulties; not least among them was the fact that the majority of the pupils were still the children of Army and Air Force personnel. These constituted a constantly shifting population on account of frequent transfers. Then there was the great preponderance of non-Christians in the school, and just a sprinkling of Catholics. Another difficulty was that the staff of the Primary and Junior school was largely recruited from the wives of officers, as they were well educated and fluent in English. So according to transfer of personnel there was also a shifting staff, that was never a good thing for any school.

Growth and Development of Education in Delhi

During these early years of the twentieth century, India continued to experience a kind of renaissance in certain areas. In fact, Delhi also was not exceptional to this renaissance in the field of education. Engineers, architects, businessmen, and others were stirred by new ambitions.

Religion, generally associated with Christian education, was also coming into its own. New Delhi then was gradually assuming the appearance of a dignified city. Revd Fr Luke had purchased there fourteen acres of land for Rs.7000 with a perpetual lease of Rs. 365 yearly. This proved to be a magnificent investment for the cause of education.

C.C. Barron the Chief Commissioner, wisely anticipating Delhi's educational needs, was particularly anxious to have the Convent school run by the Congregation of Jesus and Mary. Therefore, after the consent of Mother General, Mother Colette who acted on his advice, found a house suitable for a school. Stimulated rather than crestfallen by difficulties, this intrepid woman decided to open a day-school on 25th January,1923 in a veranda of a house close to the site where the Sacred Heart Cathedral now stands. This house-cum renovated and enlarged veranda was known as 'the Maria Bhavan'.

The repeated efforts to establish the school had the approval of Delhi's Chief Commissioner, the Superintendent of Education, and the Engineer-in-chief. The Estate Officer in Delhi lent some tents when the cold winter months obliged the nuns to vacate, in favour of the 'Old Club' not far away. Later, the summer heat forced government officers and their families to retire to the hills for some six months of the year. The Convent School was also obliged to close down, and the Log Book indicates that for the first time that its staff and pupils went to Hampton Court, Mussoorie on the 30th March, 1922 to sojourn there during these months. The Delhi nuns then gave generously of their time and experience in Hampton Court School while the staff of this school was equally helpful in the Delhi School during the winter months.

Mother Colette's entry in the Delhi School Log Book in January 1923 has the following entry: "The teaching staff of the Hampton Court School, Mussoorie, will throw their energies into this school during the winter months, and we will work in both schools. Delhi considered them as one to simplify our own work and that of the Education Department" (Chronicles of CJM School Delhi 1923, 43). For obvious reasons, the little school in Old Delhi was permanently closed on the 23rd September 1923. The nuns' every effort was then directed towards raising the standards of the new day-school on the Cantonment Road, while they resided in the house beside the Cathedral. Along with the usual subjects, Art and Music were taught satisfactorily as testified by Inspectors' Reports. It mentioned a happy atmosphere, excellent discipline and the good tone pervaded the little school. The small percentage of Indian pupils enrolled in the European section, like those in the prosperous English teaching private department under the patronage of St. Joseph, showed a marked eagerness to master the English language. Indeed, it was considered a source of much pleasure to their parents. The latter persuaded Mother Colette to continue to maintain the unrecognized department, which was happily sanctioned by Rickey, Superintendent of Education in 1925. This educational set up continued at 'the Club' till 1926.

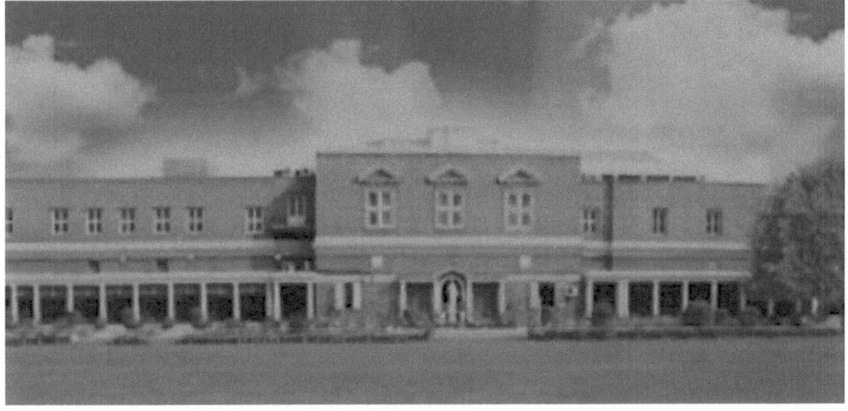

CJM, Delhi

During these early years of struggle, Barron, the Commissioner and Mother Colette could visualize the prospectus of the school with a deep satisfaction. The Army Headquarters and Telegraph Offices from Agra and Lahore were expected to be installed in the capital by 1926. Thus, hopes were entertained that an improved financial position due to an increase number of pupils bolstered up by government would stabilize the small establishment. In 1920, a fund-raising campaign entailing the organization of some successful entertainments was launched, supported by several friends of the nuns. Mother Colette also applied to the Local Government, and the Education Department of the Government of India for a building grant "for a suitable and permanent Day School, in keeping with the surrounding buildings of the Imperial City" (Chronicles CJM School Delhi, 1920, 52). This must be single-storeyed structure in conformity with the general building plans of the city; but the future of the Jesus and Mary nuns' apostolate in this area was also envisaged by laying foundations with a view to support a second floor.

Barron, the Director of Public Instruction, though cordial as ever initially, gave little hope of financial aid. Unabashed, the nuns in the community started pleading to God and the assistance of their Mother Foundress. Before the conclusion of this fervent intercessory prayer, the sanctions of a building grant of Rs. 10,000 arrived, to their unbounded joy. Major Hubens I.M.S., New Delhi's Civil Surgeon, laid the foundation stone in March 1926. These started a series of permanent structures, the teachers' residential quarters in 1928, and about three years later, a new garage and drivers' quarters were set up in1931. Along with this, some land was also acquired for a playground.

The winter of 1928-'29 saw the new attractive building swept and garnished, awaiting the pupils. Revd Mother Dorothy, Provincial Superior was among the first well-wishers and friends to appraise the work of those concerned. She had been an encouraging angel to the establishment many a time, and often when life's burdens seemed difficult. Mother Colette wrote in the school Log Book, "She is a great educationist herself, and most anxious to have a high standard of work in all the classes, as well as intellectual and good moral training" (Chronicles CJM School Delhi 1929, 65). The new Chief Commissioner Sir John and his wife Lady Thompson evinced great pleasure on seeing the new building. Its Kindergarten classrooms with their tiny occupants were especially dear to their hearts. There were repeated remarks from Sir. John to the effect that the day-school was "an ornament in New Delhi", the best he had seen in the country (School Inspection Report CJM School Delhi,

1931, 187). The same year, Her Excellency Lady Irwin and her A.D.C. were no less charmed with all they saw. It is scarcely surprising that the dauntless Mother Colette and her co-workers were so successful. Fr Luke, the priest already mentioned speaking of the same little band, remarked that they were real pioneers in the educational world, and they continue their wonderful work, becoming an instrument in bringing glory and honour to the Catholic Church there. To him Mother Colette was a person of a great enterprising spirit.

The April 1936 issue of Franciscan Annals, Agra Cathedral archives, has two short articles written shortly after she received public Government recognition for her work in the cause of Christian Education for girl children. Besides her, Mother Lucy and Mother Gregory Canty also deserved Government Awards. In the presence of Mr Parkinson, D.P.I., Armstrong, Inspector of European Schools Punjab, Rev. Mother Dominic, Provincial of the Congregation of Jesus and Mary, the nuns, staff and a throng of white-clad smiling girls, his Excellency, the Governor of the Punjab invested Rev. Mother Colette with the 'Kaiser-i-Hind' Medal at the Convent of Jesus and Mary, Lahore. On the 20th February 1936 Simla Times wrote,

> Revd Mother Colette has spent fifty-eight years of her life in the cause of education, giving freely with the full measure of a wonderfully generous heart, of her time, energy and love, to all the children who came under her care. She was a true mother to the orphans, and those unfortunate ones whose parents could not afford to rear them. Selfless, unwearying, courageous, always optimistic, a genuine friend to all in adversity, Mother Colette cannot be forgotten by anyone who ever met her. She sought no earthly honour, yet distinction was hers in recognition of her prolonged invaluable work; and the Congregation of Jesus and Mary, the missions for whose schools she had worked, all her friends, pupils and ex-pupils wholeheartedly rejoice…. ("Great Educationist" 1936)

Expansion of School Education in Hill Areas

Meanwhile, the visit of the important government officials and their appreciation for the institutions of higher learning, teachers, and pupils, who are well disciplined and well behaved, proved to be a crucial achievement of the dedicated nuns who worked untiringly day and night. In 1935, Mother Mary Xavier Weiss, an American nun became the superior of the convent at Hampton Court, Mussoorie. She was called to build Hampton Court into a model school for small boys. She catered to the needs of the physical and educational well-being of the boys. Only when this task was efficiently achieved to her full satisfaction, she turned her attention to the old house which was literally crumbling and in urgent need of repair. She commenced an era of building, repair and reconstruction in Hampton Court which altered its face to acquire a totally new look. While she was in the States, she spent time in observing a great deal of building operations, especially the use of cement, which not only provided strength to the building but also gave a clean finish that had impressed her. This knowledge proved invaluable in her task of restoring Hampton Court.

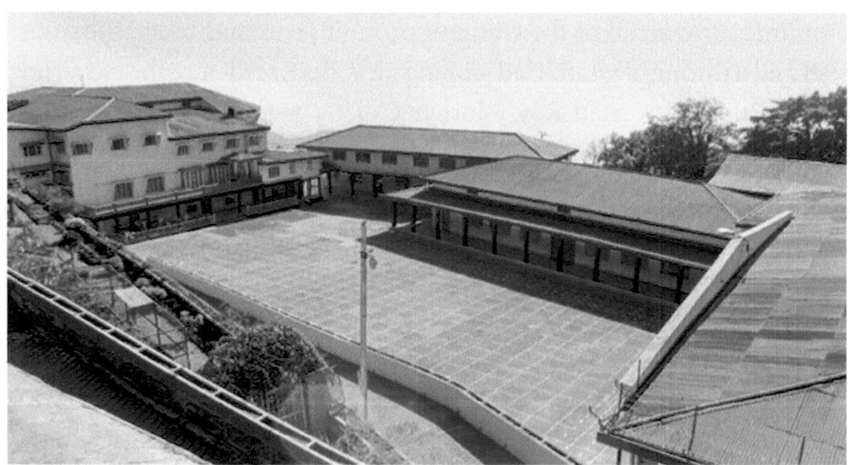

CJM School, Hampton Court

Hampton Court had acquired an enviable reputation of being compared to the best schools in the country. Indian Independence in 1947 introduced a new era in the history of the school. As the European families left regretfully, Indianisation progressed rapidly. Applications from Indian families poured in from England, Germany, Africa and even the United States. The new session in 1948 began with the changed geography of the country, which divided the people of common heritage into two separate entities - Pakistan and India. Hampton Court became a school exclusively for boys and girls from India, together with pupils from far off countries like Africa, Thailand and later on from the States, UK, and Germany. The school fulfilled the needs of the Indians working abroad not only in terms of bilingual education but also as a safeguard in terms of their citizenship rights in India.

The school gradually adjusted itself to the new era and the second house in the school compound was converted into a dormitory and other rooms were added. The school flourished and the new hall, where at present the morning assembly is held, was built. Hampton Court was a home away from home for their young children and was usually the first choice of the North Indian parents. Applications for admissions increased with every passing year. A long course has been traversed since the struggling days of the opening of the orphanage for the British children in 1922 till the period of this study, but the history of all institutions changes with changing national life. The nuns of JM, who educated children, still carry on their Founders ideals hoping that it may be their privilege and consolation to guide and educate Indian girls, to be truly worthy women of the India of the future.

Established on 6th March 1922, Hampton Court Preparatory Boys School began its life as an integral part of the educational apostolate of the JM Congregation in Mussoorie, the present-day Uttarakhand. On the day of its inception, there were sixteen boarders and six day-scholars. The members of the staff were: Revd Mother St. Colette Courane, Superior and Manager, Mother St. Imelda Carver, Mother St. Eugene Wilson, and Mother St Charles Wilmott with two secular teachers –Miss Kelly and Miss Bannister. In April 1922, the boarders increased, so did the day-scholars and the staff. They were Mother St Clotilda Daly, Assistant Manager, Mother St Emily Cooper, Sister Leocadie, Sister Julie, Miss Molly and Miss Canning. By the month of May the boarders increased to forty and over a period of time the total number of pupils rose to over a hundred. The first inspection of the school took place on 31st May 1922. The inspector of European schools Mr E. Tipple visited the institution. During his visit, there were a hundred and thirteen children on the rolls. He appeared to be satisfied with the work of the school. He praised and thanked the nuns for their dedicated work and the incredible sacrifice they made for the Indian children's education. While talking to the little boys he found that how these little ones loved the nuns and the teachers. They said the school was their home and the nuns were their mothers. This is what when Claudine meant as she said, "Be mothers to children". (*School Inspection Report, CJM School, Hampton Court* 1922).

As soon as Miss Holland's family, a colonial official had vacated the main house in the beginnings of 1923, the Congregation of JM actually took over the property of Hampton Court, Mussoorie, on 10th March, 1923 for the purpose making it a boarding school for little boys and girls up to the preliminary Cambridge class. The building, a ruin and shell of previous grandeur, was spacious, set in ideal surroundings, and commanding a full view of the Dun Valley below. In April, the staff of the school increased considerably. Revd Mother Provincial Mother St Dorothy came to visit the school. She presided over the prize giving function which was attended by a group of guests. The guests were really awestruck in witnessing such a fantastic programme performed by the children of the school. They were in praise of the management and the school staff for providing an all-round education and training to the little boys. The school continued with classes, games, and outings. After a long period of working, the school closed on 28th November 1923 for the winter actions. The winter again was undaunted, and the little band of nuns bravely faced the burden of scrubbing and cleaning the neglected house. The generosity, efficiency and hard work on their part turned Hampton Court into the fine school it is today.

In 1926, Revd Mother St Colette, who believed in approaching the highest officer in a difficulty, appealed to the Secretary of State to sanction a large grant in full or in installments in the Budget of 1927-

’28. She explained that Hampton Court being greatly in debt owing to the heavy mortgage inherited from Miss Holland, the nuns were barely able to meet the interest on the purchase loan which had crippled the institution. The interest was so high and so difficult to meet, that the institution could barely pay anything towards the loan. She evidently got her way. Revd Mother St Colette was a religious of high ideals and unyielding principles. She was also a woman with great sense of order and of what was fitting. She managed the new foundation excellently well. The boys found in her a strict disciplinarian. But the ‘motherliness’ of the Sisters, along with their sensitivity and understanding, brought great joy and peace to the little boys. Mother Clotilda’s discipline accompanied a deep love and understanding. She really loved the boys to whom she became ‘Granny’. That’s the way they called her in those years.

The move into the big house was followed by a decade of constructions, alterations, and repairs. The years rolled by when on 2nd April 1927, a severe hailstorm hit Mussoorie causing damage to the school roof. The problem was further compounded when on 28th May, the same year a terrible storm blew off the roofs of the dormitory and the school concert hall. The children were kept in the basement for nearly two weeks. The storm had taken a heavy toll as the roofs of many houses all around the town were blown off. After the children left for winter vacations, repairs were started again. Reinforcement was given to the falling walls and worn out timber poles and railings adjoining the verandahs.

It was during this time many of the countries in the world were affected by the deadly epidemic Varicella (chickenpox). India was not an exemption. Chickenpox results from primary infection with the varicella-zoster virus (VZV). It is a highly contagious rash illness that is transmitted from person to person by direct contact with patients with either varicella or herpes zoster (HZ) or by airborne spread (from respiratory secretions or aerosolized vesicular fluid from skin lesions. The average incubation period is 14–16 days. Persons with varicella are considered infectious from 1 to 2 days before the rash appears and until all lesions are crusted over. Infants, adolescents, adults, and immune-compromised persons are at higher risk for complications.

Mother Colette showed a deep concern regarding the children's health. Dr. Andreae, known for his exceedingly kind approach towards the children, was the Medical Officer-in-charge of Mussoorie. He unfailingly administered inoculation against infectious diseases such as chicken pox and typhoid. Mother kept the quarantine period of the infectious sickness very strictly, thus preventing the spreading of these germs which were rampant in those days. Her commendable disciplinarian attitude with motherly care provided the much-needed support to the tiny ones who never suffered from home sickness and separation from their parents.

The academic side of the school did not go unattended. The nuns were able to secure the co-operation of good, experienced, and well-qualified teachers, such as Miss Marcoolyn and Miss Lane Smith. Sisters, who were apprehensive at the beginning due to the complexity of cross-cultural communications, soon got over their fright, as soon as they realised how much easier and rewarding it was to teach young children. Mother Laetitia Lobo, Mother St Regis Young, Mother St Michael Williams, and Mother Pia Nazareth were the first Indian nuns who served as teachers in the early days.

In 1929, Revd Mother St Clotilda replaced Mother Colette as Superior and Manager of Hampton Court. She had Mother Eugene to assist her. Mother St Martin taught classes 1 and 2 and Sr. Leonard worked in the house. Mother St Mechtilde Finnigan replaced Mother St Imelda, bringing music and joy into the lives of the young boys. In the school there was also one of the first trained teachers Mrs. Whitehead, from St Bede's College, Shimla, who could take classes for III, IV and V Grades. She also taught drill, gymnastics, and craft to the boys.

On 24th July 1929, the school was visited by Rev. Mother Marie Des Agnes, General Councillor, accompanied by Mother Dominic Cahill, Superior of Shimla Convent. They expressed their satisfaction of the work being done and remarked on the healthy appearance of the boys. The year 1930 was a particularly important year, a turning point in the history of the school. It was the year the young Indian boys were admitted to the school, much to the happiness of their parents who had all along tried to have their sons under the care of the nuns. One of them was Stanislaus Rikh, son of Raja Francis Xavier Rikh of Tajpore. The little boys and two Sisters were already in Waverly (*Chronicles of CJM School, Hampton Court* 1930). The untiring zeal and the dedication of the nuns marked Hampton Court on the map of primary education in North India.

The children from the preparatory school automatically went on to St George's College run by the Irish Patrician Brothers. There was a healthy rivalry between Hamptonians and their Brothers in St George's in the field of sports. However, the love and affection of the nuns and the hallowed surroundings of the school of their childhood brought them back time and again, for sharing their inner thoughts and homesickness. Even today, many alumni of the school visit the campus passionately to revive the memories of their early days in school, introducing themselves as ex-students of Hampton Court, and expressing their emotions of seeing the beds they had in the dormitory and other memorable spots. One such occasion on 4th October 2013, while visiting his former school, Shri. Lucky Ali, an eminent singer, composer, and actor of the country, said "Mussoorie is a queen, and queens do not sell themselves but invite others to their kingdom." (*Chronicles of CJM School, Hampton Court* 1930). He was very emotional and full of praise to his 'alma mater' in Mussoorie.

Mother Colette, who had experienced many difficult days and had endured it all with great courage, faith, and fidelity, sacrificed her health in the process. In 1933, Mother Clotilde took charge of the school. As a nature lover she delighted in flowers, trees, birds and loved the young pupils. Mother Warrington observed that the response from the students was open, sincere, and wholehearted. Perhaps, it is, this experience of the care of the nuns made the Hampton Court students different from others in terms of loyalty, dutifulness and love for the institution and fellow human-beings.

Before closing this brief history of growth and development of this institution, some tribute must be paid to those who have guided this institution through its varied periods. There were times of struggle and times of rapid progress. There were periods of darkness when its future seemed at stake, and there were periods of great popularity and tremendous success. For each, God raised up a leader who held the torch high and called on others to follow. Of the venerable women who worked for the cause, the place of honour must be given to Revd Mother St Gonzaga, the first Superior who in a completely hidden manner and almost alone faced the storms of opposition and discouraging criticism. Looking through the old records, her name appears only once. The reason for such lapse was that all the correspondence was addressed to the Revd Chaplain who as secretary was officially recognized as head of the institution by military authorities. But it was Mother Gonzaga who stood at the helm and guided the storm-tossed vessel over those almost over whelming waves of antagonism. As a true daughter of Claudine Thevenet, she sought to fulfill the ideals of her Congregation and became a mother to her students. She carried on the work for nineteen years and the only tribute to her memory is to be found in a marble slab on the chapel wall above the vault in which she lies waiting for eternal glory.

Many other Superiors followed, and a long list of loved names comes in the records. Mother St Xavier, one time the Provincial Superior, and Mother St Lucy, a brilliant little French woman to whom all submitted joyfully. She won all hearts and was awarded the "Kaiser-i-Hind Medal" the highest award for an educationist for the invaluable services in the field of education (Cuthbert, *Echoes of Century* 82). Mother St Clementine, a gifted musician always affectionately known by pupils as 'Little Mother'. She was barely five feet tall but her forceful character and intensely kind heart made her indeed the beloved mother of the children of St Francis School. Mother St Dorothy, perhaps the most feared, yet most loved of all, a warrior in any good cause, led Chelsea for many years; first as mistress of the schools, then as Superior and Co-foundress of St Bede's College. There were many other nuns who gave all the strength and love of their young years to the welfare of St. Francis School and whose memory, because of their care of the poor and weak and lonely, lives still in the hearts of innumerable old pupils. They have all gone now to receive their eternal reward for they sought no reward during their selfless lives. A long line of venerable Franciscan priests shared in the religious and academic life of the school. There were too many to enumerate but each in his own way inspired the children with the highest ideals of a truly Christian life.

The discussion on the growth and development of the JM institutions gives a brief history of the educational achievement in North India. Though all these institutions had their origin and growth leaving milestones in the passages of history, its development never ceased to have its impact in the years to come. The educational movement under the aegis of the JM that started in 1842 in Agra went on establishing institutions throughout the country. As its span is not being limited to the spatial or temporal borders it sprang across the different regions even after independence.

The JM brand of educational institutions branched out westward to Gujarat and Maharashtra, southward to Goa, Kerala, and Karnataka, eastward to Bengal and Chhattisgarh. These institutions bore witness to the major historical and social upheavals in the modernist period. They have undergone the traumas and the excruciating agonies of the social life in the aftermath of the two Great World Wars. And these institutions left its own imprints towards the contributions in the field of women education. Along the educational development in terms of quality and excellence, the strength that gained benefits of the education is the result of the educational enterprises of these great institutions. The growth and development of these institutions left indelible imprints and institutional landmarks in terms of achievement in the field of women education and it will not go unnoticed.

Endnotes

[1] One of the four Pontifical mission societies; an international association for the assistance by prayers and alms of Catholics

[2] A prelate appointed by the Pope to serve as the Bishop for an apostolic administration. Apostolic administration can be either an area that is not yet a diocese, or for a diocese that either has no bishop, or in very rare case, has an incapacitated bishop.

Chapter 6

Higher Education, Dissemination of Knowledge and Women's Empowerment

Women constitute the most significant part of society everywhere in the world. Missionaries and various reformers like Raja Ram Mohan Roy and William Carey initiated several measures to improve the position of women in India. The congregation of Jesus and Mary being an educational congregation has done a commendable work in the field of women education in North India. The congregation came to India in such a time when there was hardly any education, even for boys in India. With the help of missionaries and other philanthropists, Acts were passed against sati, female infanticide, child marriage and polygamy. Widow remarriage was encouraged, and special emphasis was placed on education of girls, better health, and provision of opportunities for women taking up respectable jobs in order to make them economically independent.

When the JM visionaries came to India and started their educational institutions, they saw women, compared to men, were having deprived and subordinate status in terms of freedom, access to resources, and enjoyment of rights. The JMs realized that this has profound implications for women's capability to conduct their lives as autonomous and self-reliant members of the society. Subhadra Mitra Channa in her "Feminism and Empowerment in an Indian context: A critical Analysis" argues that the position of woman is not a universally uniform category, but one that is culturally and historically conditioned.

Meanwhile, the Hunter Commission viewed the progress of education in India and serious efforts had been made to develop primary schools for girls and teachers' training institutions. Higher education for women and co-education were still contentious issues. Faced with the fact that 98 percent of school age girls were not in school, authors of the Hunter Commission Report recommended more liberal grants in aid for girls' schools than for boys' schools, and special scholarships and prizes were instituted for girls. It was noticed by the authorities of the JMs, namely Mother Clare, that North India lacks good training institutes for teacher training. As soon as it came to her attention, she put all her efforts to start a good training college for women teachers.

It is to be noted that the teachers' training college at Shimla, set up by the Convent of Jesus and Mary in 1904, played a crucial role in producing teachers of high efficiency, intellectual calibre and dynamism. The JM Sisters conducted this technical college for the training of teachers and the higher education of women with the aid of Punjab Government.[1] First thing that strikes one about St Bede's College is the picturesque, almost idyllic location of its campus. Nestling amidst spruce, fir and oak trees, the institution has been a learning ground for numerous Bedians for more than hundred and fifteen years. Initially, the college had been housed in a single block with only fifteen students, who were taught a special course called Teachers Training Certificate (TTC). It was set up by Revd Mother Clare who was in-charge of Indian province. The predominant objective of this teachers' training institution was to raise the standard of education among women in North India.

The college scheme made provisions for three courses of study. According to the first provision, there was a course for girls who have matriculated or passed some equivalent examination, who intended to adopt a teaching profession. In this course, due attention was given to prepare them for their professional career. In the second provision, there was a course for girls who had matriculated and who wished to get a degree. In fact, this course met the requirements of Indian universities and was a preparatory to Course III. According to the third provision, there was a post graduate course which prepared students who had taken a degree for the Licentiate of Teaching in the Indian universities. This course covered for a period of one year. The College buildings had been carefully planned to ensure the comfort and progress of the students. It contained lecture rooms, library, museum, laboratory, music, and recreation rooms. Students' health and physical development were given special care. To that end, the hockey ground and tennis court were set up. Interestingly, 'advanced students' were expected to join the Debating Society and to take part in all that is calculated to promote the well being of their fellow students.[2]

The first set of students passed the examination very successfully, the greater number with first class honours. St Bede's reputation slowly and steadily started spreading to various parts of India. From that day onwards, it has gone from strength to strength. Today St Bede's is known not only all over India but also in other countries of the world, where the old Bedeans' good standard and success in teaching, medical, engineering, administration, politics and so on are always genuinely recognized and highly appreciated. The European students have gone but hundreds of India's daughters have found St Bede's as their happiest of homes and a beloved 'Alma Mater'. Since 1904, St Bede's and CJM Chelsea School combined to work earnestly for education in India. This and other local institutions offered outstanding and exceptional training to students, and the St Bede's college set exceedingly high standards of attainment, which made ambitious young teachers in the schools to emulate them.

The Punjab Education Department during the early decades of the 20th century set out to ensure that education in India should not lag behind the one that of the West. More frequent and searching inspections were carried on. The curriculum and syllabus of work for the classes were revised regularly. Courses in Art and Physical Training were organized, and the standard of the examinations was raised considerably. As the years went by, the number of students in St Bede's teachers' training college increased beyond all expectations. The Teachers' Training Course was continued, and both European and Indian girls who appeared for the certificate examination did exceptionally well. The standard of English in the College had always been remarkable, as the time went by many Indian parents were anxious to get their daughters all the advantages possible for an all-round training. St Bede's became one of the sought-after institutions for girl's education not only in India but also abroad. The training which was imparted at St Bede's was matchless. Studying at St Bede's was considered as a prestigious academic experience and astonishing opportunity to get perfect training for their daughters (Cuthbert, *A Pioneer* 62).

Generation after generation of students have gone forth from Bede's teachers' training college, they were trained not only in teaching but also in social decorum and manners, orderly habits, and consideration for others as well. The Latin motto, which Mother Clare chose for her beloved college, "Non Nobis Solum" [Not for Ourselves Alone], has inspired many to lead a serviceable and cheerful li fe. When the institution was celebrating its Golden Jubilee, it was found that its ex-students were working all over the world. To cope with the needs of modern times and the entry of Indian women into public life, the college has developed new activities, while continuing the valuable Teacher Training, Academic studies, University degrees, inter-collegiate debates, and declamations. These have not only brought commendation and recognition to the institution, but also prepared the girls to face the challenges of contemporary world.

In addition to the T.T.C., the students took the intermediate Arts and B.A. examinations of Punjab University. Subjects such as Philosophy, Economics, Political Science and Hindi have been the popular courses. Dramatic Art has always played a significant part in the students' education, and from time to time they have been requested to present plays at 'Raj Bhavan'. They also have held public performances at the Gaiety Theatre. The College Debating Society had a fine record and they excelled at games and physical training as well.

In 1943, a system of self-government was introduced into the College, which has continued to function to this day. Its initial stages were guided by Mother St Ursula Warrington and Revd Fr Declan O.F.M, Cap. (Cuthbert, *A Pioneer* 12). Now it forms an integral part of St Bede's tradition. The chief goal of this youth movement is to produce better and more responsible citizens by means of character training and the development of personality through self-discipline in a co-operative and coordinated student association.

It aimed at developing creative initiatives among the students and seeking to train the girls to be ever-ready to serve humanity in general and the needy in particular. The 'Ship System' as the movement is named, has an admiral who is the Head-girl. She is assisted by five captains, each representing a different form of activity. This system of self-government has been at work for many years, and it makes for real education, and draws out the inner resources of individual students. It has been a great happiness to see the ideals and aims of the system realized in so many of the students who have passed through the college.

The year 1947 saw the dawn of Independence in India, and the consequent exodus of European and Anglo-Indian families from the country. Records and registers indicate that in the early years of the College only Christian girls and daughters of the royal families availed of the education offered. After independence, a few girls from other faiths joined the College. But the number of Indian Christian girls and a few from other faiths, annually seeking admission to the training college after Independence, could have never made it an economically viable education unit, even though State's grant-in-aid continued. For this reason, and also there were no higher education institutions for girls existing in Himachal Pradesh, many non-Christian parents in North India made repeated requests to the Sisters to start classes in general education at college level. Accordingly, undergraduate, and graduate classes were introduced in 1947 itself. Owing to these requests, other graduate classes were also introduced in 1948. Mother Felix was the Principal at that time. Classes were not affiliated to any University. Students took the examination in the humanities only, and that too, as private candidates. The students of the undergraduate and graduate classes made it evident that social etiquette and cultural achievements rather than academic excellence were their main pursuits. Thus St Bede's came to be dubbed "the vestibule for marriage" ("Editor's Note" 4). Young men and their families preferred girls who are graduated from St Bede's College. After their marriage the girls came back to the college and hostel along with their husbands and children just to relive their college life and to say how much they owe to the college and the staff.

The T.T.C. continued in the college as a two-year course. As it has been stated already, the T.T.C. Part I course was purely academic. Therefore, it offered the general subjects such as English, Hindi, Social Studies, General Science, Mathematics, Physical Education and Art. The qualifying examination for the course was the same as that for the entrance to the first year of the university course. The College with the approval of the State Department of Education and Inter-State Board for Anglo-Indian Education, which prepared the T.T.C. syllabi, offered to prepare simultaneously students for both T.T.C. Part I examination as well as for the first year examination of the University. Some students took two examinations at the end of the first year of the college, and then passed on to the T.T.C. Part II classes.

After Independence, even though the College moved forward in the interest of Indian education, it still maintained a certain international atmosphere. Members of the diplomatic and other services sent their daughters to the College. There were pupils from Africa, Thailand and even from Europe and America. All these increased the opportunities to learn different cultures and their values, and also brought an international understanding among the students and faculties.

St Bede's weathered many turbulent times and faced many stirring days of history. The period of World War I may not have seriously affected educational life in the Punjab, but the day was dawning when their peaceful security would end. India had openly started its campaign for freedom and there were signs that the campaign would not be won without sorrow and bloodshed. As normalcy returned with India's Independence in 1947, the college which previously was mainly for Christian girls' opened its doors to students of all faiths. Undergraduate courses were introduced and students appeared as private candidates from the Punjab University.

The College grew in strength and stature, and then required additional classrooms. The 1950s saw the emerging modern woman of India, an awakening of an awareness that society was beginning to require of her academic achievement, and even professional training. In few years, student numbers doubled, and a new block was erected in 1964 where the Higley Library was now transferred. The new building also housed four classrooms, some administrative offices, a common room, and dormitory type hostel accommodation for an additional forty students.

Admission to the T.T.C. classes has to be restricted to forty in number, under the guidance of the Inter-State Board for the Anglo-Indian education. In collaboration with Principals and teachers of similar institutions throughout the country, along with valuable help and suggestions from the British Council, the syllabus for this course was revised and updated. The women of Himachal Pradesh had to be attracted to college education, thus began a project to introduce the teaching of Science and Home Science in St Bede's College. Financial aid was sought from the Netherlands, and in 1973 the foundation stone of 'the Marian Block' was laid.

St Bede's contribution in the field of education and empowerment of women in Himachal Pradesh, India and in the world itself has been awesome. In 1967, the management of St Bede's had to take a serious decision regarding the existence of this College. As the Church authorities and the government of Delhi approached the JM Sisters with a request to start a college for women in Delhi, they had to make a choice. The higher Superiors of JM Educational Society decided to close St Bede's and open a new JM College in New Delhi. This decision was not lightly taken, but it had to be reversed on account of petitions made by the people and the Government officials of Shimla to Bishop Alfred Fernandez. However, St Bede's being the premier institution for women in the region; an appeal was made by the then Himachal Pradesh Chief Minister, Dr. Y.S. Parmar and several local dignitaries and people, to the Bishop and the higher Superiors of JM sisters, for the continuation of the College. The appeal bore fruit and St Bede's was saved from closing down. Student numbers had dwindled somewhat, but the College soon began to revive enrolment of students , both residential and non-residential. A cottage in the school campus was acquired on loan and rent-free in order to provide extra residential accommodation.

In its new lease of life, the institution has not belied the confidence and trust of its superiors, officers of the State and all its stakeholders. The girls are prepared for career and life situation through education, extra-curricular activities, and value education, without which education is worthless. The College Motto, *Non Nobis Solum* i.e. 'Not for Ourselves Alone', continues to inspire everyone who study in this institution. The alumni of this College have made their mark in the fields of administration, business, politics, education, art, and social work. The College celebrated hundred glorious years of its dedicated service to education in general, including special areas of education, grooming young women to become good policymakers, administrators, military police personnel, teachers, artists, writers, diplomats, dedicated mothers and career women. Hundreds of young women have passed through the portals of this prestigious institution, opening schools of their own and working for schools all over India and abroad.

St Bede's College is now a well-planned, open and beautiful, and could well compare any day with any of the best university campuses of the western world with its six buildings that house almost two thousand five hundred students and seventy-five teachers. It is really a fine monument to higher education in North India. It has grown not only in size but also in significance. From 1904 to 1958 the Principals of the college were highly qualified Europeans. The college witnessed two World Wars and the struggle for Independence. The European students gave way to girls of Indian families and quite a few from princely Indian families. Daughters of the affluent families living abroad as well as the local and poor girls also were enrolled in 1950s.The poor and the marginalized girls were given special scholarships by the college authority. This shows how much importance was given for the education of the poor, especially the girls by the JM nuns. The nuns would leave everything behind and sacrificed all their comforts in order to give a quality education to Indian daughters. The girls and the parents always found a home away from home in St. Bede's.

The College library that started with 200 books has now more than fifty thousand scholarly books and has been computerized and digitalized fully. It is a treat to see rare books on display, some of them dating back to 15th century. For instance, such works as *Christmas with the Poets, A Collection of Songs, Carol and Descriptive Verses from the Anglo-Roman period to the Present*, date back to 1647. Library also maintains a 'Visitors Book' with the pictures as well as signatures of all visitors. Eminent personalities including Pandit Jawaharlal Nehru, Vijaya Lakshmi Pandit, Lord and Lady Mountbatten, Jacqueline Kennedy, Indira Gandhi, Benazir Bhuto and so on and so forth visited this institution of eminence. They were surprised and charmed to know that India possessed such an excellent institution, and as such it was noted in the Visitors Book of St Bede's College.

Historical Development of St Bede's College

In 1902, Mother St Clare Bray, an English woman with her strong, rich personality visited all the convents of JM in India at that time, and as she travelled around, her mind absorbed details and impressions which fired her zeal. She possessed a cosmopolitan nature. In the history of the Congregation she was the longest ruled General. During those 28 years as Superior General she travelled the world and was convinced about the universality of the congregation: universality of races and languages; universality of ways and means of bringing the knowledge to all, through JM education. It is worth mentioning her charismatic leadership and contributions to the history and tradition of the congregation and its great humanitarian work of education. Her cosmopolitan character was all-embracing; she was creative when it came to understanding the meaning of women education. She was passionate about the educational spirit of the congregation and the importance that its Founder had always given to the professional formation of the religious who were educators. It was her dream to create new avenues and apostolic platforms to bring Indian women into higher education. She felt the immediate need of opening a teachers' training school in Shimla. A woman of great vision and foresight, she realized that, though much good work was being done, what needed most was a training college where the women students could study and qualify under highly professional teachers. The idea of establishing St Bede's College for Women gradually took shape in her mind but nothing could be done without the permission of the Government. She spoke about this with the authorities in Punjab, the Director of Education, and the Ministry of Education as well as with the Governor. Though her distinguished personality and good manners were irresistible, and she won all hearts, she met with strong opposition as soon as the question of a Teacher Training College was mentioned. Gradually she won over the Director of Education but not so the Governor of Punjab, who had the final word. Then Mother Clare invited him to visit the Convent school in Shimla. The training college was to be built in Shimla, the beautiful Himalayan hill station soon to become the summer capital of India.

The Mother General, Revd Mother Clare having seen the establishments on her visit all over India and being much impressed by the work of her nuns, decided that it was time to complete what had begun in Chelsea, Shimla, for an institution of higher education and a much needed training college for teachers. It was not only for the teaching formation of her religious Sisters but also for secular women students as well. She was dedicated to the idea of developing Northern Indian women to be pioneers in the educational field. It is important to note that North India hardly possessed a Teacher Training Institute during that time. So much so the people of the Punjab were all looking forward for such an institution of higher education to make their daughters as good teachers and form the future citizens of our country through school education.

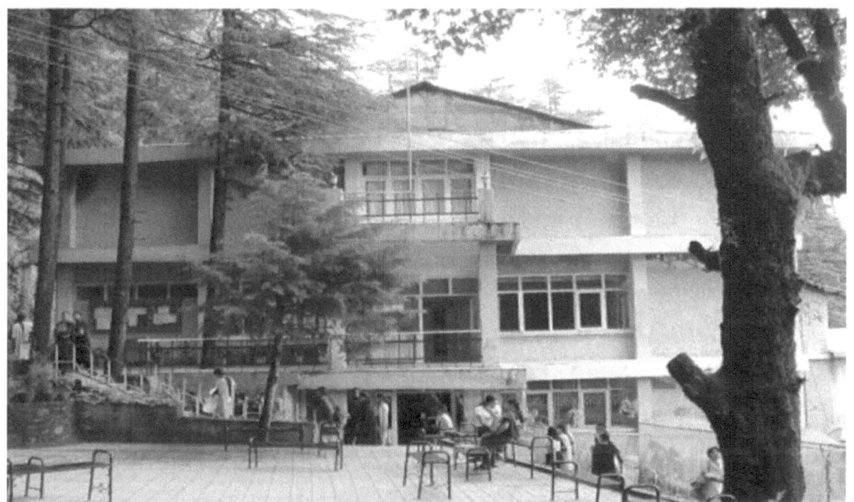

St. Bede's College, Shimla

In March 1921, Mother Clare came to India for the third time and to her satisfaction she saw the congregation in India was grown to greater heights. St Bede's college was becoming a sought-after institution for girl's higher education. The professionals, the teachers that the College sent out were employed not only in the country but even outside the country where they were given so much importance. By now the JM nuns were involved not only in education but they were contributing also to the development of Indian villages through their self-sacrificing missionary activities. It is important to mention here the political unrest that was happening in India during this visit of hers. It was the time when Gandhi was gaining more followers, without his non-violence being able to eliminate brutal reactions. His order to boycott England is particularly to be remembered. The visit of the Prince of Wales, the future Edward VIII, provoked tumultuous manifestations: riots broke out during his journey to Bombay. The nuns who went to welcome him narrowly missed being stoned; they had to abandon their special trams and return home by quiet roads, while M. Clare who had come by car with a few others, was obliged to take refuge in a private house. In 1928, she came to India for the last time and presided over in person at twenty fifth anniversary of St Bede's College, her first foundation. She was happy and satisfied to see her hard work producing good results.

Today the College, as one of the leading colleges for women in North India, particularly in Himachal Pradesh, offers a range of courses at Uunder graduation and post graduation levels. Subjects include B.Sc., non-medical, B.Sc. (Hons) in Micro Biology and Bio-technology, B.Com. (Hons), B.B.A., B.C.A., B.A. Programme courses with different combinations, and B.A. (Hons) courses in English, Economics, Geography, M.Com. M.A in English, M.A. in Geography, M.Sc. Botany; add-on certificate and diploma courses in travel and tourism, fashion designing, and communicative English and Teachers Training Course. The College regularly conducts personality development and faculty enrichment programmes that help students and teachers to upgrade themselves. The College serves as a finishing school for boarders, teaching them everything from table manners like handling cutlery, social interactions, public dealings to conversation skills (Channan, 3).

Today mentoring has become a national priority in any educational institution. Mentoring has been an age-old practice followed by the institution. The College authorities and the faculty are very particular about the formal and informal mentoring of the students. Mentoring efforts can be effective in addressing key issues and problems currently facing colleges and universities across the country, including the need to increase degree completion rates, reduce inequities in outcomes for marginalized and underrepresented groups, and broaden participation in science, technology, engineering and math (STEM) pipeline and workforce. Mentoring has long been considered a developmental and retention strategy for undergraduate students, and research suggests mentoring efforts are positively related to a variety of developmental and academic outcomes.

To evaluate the standard of higher education of the college, the members of the National Assessment and Accredited Council visited on 8-10 May 2004 for the first time. The eminent scholars from different parts of the country visited all the constituents of the college, interacted with the principal, teaching and non-teaching staff members, faculty, students, alumni, and parents. They also verified and validated all the relevant records and documents. Based on their observations the team accredited and awarded the college with an "A" Grade.[3]

The team members also appreciated the College for its commendable features . They are as follows: Making the best of the multi-institutional educational complex by resource pooling and optimal utilization strategies, with qualified and committed faculty with good rapport with the students, the college has a good record of success consistently and ranks and gold medals in the university examinations. It emphasizes with a special thrust on value education through mentoring system. Venturing into five year integrated MCA with a tie-up and affiliation of Guru Jambeshwar University was an exceptional phenomenon. It has good and well maintained physical infrastructural facilities and a conducive academic ambience, with good hostel accommodation for the students. Adequate attention is paid to ensure holistic development of student personality through a mechanism of comprehensive recording/ monitoring of student profiles every year. The college has a compassion for the poor and underprivileged. For example, fee concession both in the college and in the hostel, free remedial classes for the school children are highly appreciable. Thus, the college has earned its reputation over the period as one of the best centers of Higher education for the girls in Himachal Pradesh.[4]

The College also pays adequate attention to promote English education to equip the students to face the challenges of contemporary India. It is also considered a safe institution of higher learning for girls. Education at St Bede's is regarded as a kind of finishing school for girls who are groomed for marriage. It is to be noted here that the students are drawn largely from rural and urban-middle class backgrounds. The second visit of the NAAC team was in 2009 and the College has been awarded for the second time with an 'A'grade. The College also has been awarded 'Star College Status' from Department of Biotechnology, Government of India. Today it stands as a heritage institution approved by UGC. It was also awarded Potential for Excellence status by UGC in 2011. St Bede's College has the distinction of being the only institution of higher learning with all these academic achievements in the state of Himachal Pradesh and also in the whole of north India. The College also has received a number of awards including Dev Bhoomi Award for Excellence by Charu Castle Foundation, Department of Language, Art and Culture and Department of Tourism Himachal Pradesh, Himachal Excellence Award for remarkable performance in the field of Women's Education by Divya Himachal. It was recognized as the Best College in Himachal by the *Tribune*. It also received CMAI National Award for Best institution for Innovative and Value Based Education in Himachal Pradesh.

In 2016, the College completed three cycles of accreditation and was given an 'A Plus'(A+) grading by the National Assessment and Accreditation Council (NAAC) for maintenance of high standards in academics and extra-curricular activities (Chopra 53). Apart from academic excellence, the students were also taught the importance of social service. For instance, the College has adopted a government primary school in village Theog. The state government, through the college administration, has made a series of efforts to develop the infrastructural facilities of the school. The students visit the school fortnightly and teach them subjects like English, Science, Mathematics, Computer, and a certain crafts work. They also make the students to be aware of their hygiene, manners, discipline, duties, and responsibilities. Interestingly, the college students also celebrate national festivals like Republic Day, Independence Day and so on with the school children. This, in a way, helps both the college students and the school children to give back to society something, which they receive through education.

Despite all these strengths, the college is undergoing a series of challenges such as competition from upcoming institutions, increased maintenance of infrastructural facilities, high fee structure for self-financed courses, topographic constraints for infrastructure enhancement, unwillingness and reluctance of Government to fill-in sanctioned posts, uncertain university policies towards college, limited generation of funds to meet the growing demands of good education and so on. These challenges are due to lack of funding from the government.[5] Despite all these practical difficulties, the college stands firmly rooted on the foundation of faith, commitment, hard work and dedication without compromising the quality of education.

Higher Education in Sardhana, Meerut.

St Joseph's Girls Degree College is established and governed by the Society of Jesus Mary Sisters. The College was formally inaugurated on 15th August, 1981 as a great relief for the local parents and their daughters from Sardhana and the villages around. The girls from the surrounding 22 villages could not go to Meerut daily for higher education due to the prevalent social customs. For the sake of better safety for girls and to ease out financial problems, it was necessary to have a degree college for girls. This institution could serve higher education purposes to the girls from nearby villages. It all happened under the able guidance of the then Provincial, Sr Mary of Jesus. She was instrumental to obtain permission for a degree college from the authorities of U.P. government and the university of Meerut.

Sr Magdalene Gonsalves was the first Principal. The college offered six subjects – Hindi, English, Sanskrit, History, Political Science, and

Home Science. Though the College received permanent affiliation in 1984, the grant- in- aid was granted a year later. The college began with six faculty members, one clerk and three helpers. In the beginning years sisters Vianney and Sebastian taught History and Political Science respectively.

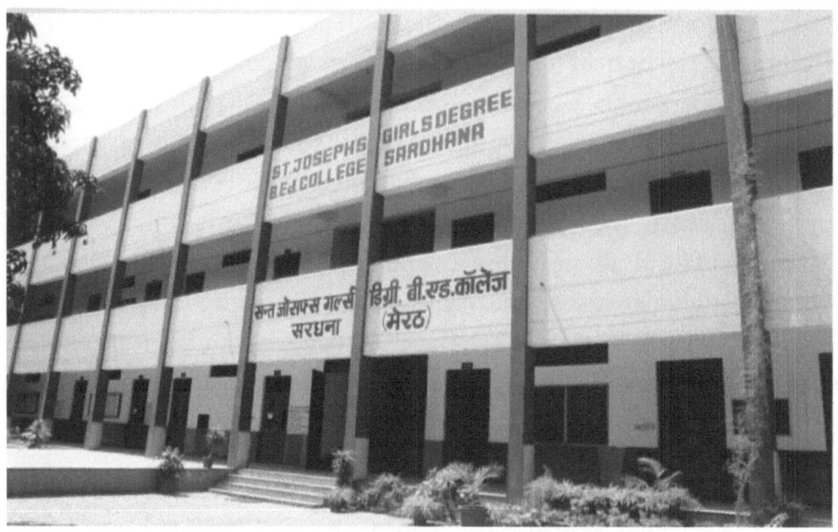

St Joseph's Degree College, Sardhana, Meerut

As time passed by, there was a felt need for B. Ed. training college for the poor girls and other girls of our locality and neighbouring villages. In 2005-2006 the B.A. section started three additional subjects under the Self Finance Scheme mainly with drawing, Sociology and Economics. The college applied for permission to start B. Ed. course from the authority of U.P. Government and CCS university, Meerut. The application was sent to the university and the team came, mean while the new building was ready. The inspection team from N.C.T.E., Jaipur visited the college in 2006. After having a thorough inspection, the team was satisfied with the facilities, and recognition was granted for one section w.e.f. 2007-2008 under self- finance scheme. The university also granted the approval for the same. Today the college has around 700 students all together. The mission and vision of the college is to provide higher education to the young girls of the locality and neighbouring villages and mould them into good human beings and responsible citizens of our country. The Sisters were of the opinion that as the girls from the surrounding 22 villages could not go to Meerut daily for higher education due to the prevalent social customs, safety and financial problems, it was necessary to have a degree college so that they could serve the girls with higher education.[6]

St Joseph's Girls Degree College was established and governed by the Society of Jesus Mary Sisters and the inauguration of the college took place on 15th August 1981. The college offered Hindi, English, Sanskrit, History, Political Science and Home Science. Despite the fact that the College got affiliation with the University of Meerut in 1984, the grant-in-aid was received a few years later.[7] The college, at present, is a Post Graduate institution. It offers courses including B.A., with nine significant disciplines, and recently added courses including M.A. in History, Hindi, Political Science, B.Com B.Ed., and so on. The college has more than 800 students from about thirty-five villages

Growth and Development of Jesus and Mary College

The Jesus and Mary institutions for higher learning in India consisted of the following colleges: St Bede's College, Shimla, St Joseph's Hindi Medium College for Women, Sardhana, Meerut, St Margaret's Training College, Bombay and Jesus and Mary College, New Delhi. The Jesus and Mary College was established in July 1968 as a constituent college of the University of Delhi. The then provincial Mother Felix was primarily responsible for the founding of the Jesus and Mary College. Even before the establishment of the college in 1968, she had worked hard in obtaining land in a suitable place in New Delhi. She made every effort in raising funds to erect what has come to be recognised as one of the most beautiful college buildings in Delhi University. The Government of India, through its Ministry of Works, Housing and Supply, offered the provincial society, a plot west of the Diplomatic Enclave, but the land was a part of an undeveloped land of three hundred and thirty acres, which meant a further delay of two years.[8] It was Mother Felix who fulfilled the long cherished dream of Jesus and Mary institution of higher education for women in the capital city of the land she had come to love as her very own (Rodrigues 2). The college offers an integrated all-round education –intellectual, cultural, social, emotional, physical, aesthetic, moral and spiritual. In the beginning, the college had only one department offering English (Hons) and B.A. (Pass) Courses with an enrollment of 116 students. The vision of the college is the creation of a just, humane, and inclusive society on earth through transformative education. As an institute of inclusive learning, the college welcomes students from all sections of society irrespective of their religion, caste, and class. Sister Marina John who was the principal of the college for about two decades said: 'We live, work, pray, play and grow together as a family. We know that it is possible to work together for common goals and we are enriched by such an experience...with a pledge to live in peace to promote humanity and fraternity' (John 3).

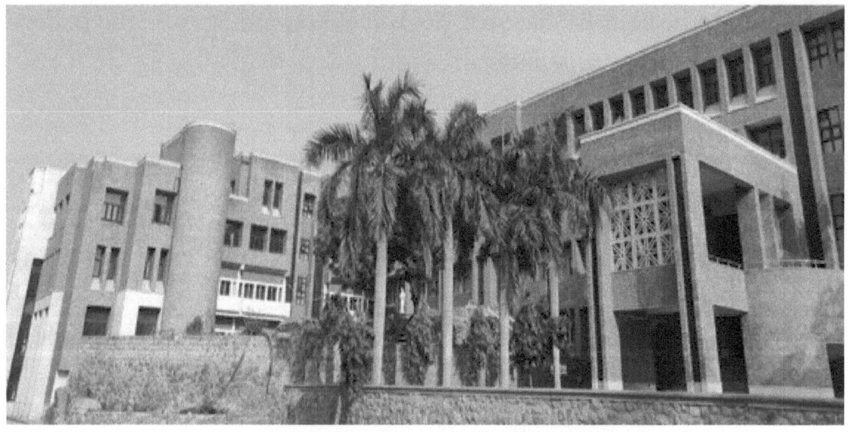

Jesus and Mary College, New Delhi

The college enables the students to realize their potential and self-worth so that they evolve as leaders and transforming agents who make a significant contribution in all spheres of national and global life. The college is committed to nurture a community of learners motivated by a passion for academic excellence. As a part of this vision, the college equips the students with the latest technological skills and soft skills making use of the learning resources available. It instills in them a sense of confidence to cope with the emerging demands of a digitalised world. It also creates and maintains an institutional ethos for multi-cultural thinking through freedom to learn and experiment. It is meant to nurture critical and cognitive faculties with a view to create an inclusive development model. As a leading liberal arts College, it makes every effort to be a pathbreaker nationally and globally in the realm of education. The college respects and promotes the rights and dignity and diverse perspectives of each individual.[9] The college not only imparts the necessary skills to the students to think for oneself, but also helps them to value themselves and the possibilities open to them. The college also makes every effort to facilitate the students to acquire the ecological awareness and the self-confidence to strive towards equality for all irrespective of caste, creed and class.[10] The fact of the matter is that educating young women involves training them in responsibility and accountability to meet the challenges of contemporary India.[11]

The larger objective of the college is 'to make God known and loved by means of Christian education'. The mission of the college is to accompany and mentor the students so that they develop as women of competence, compassion, and conscience. Empowering the students with ignited minds and hearts, the college instructs them to pursue the goal of transformation of our society. Keeping in mind the vision and mission of St Claudine, the founder of the Congregation of Jesus and Mary, the College continues to offer an integrated and all round education encompassing - intellectual, cultural, social, emotional, physical, aesthetic, moral and spiritual values.[12]

Within five or six years of its establishment, Jesus and Mary College girls could opt for many of the Honours Courses they desired, including Economics, Political Science, Hindi and Psychology. In addition to these courses, a B.Com. Pass Course and an Honours Course in B.Com. Degree was added in 1977 to attract the attention of students and to make them business-oriented.[13]

The Parents Teachers and Students Association [PTSA] in the Jesus and Mary College was formed in 1974 aimed at developing wholesome interpersonal relationships and cordial campus life. A unit of National Cadet Corps [NCC] was started in January 1974. A few girls were selected for the Air Wing, two were promoted to power flying and gliding. It should be noted that a student of Jesus and Mary College was the only Indian of her age holding a private pilot's licence.[14] The motto of National Service Scheme [NSS], 'Not me but you, provides an opportunity to help those in need, and contributes to national progress and development. Depending on local needs, skills, resources, NSS volunteers take up various projects relating to education, family welfare, arousing social consciousness, uplifting status of women and so on. A series of NSS camps were held for the implementation of various welfare programmes. These camps involved in the empowerment of young slum dwellers by teaching children basic hygiene and nutrition habits, along with creating an interest in them in activities such as sewing and knitting. In fact, for all these NSS volunteers, 'light is the task where many share the toil'.[15]

The 10th anniversary of the college was celebrated in 1978-79 when Sr Melba was the acting Principal of the College. In the annals of the history of the college, the year 1980 needs to be written in golden letters. It was in this year under the guidance of the principal Sr Agatha McLoughlin, students organized the first ever All India Cultural Festival, popularly known as 'Montage' successfully.[16] Interestingly, before the celebration of Montage, there would be three days of debates, creative writing, dumb charades, street plays and western music. With the choreography competition and the rock show as the main attractions of the festival, several college students do participate actively.[17]

It should be noted that the college established the Women Development Centre in December 1983. It included personal counselling, vocational counselling, art counselling. A series of programmes were organised to address the issues of women. There were talks on women and law, Constitution of India, and basic rights of women. The college departments coordinated and cooperated with the Centre in organizing programmes related to the issues and challenges of women. There were also exhibitions on International Women's Day. A series of shows on the issues related to the exploitation of women through the media were organized (Augustine and Balachandran 14). The Centre inculcated many novel ideas of how to involve students in exploring women's issues. Attempts were made to enable students to have direct experiences rather than remain confined to talks and discussions. It helped them to relate to some of these issues at a personal level and to understand the crucial link between research on women's issues and the movements of women activists for women's empowerment. To that end, a few areas of interest, such as the role of media in the exploitation of women, legal issues concerning atrocities on women, the impact of reproductive technologies on women and attitude towards children were identified (Batra 32). Similarly, in the academic year 1991-92, the students organized poster exhibition on the theme 'The World of a Child". It consisted of around 300 posters which covered a range of problems of children including child abuse, child labour and child education to sensitize students.[18]

The college also had a project in 1980s known as the Claudine Thevenet Outreach Programme, which promised formal and non-formal education integrated with health education and vocational training programme. Interestingly, the proposal was approved by the University Grants Commission [UGC] under the twenty-point Economic Programme. Moreover, the college was asked to take up adult education as part of implementation of the National Plan. Jesus and Mary College was allotted thirty centers of which twenty were to be organised in Indira Nagar and ten in Dakshinapuri. This project grew in response to the appeal made by the Adult and Continuing Education Centre, University of Delhi for development of formal and non-formal education among the illiterate and partly-literate within the neighborhood of the college. Similar such projects were conducted in some parts of India. For example, during the academic year 1984-85, fifteen students conducted a survey in the Indira Nagar Jhuggi-Jhopri settlement in Delhi to assess the literacy level among the adults in the area. The students visited the people, who were extremely poor and illiterates. The surveys helped them to discover that there was a problem of mass illiteracy in the area. They also found that the illiteracy was not only rampant among women, but among men and children as well. Consequently, the students felt the need for a programme to render service to the underprivileged by conducting literacy programmes, health and welfare programmes and providing economic and moral assistance. To help in formal education, the students proposed to set up literacy centers to impart reading, writing, accounting skills.[19]

The literacy programme for women took the shape of 'each one teach two or if possible three'. This literacy programme was covered completely by Doordarshan. To improve non-formal education, they proposed to promote social and cultural uplift through film shows, talks, excursions and so on. They also suggested that there was a need to emphasize the importance of responsible parenthood and set up crafts and serving centers that would aid in generating an income. This outreach programme had brought three groups of people into direct relationships - Department of Adult, Continuing and Extension of the University of Delhi, Jesus and Mary College, and the Indira Nagar slum dwellers. Therefore, the joint venture furnished several opportunities to prove that education in Jesus and Mary College goes far beyond personal pursuits.[20]

During the academic session of 1984-85, the students of Jesus and Mary College undertook a few projects, like the community development project and fund-raising project and so on. The members of the community development project, usually the third-year students had to visit slum areas, especially Indira Nagar to enlighten the women on the importance of hygiene and sanitation. The first- and second-year students taught the non-school going children. To help these children, newspaper and wool were collected. The wool was distributed to the needy in slum areas. The newspaper was sold, and the money raised was spent exclusively for the slum children (Mitra and Tripathi 7).

India being a poor country, the students felt that many people could not even afford to have a square meal a day. To begin with, the students came out with an idea to remove hunger. The main objective of Hunger Project introduced in 1989 was to banish hunger from the society. The students decided to adopt a village or to select a group of people either in a village or a city to fulfill the needs of the people. A large number of students joined the society with the impression that they would donate money, and rations to remove hunger. To that end, students collected large quantities of dal, sugar, flour, clothes, soaps, wheat and so on. These collections were handed over to Mrs. Aruna Asaf Ali, popularly known as the grand Old Lady of Indian freedom movement. During this time, she was in charge of Delhi for Bihar earthquake relief work. The students also collected rations and clothes to be distributed among the poor people in Delhi and handed them over to Mr. Romesh Bhandari, the then Governor of Delhi. Similarly, the students were highly active in collecting medicines for charitable hospitals in Delhi to cater to the news of the poor in Delhi. Similar such initiatives were made in the subsequent years with more enthusiasm, selflessness, hard work and sacrifice (Arora and Mathur 53).

The college also initiated a project, popularly known as Banish Hunger Project [BHP] with a membership of 294 students. The very first activity of BHP was collection of old clothes which was distributed to the poor through some charitable organisations. During Diwali times, grand sales were organised. The fact of the matter is that all the articles were made by members who had come out with creative products such as decorated 'diyas', stuffed toy, cakes and so on. The students, through the project, sponsored five children during the academic years 1991-92, helped poor families through the Wincent De Paul Association, a Delhi-based international voluntary Christian organization working with the poor and disadvantaged. The students also helped in the education of poor children of Sardhana, near Meerut in Uttar Pradesh (Thomas 10).

When Sister Melba Rodrigues was the Principal, the College completed 25 years of its educational service to the society in 1993. The college celebrated the whole year with a series of cultural, academic, and other programmes as part of the Silver Jubilee Celebrations. Interestingly, a play on the life of Claudine Thevenet directed by Prabha Tonk was also staged. In just twenty-five years, the College evolved into one of the premier institutions of higher learning in Delhi University.[21]

The College added one more feather to its cap by introducing a Bachelor of Elementary Education (B.El.Ed.) Programme in 1994 in collaboration with Maulana Azad Centre for Elementary and Social Education [MACESE] and Central institute of Education, (CIE), University of Delhi.[22] In fact, the Jesus and Mary College was the first institution to initiate the experiment. Consequently, the B.El. Ed. programme became a historical reality. There is always a passion for admission to the four-year integrated programme for elementary teacher education. Since it was introduced for the first time in Jesus and Mary College, as usual, parents had several questions to ask about the programme and its future. When parents approached the college with a series of clarifications, the third-year students of B.El.Ed. programme participated enthusiastically and convinced them of the challenges that awaited them after their graduation. The first-year students had language, mathematics and other subjects like theatre and craft as a part of working with children. The second-year students had a feel of issues more linked with teaching children. They attended workshops for story telling and self-development. The third-year students had new courses related to pedagogy and school. They visited several schools as part of their field visits. They travelled out of Delhi and spent time in innovative school programmes aimed at making schools relevant and interesting for the students and the community (Sarangapani 59).

The JMC students excelled in various extra-curricular activities like debating, elocution, Indian music, western music, dramatics, creative writing and other competitions.[23] The students actively participated in debates, conducted by different colleges of Delhi University, and brought laurels to the college by winning prizes. The themes for debate centered largely on politics, media, literacy, leadership, the idea of God, gender, and women empowerment. Topics such as "Women in India are still second rate citizens", "Euthanasia should be legalised", "India's poor development is attributable to a perverse streak in the Indian psyche", "America's intervention in the Gulf War is moral", "A Free Press is a Gutter Press", "Literacy is a Prerequisite for Democracy", "Even the Gods must change with Time", "The leadership of the intelligentsia has failed –if it ever existed", and so on attracted a great deal of attention of students. Similarly, Annual inter-college Claudine Thevenet Debate, one of the popular most popular debating competitions, used to get publicized by *Hindustan Times* every year.[24]

The college gave extraordinary importance to extracurricular activities to discover the potentials of students. For the first time the college received the Vice Chancellor's Trophy and was declared the best college in Delhi University in women's sports competitions. The college had the unique distinction of getting this Trophy continuously for more than twenty years (Chander 55). Interestingly, even before 21 June was declared as the International Yoga Day, Jesus Mary College made every effort to disseminate the idea of Yoga among students, teachers, and the general public. In fact, the college set up Yoga Sadhana Kendra in July 1988 when Sister Dorothy was the principal. The college taught that Yoga is not a religion, but a Sadhana implying devotional practice –an open, generous, liberal, and positive attitude in respect of life. Therefore, barriers of religion did not bind or control the practice of Yoga and followers of any religious faith could practice it. The Yoga Sadhana, introduced in the college aimed at a radical change of consciousness, so as to lead the participants to a state of unconditional peace, freedom, and joy. It should be noted that in the ancient times, Yoga was an integral part of students' curriculum in India. Unfortunately, however, this system received a major setback owing to a long period of foreign occupation. After India's independence, the Ministry of Education made regular efforts to revive the teaching of Yoga Sadhana, by introducing it in the general curricula of schools, colleges, and universities, keeping in view the better health and happiness of future generations. Yoga cultivates the ability to adapt to the circumstances surrounding them and their way of living.[25]

The Yoga learners [Sadhakas] acquire skills in learning the techniques of concentration, contemplation, and meditation to experience peace, quietness and silence of the inner mind. In addition, the Sadhakas also learn the methods of performing Pranayama to purify and clean vital energies. To keep the body fit, the students perform the simple Yogasanas like Talasana, Gomukhasana, Shavasana and so on. Daily practice of Yoga Sadhana helps people to develop the attitude of a detached onlooker towards petty sorrows and griefs in and around them. This facilitates the learner to be a better student, a better teacher, a better worker and a better person in general. Above all, the college attempts to educate the students the significance of Yoga to maintain elasticity in the body even in advanced age, when stiffness generally sets in (Shardha 33).

The college, thus, attracted a great deal of attention from the people cutting across religion, region, and caste for a variety of reasons. The road in front of the College was named as Jesus and Mary College Marg. Mrs. Sheila Dixit, the former student of Jesus and Mary School and the then Chief Minister of Delhi, played a significant role on this crucial occasion. The fourth Archbishop of Delhi Alan de Lastic graced this remarkable occasion. The JMC community considers this a proud moment in the history of Delhi because it is the only institution in the national capital to have a crucial identity to have a road in its credit.[26]

Today the Jesus and Mary College, with a huge library, having scores of books on history, English, Hindi literature, psychology, economic, business, elementary education, caters to the needs of more than 3200 students. The college has, at the present, ten Honors programs and B.A. restructured programmes (with 13 subject combinations) and Post graduate courses in English and Hindi. Besides, the college also has four-years integrated degree-cum professional course (B.El.Ed.), two B.Voc. (vocational) degrees in Health Care Management and Retail Management and Information Technology. The college has an imposing library building and stands as a testimony as a treasure house of information.

The library occupies three floors of a four-storeyed building, which is fully air-conditioned and fully automated by Troodon Software Package - an integrated multi-user library management system.[27] The college library also has membership with the British Council Library. It is also a member of N-List [INFLIBNET] in which the user can easily access 6000 journals and 97000 e-books anywhere with their ID and password, and the college is in the best ten users list. As per the latest record, the college has 7301 books on Commerce, 2,954 on Economics, 1121 on Elementary Education, 6239 on English, 10298 in Hindi, 6229 on History, 1845 on Mathematics, 1001 on Philosophy, 100 on physical education, 3622 on Political Science, 3273 on Psychology, 6095 on reference and general sections, 2959 on Sociology, 78 books on Spanish and French combined. The college has been updating scholarly books and journals every academic year to cater to the needs of students and teachers.[28]

These books are beneficial for students, and teachers in developing and maintaining their potentials. The crucial role and the significance of libraries in education has been very well emphasised in all the educational commissions appointed by the Government of India from time to time. The college provides necessary resources for study and research in the fields of special interest to the college. It facilitates the teachers in developing their areas of specialization and provides basic assistance to readers to indulge in reading for delight, self-exploration, and shaping of intellectual inquisitiveness. The college has been accredited by the National Assessment and Accreditation Council with 'A'Grade in 2014-15.

Jesus and Mary College recently celebrated its Golden Jubilee in September 2017. The President of India Shri Ram Nath Kovind was the guest of honour. While addressing the gathering, the President applauded the persistent efforts of the college to update its campus for the new generation of students. He pointed out that India is in the midst of multiple transitions and transformations, thus it is crucial to harness the energy of our young people and use it to make our country a developed society. Underlining the importance of women's education, the President remarked that an educated woman contributes to the economy and at work. He also noted that every educated woman ensures that other children in her family are educated. He underscored that the next generation is made responsible and educated predominantly through the education of women. Applauding the transformative education offered by Jesus and Mary College, and emphasising on the needs for dynamic change in education, the President said: "We need to upgrade our higher educational system to the extent possible. Our education infrastructure, curricula and modes of teaching have to be upgraded and should be made dynamic enough to constantly embrace change" (Times of India, 20 September).

Endnotes

[1] Gazetteer of the Shimla District, 1904, Punjab District Gazetteers, Vol. VIII A, Indus Publishing Company, New Delhi, 1904, pp. 116-117.

[2] Gazetteer of the Shimla District, 1904, Punjab District Gazetteers, Vol. VIII A, Indus Publishing Company, New Delhi, 1904, pp. 115-116.

[3] The official website of the college: http://www.stbedescollege.in/Bedes4/NAAC.html, accessed on 23 June 2017.

[4] The official website of the college: http://www.stbedescollege.in/Bedes4/NAAC.html, accessed on 23 June 2017.

[5] The official website of the college http://www.stbedescollege.in/Bedes4/NAAC2015.pdf, accessed on 23 June 2017.

[6] http://stjosephscollegesardhana.com/History.aspx. Accessed on 16 June 2017.

[7] http://stjosephscollegesardhana.com/History.aspx. Accessed on 16 June 2017.

[8] First JMC graduate [name not mentioned], 1970-71, The Violet, Issue No. 3, March 1992, New Delhi, 1992-1993, p.5.

[9] The official website of Jesus and Mary College www.jmc.ac.in. Accessed on 19 June 2017.

[10] For details, see the official website of Jesus and Mary College www.jmc.ac.in. Accessed on 19 June 2017.

[11] Spectrum, Jesus and Mary College, New Delhi, 1991, p.1.

[12] Spectrum, Jesus and Mary College, New Delhi, 1991-92, p. 2

[13] The official website of Jesus and Mary College www.jmc.ac.in. Accessed on 19 June 2017.

[14] The official website of Jesus and Mary College www.jmc.ac.in. Accessed on 19 June 2017.

[15] The official website of Jesus and Mary College www.jmc.ac.in. Accessed on 19 June 2017.

[16] *Jesus and Mary College Magazine*, 1984-85, New Delhi, p.97.

[17] The official website of Jesus and Mary College www.jmc.ac.in. Accessed on 19 June 2017.

[18] Spectrum, Jesus and Mary College, New Delhi, 1991-92, pp. 16-17.

[19] *Jesus and Mary College Magazine*, 1984-85, New Delhi, p.111.

[20] *Jesus and Mary College Magazine*, 1984-85, New Delhi, p. 111.

[21] The official website of Jesus and Mary College www.jmc.ac.in. Accessed on 19 June 2017.

[22] The official website of Jesus and Mary College www.jmc.ac.in. Accessed on 19 June 2017.

[23] *Jesus and Mary* College Magazine, 1984-85, New Delhi, p.96.

[24] *Spectrum*, Jesus and Mary College, 1991, New Delhi, 1991, pp-29-30.

[25] The official website of Jesus and Mary College www.jmc.ac.in. Accessed on 19 June 2017.

[26] The official website of Jesus and Mary College www.jmc.ac.in. Accessed on 19 June 2017.

[27] The official website of Jesus and Mary College www.jmc.ac.in. Accessed on 19 June 2017; Dimensions, Jesus and Mary College, New Delhi, 1997-98, p.52.

[28] Interview with the college librarian dated 22 June 2017.

Chapter 7

Inclusive Education and Women's Empowerment

Women education in India is still - as for many years past - in a state of flux and fluidity. Initially, it was patterned after the English tradition to train students either for services or in the learned professions. Drawing a tremendous amount of inspiration from the Foundress of the Congregation of Jesus and Mary, St Claudine Thevenet, the Sisters started serving the cause of women's education ever since the inception of the Congregation in 1818 in France and 1842 in India. For them, education is the process that liberates mind. Of course, it is the liberation from all forms of darkness and ignorance of political and cultural slavery. Education is a powerful tool for the empowerment through which social justice is ensured, equality is asserted, and fraternity is established. It is in this context, JM missionaries can be identified as pioneers of modern education, particularly, women's education in North India. They provide equal opportunity of education transcending the boundaries of caste, creed, religion, and class.

Many schools, colleges, and other formal and non-formal educational institutions run by the JM Sisters, and their long lasting and devoted service to the poor and the needy, have received a wide range of respect, recognition, and appreciation. The JM institutions prepare, and train future citizens endowed with a deep sense of responsibility, morality and spiritual ideals together with a solid training in academic, intellectual and character formation. By stressing the humanistic aspect in education, aiming at the harmonious development of all human faculties, the body, mind and spirit, the JM institutions are, indeed, making a very valuable contribution to the nation building, so keenly desired in this country.

The JM institutions of higher learning have a unique way of imparting knowledge to students. What distinguishes these institutions from other institutions of higher learning, particularly with special reference to India is its path breaking academic ambience, coupled with values that can be traced back to the deeply embedded Catholic tradition. Pope Francis has aptly pointed out, in his address to the Association of Catholic School Parents in Italy in 2015, that the idea of education in the fullness of humanity and it should be the driving force of Catholic educational establishments. In fact, the JM institutions continue to serve humanity with value-based education. Its predominant objectives are centered-around individual formation and nation building, and empowering women, poor and marginalised in order to bring them to mainstream from the periphery levels. No academic scholarship, which attempts to document educational growth and development in India, can ever downplay the crucial and historical role played by the JM institutions.

The JM Institutions have been rated remarkably high for the qualitative impact that they have had on its pupils, society, polity, governance and so on. Thousands of alumni spread all over the country and abroad have repeatedly testified that high academic standards have been maintained; spiritual and moral values stressed, and a secular outlook fostered in the JM institutions. Admission to JM institutions is open to everyone irrespective of caste, creed, religion, region, and language. At the same time a preference is given not only to Catholics but to the economically and socially disadvantaged sections of society. This study analyses and critically evaluates the deeply embedded educational practices which have been cherished by the Indian society from time immemorial. It also investigates how the JM educational institutions attempted to achieve efficiency in the field of women education through quality, transformative and world-class education.

The JM Congregation believes that a quality education imparted on time makes women empowered, and the process of women's empowerment is multidimensional which enables them to realize their full potential in all spheres of life. The society gives women a subordinate status, and due to that they may miss opportunities and have become victims of deprivation, discrimination, and atrocities. Empowerment is an active process with which women realize their full identity and potential. Education in JM institutions aim this empowering process as the surest way of realization of their potentials.

Paradigms of JM Institutions

Claudine Thevenet, having experienced God in herself, tried to bear witness to the goodness of God which permitted her to remain on her feet. This founding vision left an indelible mark on the lives of many generations throughout the world for almost two hundred years. It is this experience that Jesus Mary educational institutions impart to their pupils everywhere. JM Educational institutions play a significant and dynamic role in the formation of the character of young women. The academic exposure in the JM institutions ensures self-esteem, self-respect, and confidence, building in them a positive image by recognizing their extraordinary contribution to the society, polity, and economy.

It should be noted that the JM educational institutions have brought a social awakening and awareness amongst young minds and families in the society. These institutions also continue to show the students the path to intellect and to help them rediscover their own self through self-introspection. Consequently, the students are able to make intelligent choices in order to empower themselves. These institutions continue to appeal to the students to rise above the self-centered system by transcending the boundaries of 'I', 'me'and 'myself.' This self-realisation and people-centric attitude becomes possible largely due to the value-based education. These institutions continue to display functional literacy, empowerment, gender sensitivity, holistic and conducive environment for a dignified life.

For JM institutions, education is a tool for opening up the opportunities for women to enter the world of productive work, to participate in development and to change their lives. JM Sisters believe that when women are educated, they can become potential means of resources for their general well being. It comes to the level of personal empowerment that makes them self confident and gives them better decision-making power. It also inculcates a scientific temper in their attitude to life and enhances the quality of their life. Empowering women presupposes a positive change in perception of our society. Women's development is an essential component in every aspect of development. Nelson Mandela asserted that education continues to be the most powerful weapon to change the world. The JM Congregation certainly influenced Indian society through its transformative education by demonstrating the all-pervasive, inclusive, and egalitarian ideals of its foundress, Claudine Thevenet.

Investing in women's capabilities and empowering them to exercise their choices is not only valuable in itself but also the surest way to contribute to economic growth and overall development. In spite of various efforts to equalize opportunities, gender disparity continues to exist. Education helps women to resist exploitation, besides, of course, empowering them to be self reliant. Women's literacy is essential for economic vitality and independence. Acquisition of knowledge is one of the prerequisites of human development. Education increases women's awareness about their rights and capabilities, and the understanding as to how the socio-economic and political forces affect them. An educated and independent woman takes decisions concerning various aspects of her life. Women are allowed to participate as equal partners in the process of national development only when they are provided equal opportunities.

Empowerment implies greater access to knowledge and resources; greater ability to plan one's life; greater control over circumstances that influence one's life and greater freedom to overcome the restrictions and constraints imposed by customs, beliefs, and practices. Women's empowerment can be attained only through meeting their needs and interests. Education thus is a pathway and has been recognized as a major instrument which societies can use to direct the process of change and development towards desired goals.

Today all development agencies agree on the importance of educating women in order to promote and maintain family, health, nutrition, and general well-being. The JM educational institutions train women in such a way that they apply their acquired knowledge to the pursuits of daily life and match them for the position they have to fill. The JM educational institutions viewed that the women's education should always be directed towards their holistic development. As a potential instrument for change, education persistently prompted women to see the world through new perspectives. Intriguingly, education created new avenues in dealing with the emerging challenges at the global, national, and local levels. This in turn, emboldened the women to deal with issues like family planning, maternal mortality, and morbidity rates scientifically and courageously. The profound increase in women's education empowered them to be efficient decision makers in the society

For a Congregation which has a tradition in providing both basic and professional education for a period of 200 years, it is the right time to look into its history and see how far it has fulfilled its vision and mission in the field of education. It naturally attempts to answer to certain critical and specific questions like what was the most important contribution that the JM institutions have given to the society? What ways the education, training and experience in the institutions are helpful to the people in the society? And to what extent JM institutions contributed to the building up of individuals in terms of their leadership, commitment to the family and nation, and dedication for the general welfare of the people? The above questions also imply the relevance of their vision and mission to the present society.

It presumes, however, that broad results would be useful to make necessary steps for improvements in areas that need specific focus of the JM management. The survey intends to obtain insights into the progress of the JM institutions on these frontiers. This is critical because there have been no prior attempts to do either a qualitative or quantitative study of them even on the limited basis. This present attempt, however inadequate, may at least be able to suggest about the major contributions of JM institutions in the educational field.

The survey was attempted with certain criteria of success in educational institutions or measures of accomplishment under five major heads: Personal fulfillment and family, educational achievement, occupational intent, economic uplift and social acceptance. The survey used a questionnaire cum personal interviews of key informants at JM educational institutions in North India to understand the achievements and contributions of JM educational ministry towards women's education.

The questionnaire was duly prepared with the guidance of experts, and after a pilot was conducted to eliminate irrelevant and repetitive questions, the questionnaire was finalized with five areas stated above. The questionnaires were administered to the teachers, students, principals, alumni, and general public to get a cross sectional view.

Methodology and Procedure

The method used was both that of a questionnaire sent to each to be filled out at one's convenience and returned within a month's time and personal interviews. A total 240 questions[1] are grouped in the questionnaire under five heads for different category of people assigning each question certain value points. The most relevant and significant questions are selected and assigned to each group. Each question in the questionnaire is assessed in terms of its 'Yes' / 'No' response. The positive answer to a positive question [2] is assigned with two marks and the negative answer to a positive question is assigned with one mark. On the other hand, a positive answer to a negative question [3] is assigned with one mark and a negative answer to a negative question is assigned with two marks.

A participant who answered 'Yes'to more than fifty percent of questions in the questionnaire is considered as having positive attitude, thus having positive achievement towards the subject in consideration. A participant who marked 'No'to more than fifty percent of the questions is considered as having negative attitude towards the subject in consideration. No compulsion was placed upon participants in connection with this survey, their cooperation being entirely voluntary.

Questionnaires were distributed both directly and through mail and collected by the members of the student committee in each institution, which has been organized by representatives of the student committee. They were returned to the representatives. As a part of the study the other information already available through other sources such as academic records and Log Books have been made use of. Every student will be assigned a number, and the desired information from other sources will be catalogued for the purposes of this study under the respective numbers. Then the questionnaire data when received also filed by number, thus bringing all related data about each individual together, without necessitating the use of one's name for identification. This method requires that every student fills out and returns the questionnaire sent to him/ her in time.

This questionnaire aimed (1) to collect factual data of importance to future educational and administrative policies of JM institutions; (2) to secure reliable information about the JM institutions and their mission of education in North India; (3) to give an opportunity to the groups concerned to express themselves on various issues related to them; (4) to determine whether their opinion on such questions can, as a practical matter, be thus analyzed and utilized advantageously as a part of evaluation; (5) to ascertain whether a need for further reflection is needed for JM institutions' future mission policies in education; and (6) if so, towards what specific problems, if any, such future studies might profitably be directed.

The data sought can only be collected from individuals but will be dealt with entirely as a group study. Statistical group studies have been made, but of course this would involve no consideration of individual cases. The data will be of value in proportion to the thought and attention expended thereon by students. All the questions raised may not be of equal interest or apparent value to all students. It is obviously impractical to try and list the motive for every question. Therefore, the motive behind every question is to be taken for granted, even though the practical significance of some of the issues may not be obvious.

When the questionnaires were administered to the students and other stakeholders, response rate was expected to be between 20 and 30 percent; but the actual response rate exceeded and was found to be around 50 percent. As the questionnaires included both structured and open-ended questions, the data was found to be relevant and useful. The responses received were both voluntary with no compulsion on their part.

The success of the study as a whole and the reliability of the data were both dependent on the development of a favourable student attitude toward the project. Analyses of answers to the various questions indicate that such information as was obtained probably reflected, as well as might be expected, a serious intention to be accurate. Some of the questions yielded objective data and others, subjective opinions. Certain of the subjective questions were themselves put into the blanks partly for the purpose of stimulating the students in the undertaking as a whole. The answers of students to such questions may not be regarded as necessarily significant. Yet, in offering an opportunity for the expression of opinion on topics of genuine interest is proved to be useful. The inclusion of such questions had a beneficial effect on the study as a whole. Certain questions on personal data were reflected in only a few instances. In most cases the participants either became sufficiently interested in the survey to cooperate whole-heartedly and devote time and effort on their answers to the questions. If they were not of genuine interest in it, they made no return of the questionnaire.

The results are based on 3401 respondents of the classes X, XI, and XII of the student body, teachers, alumni, principals and general public related to JM institutions during 2006-'07; while the total number of returns, 2466, represented 74.9 per cent of the questionnaires sent out. The non-student body of 884 respondents with teachers, alumni, principals, and general public, represented 704 with 79.6 percent of the blanks sent out. The smallest number of replies received to any particular question was irrespective to family matters and one's own personal attitudes, since some students were unwilling to answer these questions because of their personal nature. Even these figures, however, represent a good return while over 70 per cent of replies were received in answer to most of the queries. The following table shows the number of blanks sent out and returned from the students:

Name of the Institution	*Sent Out*	*Returned*	*Percentage of Return*
ST PATRICK'S, AGRA	302	241	80
ST. JOSEPH'S AGRA	581	424	73
CJM WAVERLY	35	30	86
ST JOSEPH'S SARDHANA	465	312	67
CJM SHIMLA	94	73	78
ST ANTHONY'S AGRA	285	197	69
CJM DHERA DUN	311	233	75
ST BEDE'S SHIMLA	490	328	67
CJM AMBALA	259	181	70
CJM DELHI	553	426	77
CJM HAMPTON COURT	26	21	82
TOTAL	3401	2466	74.9

Table I: Number and Percentage of Questionnaires sent and returned: Classes X, XI and XII of the year 2006-07

The number of forms sent out is less by about a hundred than the total number of students enrolled according to the Admission Register, at the opening of the academic year 2005-'06. Illness, absence, or mistakes in delivery account for the remaining small discrepancy between the 3401 given above as sent out, and the actual net total of students at the time of the survey.

Strategy of Analysis

In analysing the questionnaire, an important problem came out of the fact that different numbers of replies were received to different questions. The obvious merit of this plan is that answers from exactly the same group of individuals would be utilized in every part of the process. The group studied would be uniform throughout and each phase of the survey would, therefore, reflect the views of the selfsame body of students. This original plan would necessitate discarding a large number of answers and thus lessening materially the number of cases on which any conclusions could be arrived.

Since some questions were left unanswered by certain students and different ones by others, it is evident, while the total number answering different questions varied, that no constant error of selection was under those circumstances likely to affect the data. Furthermore, the group as a whole was sufficiently large and homogeneous to warrant the assumption that the students answering any given question fairly represented student opinion in general.

After careful consideration and actual analysis of the various groups, it was decided not to follow the method of selecting one absolutely uniform group and limiting the entire analysis to that particular body. There seemed after all to be so little to gain in reliability from this method. The other unavoidable sources of error in an investigation of this sort are ruled out on the basis of a strict methodology adopted in the investigation.

Consequently, a more justifiable method to use in this case was that of utilizing every possible answer in analysis of each question. This method implied to give more truly representative results, based on a larger number of cases. In most cases the numbers of questionnaire answers, both positive and negative, were sufficiently specific to be utilized in the analysis. The following table shows the number of received responses and the analysis of the results in terms of positive and negative and their percentage.

Name of the Institution	*Number of Received Response*	*Positive Response*	*Negative Response*	*% of + ve Responses*	*% of _ ve Responses*
ST PATRICK'S AGRA	241	190	51	78.8	21.2
ST JOSEPH'S AGRA	424	345	79	81.4	18.6
CJM WAVERLY	30	20	10	67.7	32.3
ST JOSEPH'S SARDHANA	312	276	36	88.5	11.5
CJM SHIMLA	73	59	14	80.8	19.2
STANTHONY'S AGRA	197	144	53	70.0	30.0
CJM DHERA DUN	233	196	37	84.1	15.9
ST BEDE'S SHIMLA	328	289	39	88.1	11.9
CJM AMBALA	181	134	47	70.0	30.0
CJM DELHI	426	367	59	86.6	13.4
CJM HAMPTON COURT	21	18	03	85.7	14.3
TOTAL	**2466**	**2038**	**428**	**88.5**	**11.5**

Table II: Number and Percentage of Responses to the Questionnaires-Classes X, XI and XII of the year 2006-07

At a glance, this table gives an idea about each school in terms of its participation and cooperation. It also shows a comparative analysis in terms of its results from each school. Out of 3401 sent out questionnaires we got 2466 returned forms having a percentage of 72.5 returns. The total number of positive responses is 2038 in the total of 2466 returns. It forms the 88.5 percent of the total returned questionnaire.

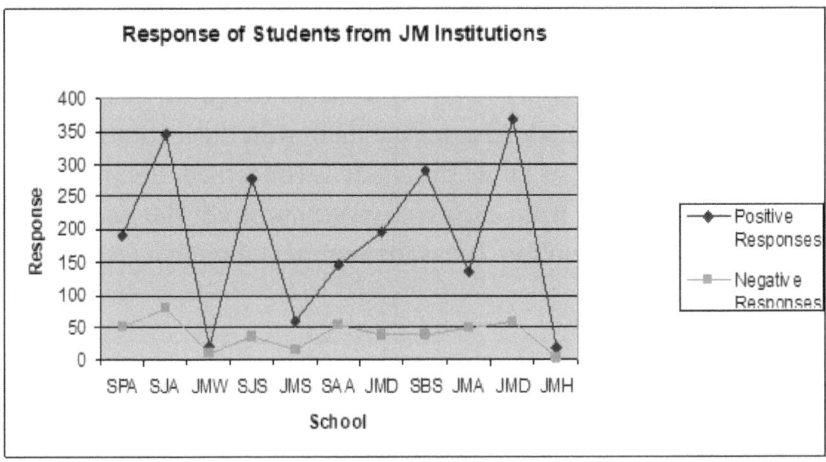

Figure - 1

Figure–1 shows the graphical presentation of the positive and negative responses of the student community in JM institutions. It is evident that the positive responses of the students are high in comparison with the negative responses. It is to be noted that there are only two institutions that come close in its negative and positive responses. CJM School, Waverly and JM School, Hampton Court have less number of students participated in the questionnaire.

Category of participants	*Number Of sent / Received Responses*	*'YES' Responses*	*'NO' Responses*	*% of Positive Responses*	*% of Negative Responses*
STUDENT	3401/2466	2038	428	82.7	18.3
TEACHER	140/121	106	15	87.6	12.4
EX-STUDENT	542/480	394	86	82.0	18.0
PRINCIPAL	12/10	08	02	80.0	20.0
GENERAL PUBLIC	190/93	79	14	84.9	15.1
TOTAL	3931/2804	2303	491	83.3	16.7

Table III: Category, Number and Percentage of Responses to the Questionnaires

Table III shows the details of the non-student body that represented in the questionnaire along with the total number of positive and negative responses. Since the non-student body is scattered in such way an attempt has not been made to associate them with the institutions they represented. And also, as far as this study is concerned, the individual representation of data from each college/school is not the issue under the preview of consideration. It has the representation of a total of 71.3 percent of returns.

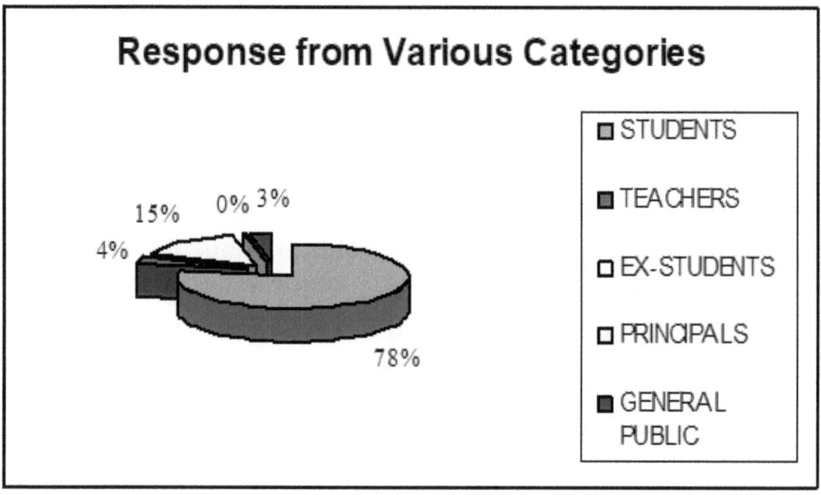

Figure - 2

Figure -2 is the graphical representation of the responses of the various categories of people took part in the survey. Out of the 2804 total number of participants in the survey, 2038 participants are students. It comes 78 percent of the total number of participants and the largest fraction in the group. There are only 10 Principals participated in the Survey. Since it is below 0.5 percent it is rounded to zero.

In the following table (Table IV) 'Yes'and 'No'responses are assessed in terms of achievement on the basis of the assigned value points. The questionnaires with fifty percent and above value points for the 'Yes' responses are considered as having a positive achievement. Since the questions are grouped under five categories of achievement the number of 'Yes'responses shows the achievement in that given category.

Category/ achievements	*Self/Family*		*Economic Status*		*Occupational*		*Social*		*Educational*	
	yes	no	yes	no	yes	no	yes	no	yes	no
Student	462	54	302	142	374	128	419	78	481	46
Teacher	16	04	30	02	24	01	21	06	15	02
Ex-student	73	18	61	21	84	15	80	12	96	20
Principal	02	01	01	00	01	00	03	00	01	01
Public	18	02	11	03	16	03	08	02	26	04
Total	**571**	**79**	**406**	**168**	**499**	**147**	**531**	**98**	**620**	**73**

Table IV: Conversion of Number of 'Yes'and 'No" Responses into the Areas of Achievement by different Categories

Figure-3 marks the positive responses of the various categories in terms of achievement. The student community is the largest group of participants and they have the highest level of achievement in educational status with 481 positive responses. The next highest number of positive responses in the student community finds in self/family achievement area with 462 positive responses. The other areas are also not that far from its highest scores as far as the student community is concerned. The next highest positive responses find in ex-student category. Though, in comparison with the number of the students, the ex-students are less in number they have highest achievement in educational area.

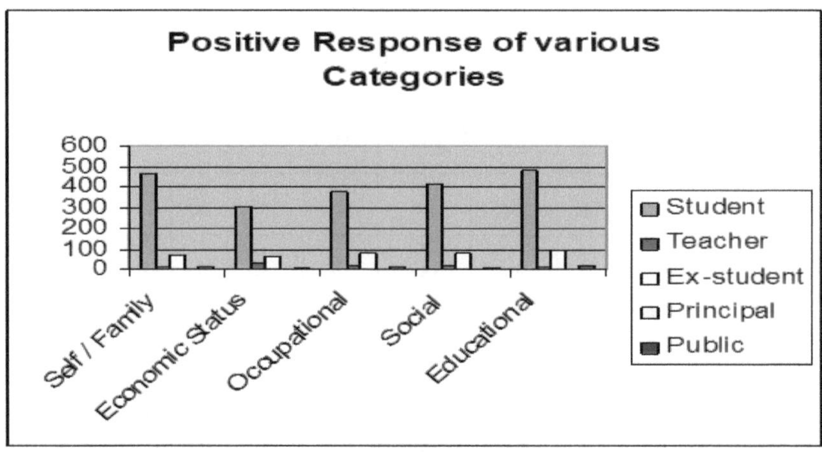

Figure - 3

Though figure 3 shows the data of each category in relation with the assigned areas in focus, it doesn't give the actual percentage of achievement in each area. The achievement of the JM institutions, in terms of contributions in the field of education, being the focus of the study, no analysis is done on the data that gave 'No' responses. The following table gives the clear picture of the focus of the study showing achievement in each area by different categories.

Area of Achievement Categories	Students' Reported Achievement in %	Teachers' Reported Achievement in %	Ex-students' Reported Achievement in %	Principals Reported Achievement in %	G. Public Reported Achievement in %
SELF / FAMILY	22.7	15.09	18.55	25.0	22.78
ECONOMIC	14.6	28.31	15.48	12.5	13.94
OCCUPATIONAL	18.6	22.64	21.31	12.5	20.25
SOCIAL	20.5	19.81	20.30	37.5	10.12
EDUCATIONAL	23.6	14.15	24.36	12.5	32.91
TOTAL	**100**	**100**	**100**	**100**	**100**

Table V: Area of Achievement, Reported Number and Percentage of Response to the Questionnaires

Figure - 4 shows the pie chart presentation of students'achievement in various areas. Achievement in the area of educational status is the highest in comparison with other areas. Occupational intent is the lowest and everything has been distributed from 19 percent to 23 percent.

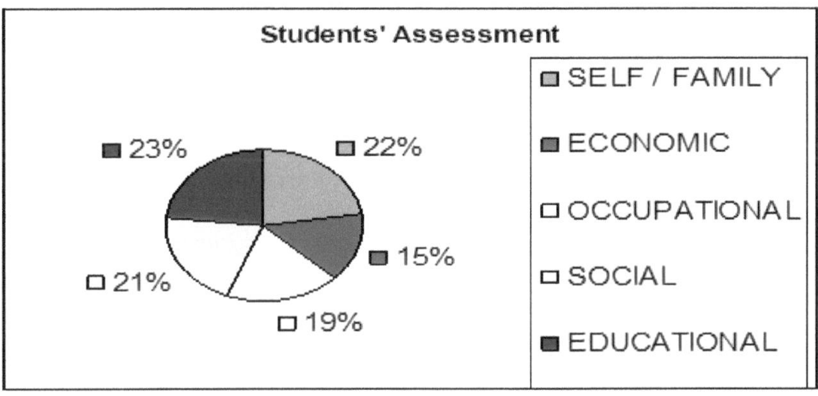

Figure - 4

Figure -5 is the pie chart representation of the achievement by ex-students in different areas. Achievement in the educational area appears to be the highest for the ex-students. Occupational and social aspects come closest to the educational status. Everything has been distributed from 15 percent to 25 percent.

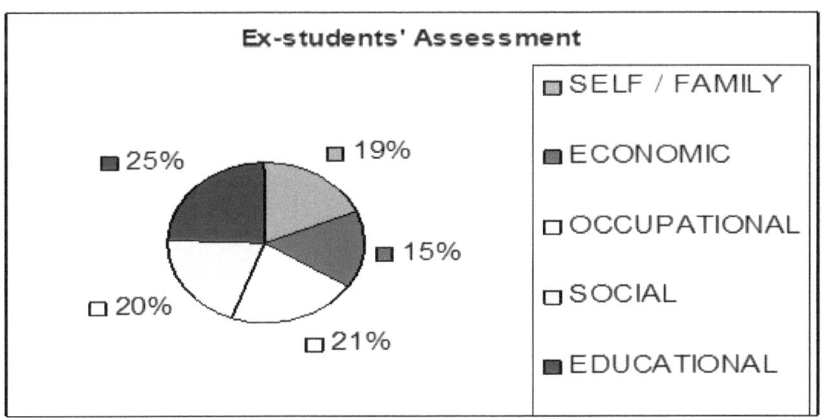

Figure – 5

Teacher assessment of JM institutions is presented in Figure - 6. It shows a marked difference in achievement in the area of economic status. The data has been distributed from 14 percent to 28 percent.

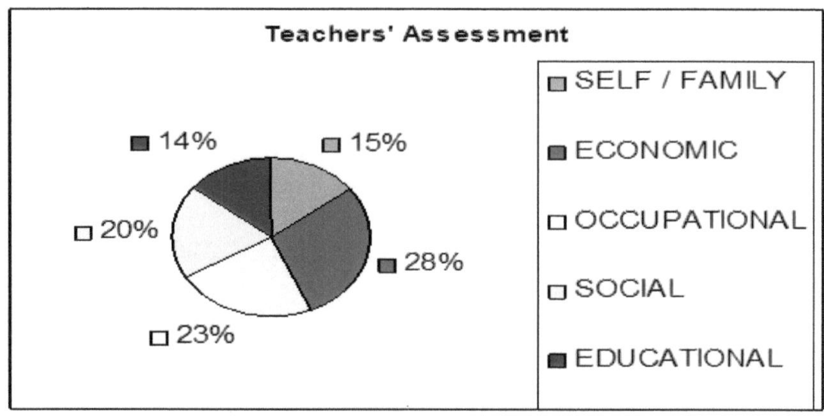

Figure – 6

Though small in number the Principals'category shows the highest achievement in the area of social acceptance. Since it falls below 0.5 it has no significant measure in the graphical presentation in comparison with the rest of the groups.

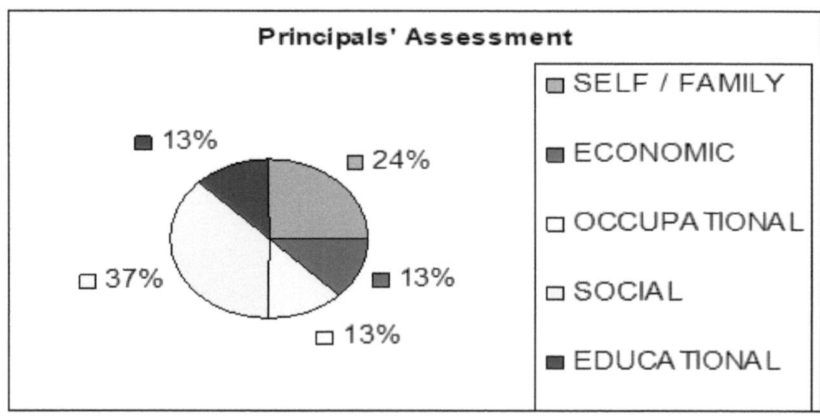

Figure – 7

The general public has assessed the JM institutions in varying degrees. In the following figure – 8, the highest level of achievement is shown in the area of educational status. And the lowest is marked in the social acceptance with 10 percent. However, it has remarkable achievement in comparison with rest of the groups.

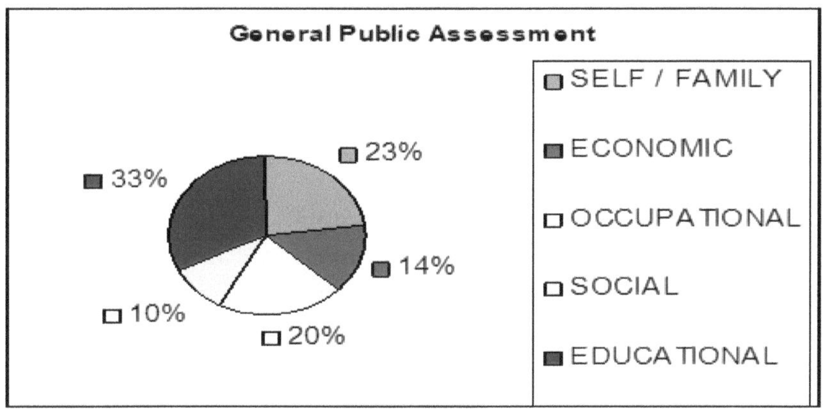

Figure – 8

Interrelationship between the Groups and Categories

As the questions gave insight into the working of the different areas of the focus of the study, it looks into the influence of one over the other. As a result, the possibility of a significant interrelationship between the personal fulfillment and family, educational achievement, occupational intent, economic status and social acceptance in groupings was also taken into account. Since the student body forms a major part of the representation, the influence of different aspects on each other cannot be ruled out. It assumes importance especially with inclusion of the subjective responses in the analysis of the data. The non-student body being the representatives from different groups they need to be analyzed separately. The same kind of interrelationship also can be noted with regard to the data availed from the non-student body.

Economic Status and Occupational Goal

Although variations in external conditions are not so readily measurable, they obviously show the influence of academic achievement for economic progress to a considerable degree. Indeed, the academic achievement of some ex-students indicates that a part of their total possible effort is rewarded at an institution which prides itself on high academic standards. Being students at the JM, learing in school and college subjects, coaching for examinations, outlines of courses–all these enable the students with a sense of achievement, without such environment they might not themselves be sufficiently able to attain.

Many students in good standing today would not even have succeeded if they had not been in institutions of JM and recieved special assistance at step after step of their school and college course. Every year the institution is asked to recommend pupils already in schools/colleges who are trying to get in, whose teachers gladly offer special coaching. Furthermore, personal interviews show that the environmental factors play a crucial role. In some cases, the environmental factors including the social background distinctly helpful to pupils and in others, these factors play a negative role for their academic advancement. No doubt other external factors are also significant.

Environmental factors are also extremely difficult to compare and evaluate in this respect. To some extent the effect of environment is being considered in this study, as we compare students from different social and economic levels and from families with somewhat different educational background. The occupation and income of families is one of several external factors considered. And in this connection, as it is evident from the personal interview, with respect to those students, one or both of whose parents have themselves had a training in JM institution had certain positive impact in their life.

Certain differences noted for groups compared in respect to family that had education in JM institution and the consequent family occupation will indicate that there is an outcome of economic achievement. Data from the investigation offer, in fact, with respect to variations in the following types of external factors of influence: Family income, degree of self-support, family occupation, family education, family influences, reasons for coming to college, degree of student's orientation and intended occupation.

Among these external conditions, especially on the economic one, considerable information is available from the personal interviews, questionnaire survey and from the records of the admission register. It gives the information on the finances and the annual income reported by the parents when the interview was conducted. Therefore, we have objective and reliable data upon which to base the achievement in respect to economic factors to the people who are associated with the JM institutions. The interview data furnish other information, such as the amounts reportedly spent by these students. For instance, the degree of self-support is obviously related to family income and their annual expenses are controlled by the total amount at one's disposal. Some of the factors which make the family influence complex are observed. We can, therefore, see the apparent correspondence between such related factors.

We thus find certain tendencies in academic achievement apparently related to students' economic status whether that be measured by family income, annual expenses, or self-support. In order to find a basis for determining objectively the factor of economic status, the relationships between each of these three factors which make it up, were analyzed from the answers in the interview. The primary purpose of this was to investigate the interrelationship between economic factors, in order that they might be methodically combined.

The general method was that of rating students in one of the categories according to the combined effect of all factors. It is objectively combined and assessed according to a schedule determined. This redistribution of all such cases was made on the basis of the resultant of financial criteria, reduced to one common expression in the factor of economic status. This procedure serves two purposes. First, it enables us further to analyze the student groups. Second, having a definite economic status rating for each student permits to adjust other groups, on the basis of relative economic status. This procedure, therefore, gives us certain insights to the factors which we are attempting to investigate:

1. The data gathered through the personal interview and questionnaire show definite objective evidence of the marked variation in economic status within the JM students. In fact, since there is no direct selection on any economic basis among applicants for admission to JM, the range of variation from complete poverty to affluence is a much wider one than is the range of potential ability used as criteria of selection.
2. We have separately observed in the personal interviews the variations in family income, in annual expenses, and in degree of self-support and found mutually corroborative evidence that economic advantage is positively related to academic achievement.
3. The influence of economic factors has been combined into Economic Status. On this basis, each of the students for whom definite objective data were available was individually classified in one of the categories which represented a progressive economic status series.
4. The tendencies noted with respect to economic status appear with such consistency to justify and reach a definite conclusion that the academic success of students in JM institutions has positively contributed to their financial status in life.

Personal Fulfillment and Family Background

Another set of external factors reflected in the questionnaire makes up the complex family environment. Differences of this nature reflected in the questions given were somewhat uncertain of analysis because the environmental effect on personal fulfillment and family itself is the resultant of various factors. Any attempted classification based on different total sets of such factors is difficult. We have, in fact, no exact or wholly objective criteria by which the significance of such differentiations can be assured.There is a classification based upon parents' occupations, and the question of relationship between college-trained parents and their daughters' academic achievement. Certain questions in the personal interview made possible to get an idea of the records of several groups of students.

The students replying to this set of questions were classed according to parents' reported occupations. It is interesting to note in the interview that the daughters of professional fathers (teachers, lawyers, doctors, and engineers) are distinctly superior in ratings, stand on the whole higher in their college studies. There are differences noted between business and professional men's daughters remain relatively unchanged. The somewhat superior academic records made by this group suggest superior academic motivation possibly because of intellectual emphasis in the family background of these students.

Further, adjustment of these groups with respect to their economic status shows comparatively little variation. The sons of professional men retain, as a group, superiority in academic records, and thus led to the conclusion that a small but reliable difference exists between these groups. So, we are justified in considering even this small difference as significant. The records of outgoing students of JM shows relatively little difference in academics between the daughters of college graduates and those whose parents did not go to college. And it deals primarily with the relation between various criteria of success and size of families; the interview offers no data strictly comparable with ours as to relative performance of the total 'college-parent'and 'non-college-parent'groups. It is, however, interesting to note that the daughters of graduates are the more prominent in extra-curricular activities and showed probable success in life.

The data from personal interview shows that daughters of graduates tend to do better academic work if they come from large families; while for students whose parents did not themselves go to college this relationship is reversed to a larger extent. Assuming that the college graduates represent the wealthier family group, a possible explanation of these findings, suggested by data from the personal interview, would be (a) that students from the JM trained families are somewhat more seriously motivated; but (b) that students in the non-JM-trained families of presumably lower income suffer from an excessive financial burden, which tends to counteract their possibly greater incentive. While from the group representing higher educational and economic levels, the student from a small family does not do as well as the one who, from a large family, is spurred by greater competition.

Influence of Occupational Goal

As the influence of different areas and groupings are at work, this section focuses on another occupational aspect –that of the student's own goal. The personal interview revealed that the uncertainty of one's own occupational decision somewhat showed the reliability of any apparent connection between the student's own purpose and her academic career. There are sources of error in students'subjective estimates of what career they expect to follow, or of what purpose they themselves chiefly had in mind when coming to JM school/college.

However, such subjective estimates may subsequently appear in the light of occupations and interests actually undertaken in the future. It is, nevertheless, obvious that what any student, before completion of her studies, thinks she is going to do may affect her point of view and degree of motivation during her course of studies. Whereas what she actually does later can have no retroactive effect upon her earlier plans. Therefore, such early views, however uncertain, are that the student actually holds during the period of her life is worth considering. Consequently, whether or not they subsequently become modified, theirs is the occupational influence working upon her student days.

Influence of Social Acceptance and Personal Fulfillment

Personal interview holds the view that those who came to JM institutions with some definite aim, giving the question of a life career, and who kept their aims in mind, made definitely superior academic records. Those, on the other hand, who had no such purpose made distinctly lower records. Similarly, analysis of the relation between parents' occupations and students' degree of orientation revealed surprisingly little relationship between these two factors. This strengthens the probability that the direction of a student's own occupational purpose is related to the consistency with which that purpose is held. The students with definite professional leanings find more meaning in curricular work and have more appreciation of its values than do those who come to college either with no definite career in mind or merely with a general expectation of entering some phase or other of the great field of business.

The answers in the interview show that such influences as family occupation or tradition, knowledge of a definite position awaiting the student after studies, and attainment of unhampered choice of an occupation, all give evidence of exerting effect upon the academic records of JM students. We may infer that students who know what they expect to do are academically focused than those uncertain as to their life purpose. Perhaps because of some specific aim which seems to characterize them, those planning to enter the professions tend to stand somewhat higher academically than do the prospective businessmen.

The personal interviews have similarly found that economic factors affect achievement, and surprisingly enough that economic advantage is not directly but inversely related to students'classroom averages. Those most handicapped financially, personal interviews revealed, make better scholastic averages than do those of greater means. The various other influences were first analyzed in their original state. While such adjustment tended in some instances to reduce the differences appearing before the process of equating had been applied, in no case it eliminated them entirely.

These observed differences were generally small but, as was emphasized earlier, in a study of this character almost any consistent difference is significant. Since the size of the groups and the manifold influences at work, it would make the assessment highly improbable. In this connection it is clear that the poorer students had already been weeded out by the process of academic selection. Many had fallen by the wayside from each class studied. The student body at the time of the survey, therefore, represented an even more highly selected group academically than that resulting from operation of the system of admission by college examinations. Therefore, the differences noted from within this highly homogeneous group are probably of true significance.

Implications of these Findings

The purpose of this has been to organize evidence, both objective and subjective in nature, upon which certain analyses will be based. The number of cases investigated varies for different topics in accordance with the number of replies received to the different questions. Over 80 per cent of the students responded to the more general topics and 45 per cent even to the questions of a personal nature in their personal interviews. Those cooperating in the survey and the interview represented a group somewhat superior to the average, but for the following reasons this slight favourable selection in no way impair the reliability of the data: a). The subjective opinion and judgment of the superior students would presumably have more significance b). The groups subsequently to be compared are subdivisions of the total number cooperating in the survey. Therefore, the slightly superior students are compared in various respects with each other, and not except in a few particular instances with the participants as a whole.

Accordingly, it is justified in concluding from the evidence that the data based upon is evidently interested. The replies from a major section of JM educational institutions, voluntarily cooperating in the survey, accurately represent student opinion. Again, it is emphasized, however, that minor irregularities and the interplay of conflicting influences, because of the number of cases involved, will tend to obscure rather than to exaggerate any group differentiations. Accordingly, we must depend upon the data presented by consistent, though small, differences in our search.

Taken all together they show primarily the importance of purpose which, in one form or another, they all express a certain sense of achievement as the underlying motive. These deductions seem to offer ample justification for the often-repeated criticisms which have been showered upon the typical course of study in JM educational institutions. The test of the abiding influence that the JM institutions exert on its students is the performance of the student after they leave the portals of their institution. When educated young men and women assume positions of responsibility in society, they are often influenced by the value systems they imbibed in their school and college days. If the institution has succeeded in deepening the spirit of service in its young women, they would stand for justice and human rights when occasions arise. It is this aspect of the formation offered by JM institutions in North India that we analyse in the question on the performance of the old students of JM institutions. As the effect of the values the students have imbibed in JM schools and colleges can be measured in terms of their performance in their personal and social life after they leave the institutions.

As far as limitations of the data, an attempt has been made to integrate the various findings. Answers to the questions raised in the beginning of this chapter focused on personal fulfillment and family, educational achievement, occupational goal, economic uplift, and social acceptance show the impact of JM institutions in the North Indian society. The most important of these influences is upon educational achievement and this is measurable to a considerable degree through questionnaires and personal interviews.

Something very remarkable about this study is that it has elicited profuse positive comments from good section of our respondents. With very few exceptions, the comments have been highly appreciative of the role played by JM institutions in this regard. There are typical and significant contributions JM institutions have made to the country. They have been pioneers in the field of women education in North India. Through their education they have been forming outstanding citizens in all walks of life throughout the country. They have produced many distinguished intellectuals, professionals, administrators, political and national leaders like doctors, lawyers, teachers, members of the administrative service, government officers, army personnel and entrepreneurs in industry and business.

The JM institutions have formed men and women of integrity, self discipline and moral caliber who have become shining examples and an inspiration in public life. They have spread the noble ideals of selfless service, social justice, hard work and commitment by upholding high academic excellence. It will be pertinent to share of a few of the JM pupils and members of the faculty whose success stories in real life is reflective of achievements. For instance, Ms. Sheila Dixit, the then Chief Minister of Delhi, Ms. Shailaja Kumari, the former Deputy Minister of Education, Priyanka Gandhi, a politician, Mrs. Ritu Marwah, Dy. Director of Education, Delhi, and Aruna Roy are but a few. Aruna Roy, an Indian political and social activist served as an officer in the Indian Administrative Service from 1968-1975 and went on to set up the 'Mazdoor kisan shakti sangathan'. Mrs. Sangeeta Singh, MP, Lok Sabha, Aung San Suu Kyi, Nobel Lauret and socialist in Myanmmar, fighting for the peoples'rights, were some of the JM pupils who brought name and fame to the JM institutions for their achievements in administrative and social fields.

Jesus and Mary College is known for its exceptional academics and extra-curricular activities. In fact, this college is the 'alma mater' of several crucial personalities including Neha Dhupia, a renowned model and Bollywood actress, Ambika Anand, TV anchor and the Editor in Chief, Fashion at NDTV Good Times, the lifestyle channel of NDTV, Sushmita Mukherjee, a senior Bollywood and television actress, and Hasleen Kaur, a model who was crowned Miss India Earth and eventually participated in the Miss Earth pageant in 2011.

Interestingly, a large number of JMC students became influential citizens of the country in the field of politics, teaching, publication, journalism, sports, creative arts, entrepreneurship, and business. For example, Mazel Ampareen Lyngdoh, became a prominent politician from Meghalaya who served as a Cabinet Minister in the Government of Meghalaya, representing the Indian National Congress. Namita Gokhale became a distinguished writer, publisher and festival director. In fact, she has authored more than sixteen books including the latest panoramic historical novel "Things to Leave Behind," published in November 2016. Nistula Hebbar became a leading journalist and editor who worked in leading national dailies including *The Hindu*, *Times of India*, *Financial Express*, and the *Economic Times*. Radhika Madan became a popular television and film actress who won the 'Best Debut' Award at Zee Gold Awards 2015. Similarly, Sandali Sinha became an influential Bollywood actress and model known widely for her portrayal of Pia in the romantic hit *Tum Bin*. Ankita Shorey became a popular model who was crowned Femina Miss India International 2011. Rini Simon Khanna became a noted Indian television news anchor who worked with state-run Doordarshan. Several sports women continued to bring aura to their alma-mater, most importantly, Apurvi Singh Chandela became a noted sport shooter who won the gold medal in the 2014 Commonwealth Games in Glasgow, Scotland. Similarly, Manika Batra became a table tennis player who has been projected as the top-ranked female table tennis player in India and also ranked 58th in the world.

Ms. Sonia Verma, news reader and executive editor NDTV, Sushma Seth and Divya Seth, theatre and television personalities, Bubbles Sabharwal, a veteran in the children's theatre, Shikha Swaroop, Poonam Nath, Lovleen Mishra, and Aita Wahi, cinema and television personalities, Monisha Naguni, journalist in *Hindustan Times*, Vinita Dawra Nangia, Senior editor in *Times of India*, Nona Walia, Editor *Saturday Times*, Nalini Singh, Journalist, Komal G.B Singh, news reader, Sujata Madhok, Indian activist and developmental Journalist, specializing in women's issues, Nalini Singh, Head girl and sister of Arun Shouri, journalist, Nandita Veermani, classical dancer, were a few of the JM pupils to name who proved the mettle, and became shining stars in the horizon of the television and communication media.

Dr. Gurshan Kaur, radiologist, Dr. Alka Pande, art curator, Shalini Verma, engineer, Ritu Malhotra, fashion designer, Henna Wadhwani, graphic designer and stylist, India Today Group, Anjalika Kripalani, interior decorator, Dr. Shika Bansal, dermatologist, Maulana Azad hospital, Dr. Seema Joshi, Asst. Professor of Medicine, University of St. Lousie, Missorie State, USA, Prof. Aruna Broota, clinical psychologist, Dr. Geeta Mehdiratta, gynaecologist, were a few of the JM pupils who excelled in the professional field of medicine and engineering. Ritu Dalmia, chef, Mrs. Deepa Joshi, teacher, Payal Kapoor, art curator, Priya Jain, and Pooja Jain, business women, Queenie Dodhy, Pooja Juneja and Shibani Sachdev, jewellery designers, Shabam Khanna, entrepreneur in biotech cosmetics and Anjana Bhargava, fashion designer, were the JM pupils who proved their creative acumen in the field of art and entrepreneurial fields.

The JM institutions prepare young women with a sound humanistic, scientific, and spiritual training capable of hard, sustained work for society. They are imparting right education to the nation. They also give a balanced view of life, sense of dedication, duty, and respect for men where one learns justice to one's neighbour. In the midst of the indiscipline, strikes and lawlessness prevailing in other schools and colleges, JM institutions present a picture of comparative peace and successful academic endeavour. Finally, they train the Indian girl to be a woman, wife, and mother with a sense of responsibility and commitment to justice.

Their meritorious efforts have been amply rewarded, and the awards and recognitions stand as icons of achievement and performance. Here a few of such recognitions are acknowledged to show the JM legacy of excellence in the field of education. 'Shresht Shree Award' was presented to Revd Sr Lucy D'Souza, the Principal CJM Delhi, for her meritorious service in the field of Education for year 1996-97 by Delhi Citizen Forum for Civil Rights. Her outstanding services, achievements and contributions were acknowledged in presenting her 'Indira Gandhi Priyadarshini Award' on the occasion of International

Women's Day on 8th March 2002, New Delhi by Shri N.D. Tiwari, the Member of the Parliament. She was also the recipient of "The Best Citizens of India Award–2002", "Bharat Nirman Talented Ladies Award for Education–2003", "Rotary Club award for Education : 2003–04", and "Global Human Rights protection Award– 2006" for her extraordinary work in catering to the various needs of the students whom she has nurtured towards a progressive future. This helps them to function as wise and positive citizens who can craft a particularly good career for themselves. She has been involved in the field of education and administration in the Convent of Jesus and Mary School in Pune, Mussorie, Shimla and Delhi.

Dr. Vandana Shiva, a JM alumnus, is a physicist, eco-feminist, environmental activist and the author of over 300 papers in leading scientific and technical journals. She has participated in the non-violent Chipko Movement during the 1970s. She is one of the leaders of International Forum on Globalization and an Executive Member of World Future Council, Germany. In 1991, she founded 'Navadanya', a national movement to protect the diversity and integrity of living resources for the promotion of organic farming and their fair trade. In 2004, she started Bija Vidyapeeth, an international college for sustainable living in collaboration with Schumacher College, U.K. For her contributions to deepening the ecological paradigm, and for linking research to action, Dr. Shiva has received many awards like "Order of the Golden Ark" by his Royal Highness Prince Bernhard of the Netherlands, Global 500 Roll of Honour, 1993 by UNEP, Earth Day International Award, 1993 by Earth Day International and alternative Nobel Prize, Right Livelihood Award.

Dr. Meera Shiva, a Medical Doctor, Archana Puran Singh, Hindi film actress, Ms. Prarthna Gahilote, reporter with CNN-IBN, Dr. Suman Nangia, member of the International Council of Psychologists- affiliated to the UNO, Ragini Chopra, manager, marketing S.E. Asia, Oberoi hotels, Shweta Singh, a commercial pilot who won 'Miss. Best Smile'in Miss India contest, Bharti Bist, Indian Army, First lady officer to pass out of O.T.A. Chennai, Arti Chopra, Capt. Indian Army, Dr. Sarwat Rehman, author, B. Gill, gold medalist in high jump at Nationals, Veenu Phadke, Asia No.4, India No.3 table tennis champion, and Dr. Antara Majumdar, Senior Research Biostatistician with Bristol-Myers Squibb, U S A, were alumni of CJM Dehradoon.

St Bede's College continued to produce leaders of eminence in different fields, particularly politics, bureaucracy, army, journalism and film industry, For example, Preneet Kaur became a powerful politician who served in the Government of India as a Minister of State in the Ministry of External Affairs from 2009 to 2014. She is the wife of Amarinder Singh, who is now the 26th Chief Minister of Punjab. Shazia Ilmi, a television journalist and anchor at Star News, later became the spokesperson for the India Against Corruption movement led by Anna Hazare in 2011 and 2012, has joined in full-time politics under the leadership of Indian Prime Minister Narendra Modi. Pratibha Singh, a leading student politician became the member of the 14th Lok Sabha of India. As the wife of Virbhadra Singh who was the then Chief Minister of Himachal Pradesh since 2012. Pratibha represented the Mandi constituency of Himachal Pradesh and is a member of the Indian National Congress.

Similarly, the college also produced bureaucrats like Meera Shankar. In fact, Meera had served as India's Ambassador to the United States of America from 26 April, 2009 to 2011. It has to be stated that Meera was India's second woman ambassador to the United States of America, Vijaya Lakshmi Nehru Pandit being the first. St Bede's college produced eminent artists. For example, Persis Khambatta became a leading Indian model, actress and author who is known for her role as Lieutenant Ilia in the feature film *Star Trek*: The Motion Picture. Another significant artist in the film industry is Ish Amitoj Kaur. She is a filmmaker who resides in the U.S. and she is known widely for her films *Chhevan Dariya* and *Kambdi Kalaai*. Over a period of time she became popular for her unique theater in therapy techniques that she has evolved while doing theater workshops with children. Priya Rajvansh was yet another influential film actress, who is known for her thrilling performance in Hindi films like *Heer Raanjha* and *Hanste Zakhm*. It is to be noted that Kalpana Kartik who starred in six films in the 1950s attracted a great deal of attention all over India as an influential actress and as the wife of film maker Dev Anand. Similarly, Rubina Dilaik also became a thought-provoking actress and fitness spokesperson who gained recognition by playing Radhika, the main character in the TV series Choti Bahu.

Principals of JM Colleges received a number of awards for their contribution to higher education. Sr Melba Rodrigues, the Principal St Bede's College, Shimla, was honoured with "Mahila Shiromani Award for Distinguished Contribution in Education" in 1993, "IndhirapriyaDarshini Gandhi Award for Outstanding achievement and Contribution in Education" in 1994 and "Spardahashree Award for Cultural Organization" in 1995.

It was Sr Molly Abraham's tenure as the Principal of St Bede's, the college got re-accredited with 'A' Grade in its second cycle by the National Assessment and Accreditation Council of India in 2010. Based on the performance and the progress made by the college, it was evaluated and upgraded to *Star College status* in 2009 by the Department of Biotechnology of the Government of India. In 2011, St Bede's College was selected under the scheme *Centre with Potential for Excellence* (CPE) by the University Grants Commission. During her tenure *Journal of Research: The Bede Athenaeum*, a research journal of international repute, began attracting a wide range of scholarly attention cutting across academic disciplines. She is the recipient of Best Administrator's Award for Women (Best Administration and Students' Welfare).

Jesus and Mary College in New Delhi is known for its academic excellence and the role played by the principals, teachers and administrative staff is exceedingly crucial. For instance Sister Marina John, who worked as the Principal of the college untiringly, is the recipient of innumerable awards of recognition such as Shresht Shree Award, Delhi Citizen Forum for Civil Rights 1999-2000, Shrimani Award 2001,

Priyadarshani Award in November, 2003 for her outstanding services, achievements and contribution in the field of education.

St Bede's College produced innumerable influential personalities such as Purnima Chauhan, special secretary irrigation and public health to government of Himachal Pradesh, PretiZinta, actress, Harinder Hira, Parminder Hira and Usha Vohra, IAS officers, Meera Mukherjee, environmentalist, Bonny Sodhi, an NGO for street children and women, Puneeta Bhardwaj, Himachal Pradesh Service [HPS], Satwant Atwal Trivedi IPS, Anjana Kuthiala, artist and former Miss India, Preeti Kansal, works with an NGO and SOS children's village, Sulakshna Bramta, theater, TV and radio artist, Ruchika Mehta, editor of Life Styles, *Hindustan Times*, Charu Dada, business woman, Ms. Malvika Pathania- politician and Monica Seth, hotelier. They were some of the outstanding pupils of St Bede's College who became the agents of radical and constructive changes in society. They are not to be considered as isolated cases showing excellence, but they are the slices of the larger segment of the JM tradition.

The memorial stamps released on various occasions commemorating the valuable contributions and landmarks show the uniqueness and recognition of the JM tradition of education. At the stamp releasing ceremony on the occasion of the celebration of 150th year of JM service to the nation Sri. B.B. Kapur, Postmaster General, Agra said on 11 November 1992:

The special Postage stamp being issued today is to commemorate the 150 years long service through dedication and self denial put in by the Sisters of the CJM. The indomitable courage and fortitude shown by St Claudine Thevenet was certainly not in vain and the good work done by her successors in this Congregation will certainly be remembered for long here in India. The special Postage Stamp issued by the Department today will further help to perpetuate the memory of that brave young French Lady and will also ensure that the Sisters of CJM are forever held in high esteem in the entire country (qtd. in Smith, "One Fifty Years of Service" 5).

Mr. S.C. Dutta, Deputy Director General of Posts (Philately) Government of India expressed the special appreciation that the Department of Posts felt, in being associated with the Jubilee. He said, "The stamp depicted the fire that burned in the heart of Claudine Thevenet. It was not one that consumed but illuminated. The Congregation has achieved much in the 150 years and this occasion signifies a recharter to continue the good work" (qtd. in Smith, "One Fifty Years of Service"5). Similarly, on 23rd October 2001, on the occasion of the centenary celebration of CJM School Dehradoon, the Department of Post recognized and honoured the CJM presence in the country with the release of the First Day Cover. Releasing of the Stamp and the First Day Cover on the occasion of the centenary celebrations of St Bede's College, Shimla was another glorious milestone in the history of the Congregation of Jesus and Mary for their contribution in the field of women education in India.

At the same time, the JM institutions have been criticized for the role they have played in developing an elitist mentality and elitist groupism wherever they have been operating. Nevertheless, their positive contributions far outweigh the deficiencies for which they have been criticized. In an interview one of our respondents has illustrated the above points through the thoughtful remark: "JM institutions have given to the country good citizens, men and women of good character, culture, academic excellence, and intellectual caliber who have adorned seats of learning, offices of high responsibility in administration and public life"(qtd. from the personal interview that formed a part of the Survey). She added that it is always publicly acknowledged that Christian institutions are lighthouses of education, regarded with respect and admiration. Critical evaluations of these achievements and an analysis of each section are given separately as concluding remarks. The recommendations highlighted in the study will prove effective guidelines for further research and formulation of future policies in the JM mission of education.

Endnotes

[1] There were hundred questions for students under five different themes such as personal fulfillment and family, educational achievement, occupational intent, social acceptance and economic status, forty questions for teachers with similar such themes, fifty questions for former students and fifty questions for general public with similar themes.

[2] The term 'positive'is used here to get to know the actual benefits of education received by students.

[3] The term 'negative'is applied here to have a critical approach towards the idea of quality education for the edification of students and improvement of educational institutions.

Concluding Observations

The study argues that the seed for women's education in North India was sown in 1842, much before both Mahatma Jyoti Rao Phulle and Savitribhi Phulle jointly opened a school for the 'untouchable'girls in 1848. When there were a series of vicious campaigns launched by the orthodox upper caste Hindus that education to girls was their exclusive possession, the Catholic visionaries began to initiate empowerment-oriented quality education. In fact, the educational institutions established by the JM missionaries were opened for all girls irrespective of caste, religion, and class. Social injunctions which believed that women and the Shudras were not entitled to education underwent a series of changes as Indian society evolved. Nevertheless, educational institutions established by JM visionaries in North India continued to be critical of those social injunctions. The JM visionaries believed that if women are given proper education from young age men would never have been able to be so partial and deceitful. Incontrovertibly, the JM institution could possibly be the earliest, path-breaking, and historic initiative in North India in the field of girl's education.

Relying heavily on the theoretical formulations of scholars such as Sabyasachi Bhattacharya, Hayden Bellenoit, Tim Allender, Krishna Kumar and others, this work concludes that the Catholic visionaries were able to thrive in knowledge production transcending the spatial metaphor centre-periphery binaries (Allender 227). Well engaged with communities of different cultural traditions, these indomitable visionaries could transcend the deeply embedded formal colonial divides of caste, class, gender and race through empowerment-oriented quality education to all sections of people.

This study argues that the historic implications of French revolution on Catholic visionaries, and the emphasis of Catholicism on quality education influenced substantially many aspects of traditional ethos, gender, and literacy in North India. It asserts that the educational obligations were not so explicitly pronounced on the socially disadvantageous sections until they had Catholic visionary encounters as the affluent sections continued to claim exclusive possession over right to education.

Hayden Bellenoit in his most recent work Missionary Education and Empire in Late Colonial India, 1860-1920 argues that despite there were a series of challenges due to the presence of colonial British, the visionaries were able to successfully execute their mission of women empowerment through world class education. This became possible partly because of the fact that the children of foreign origin were also taught by these visionaries in their educational institutions and partly due to the colonial presence, which to a larger extent, provided them adequate protection, public space, and maneuverability.

Carrying forward the convention initiated by the missionary educational institutions during the colonial times, North Indian States are poised to emerge as the 'educational hub'of the country. The historic contributions made by the educational institutions of the Congregation of Jesus and Mary attest to its persistent endeavour to the quality of education. The vision and mission of Claudine Thevenet, the Foundress of the Congregation of JM was realised when St Bede's College was set up in 1904 by Mother Claire to raise the standard of education in north western India. Even at a time when the effects of the World War II were explicitly felt in some parts of North India, the war did not seriously affect the college due to a variety of reasons. The ways in which the college had an international atmosphere, incorporating students from Africa, Thailand, Europe, America and so on, suggest that the college rose to an institution of eminence for Catholic higher education. After

India got independence, the students of foreign origin, along with their parents left India and the college which was mainly for Christian girls opened to all faiths.

Thus, the college underwent a series of challenges from within and outside. It is to be stated here that the college had its centenary celebration in 2003. Interestingly, a Postage Stamp and First Day Cover was released by the Postal Department of the Government of India in recognition of the contribution made by the college in the field of higher education. On 30 September 2003, when St Bede's College, Shimla celebrated its Centenary, the 'Ex Corde Ecclesiae Medal'[1] [From the Very Heart of the Church] was awarded to St Bede's College, Shimla by Msgr. Guy Real Thivierge, General Secretary of the International Federation of Catholic Universities. On that occasion, in the speech he delivered on behalf of the International Federation of Catholic Universities, he said:

> The Board of Administration decided and voted for it, to award its medal of honour called 'Ex Corde Ecclesiae'which means 'From the very heart of the Church'and it is our document of reference when we talk about Catholic higher education. So, we have decided to award the Medal to St Bede's College, Shimla. It is not something that we do easily; we must have very good reason to do so. For instance, we are celebrating one hundred years of commitment to training, commitment to service, commitment also to the communication of the highest values to students but not only to students, to a region, to a country but also to the rest of the world (quoted in Centenary Celebration 4).

On another occasion, Shri Virbhadra Singh, the then Chief Minister of Himachal Pradesh, in his inaugural address to a four-day assembly of the Council of Bishops of the Church in North India, appreciated that: "The institutions set up by the missionaries had been a source of inspiration for the state and the country" (quoted in Tribune 7).

The educational institutions set up and managed by missionary organizations had motivated the government to build quality infrastructure in its schools and colleges. On the same occasion, Virabhadra Singh said that Himachal Pradesh boasted of a number of famous educational institutions which came into being during the colonial times. Located mostly in Shimla, Dalhousie, Kasauli and other hill stations these institutions are still catering to the needs of young women by imparting quality-oriented world-class education. These institutions had produced innumerable personalities of high repute who excelled in various fields and brought laurels to the state and the nation.

Furthering the cause of women's education has been considered a contribution of no little worth, for which the JM institutions have been highly complimented. Above all they have been acclaimed for the quality education they have been imparting all over the country. In order to understand the efforts of the Congregation of Jesus and Mary in the education of women in the country, a view of the progressive development of women's education would prove to be of great help. In ancient India, among the Vedic Aryans, women enjoyed equality of status and educational opportunity with men. Women in ancient India enjoyed a much higher status than they came to have later. They had a position of honour and authority in the family. Unfortunately, however, the right to study religious scriptures including Vedas came to be abruptly denied to women, as Manu, the great Hindu Law giver, denied them all rights to independent action. Thus, in the medieval India, the status of women received a great set back and their education was almost totally neglected and uncared for. Whatever little education they received had purely cultural and spiritual value.

With the coming of the Muslims, the 'pardha' system became a widespread phenomenon. Most of the women were forced to be confined to the four walls of their houses and seclusion of women became the order of the day. When the Europeans came to India, there was practically no inclusive schooling system for the education of boys and girls, though the dancing girls who were attached to temples had the right to educate themselves informally from the learned Brahmins. Even music, dancing and reading came to be associated with women of 'bad character.'It is true that they did not receive literary education, but they were taught all the household chores. A few girls from affluent families were taught by tutors to read and keep accounts.

At the beginning of the 19th century, the British were confronted with the task of forming and improving the system of education, with the hope that it would raise the social, economic and political status of women. Several modifications were made in the Indian educational policy, in favour of women. Fee concessions and special scholarships were offered, and the grant-in-aid system was made more favourable to women and their empowerment. During this period, a series of socially embedded customs, conventions, and practices did not allow the girls to attend schools. It should be noted that the widely prevalent practice of child marriage played a crucial role in discouraging them to study and write. Due to patriarchal oriented customs, traditions, practices, conservative ideologies, and religious beliefs, women's status has, through ages, been considered to be lower than that of men. During the rule of Lord William Bentinck and Lord Dalhousie, there was a little improvement in women's education. Raja Ram Mohan Roy and Ishwar Chandra Vidya Sagar, Mahatma Gandhi, and Jawaharlal Nehru had been emphasising on the importance of women's education and freedom but still the educational condition of women was extremely depressing.

With the inception of JM institutions in North India in 1842, the history of women's education began with a renewed dynamism and vigor. It was at the request of bishop Borghi of Agra and his successors, as well as due to the appeal of the people of Agra, the JM Sisters came from Lyons, France to India to start their educational institutions at different places in North India. It was the mission and vision of St Claudine Thevenet to teach, train and enlighten the minds of young girls, so that they could lead a life with dignity which is fruitful, spiritual, purposeful, positive, and constructive. This vision was further unfolded by her faithful successors who despite facing perilous journey on land and sea, arrived on the Indian soil with a noble cause of empowering women.

The pioneers of JM institutions did not have a short-sighted vision. When they responded to the persistent request of the people of India to open schools for the children of those different areas in North India, they realized that this was the best way of leading young minds from different forms of ignorance to knowledge and wisdom for they had an unshakable conviction that education was the most effective means of transforming a society from within. The Catholic women missionaries did not allow themselves to be disheartened, demoralized and deflated by innumerable challenges and hindrances. The available literature suggests that education has been so dear to their hearts. This is evident from the fact that the JM visionaries made every effort to make education as a tremendously rich tool for the preparation of pupils to be dynamic citizens in the modern, complex and democratic societies. In fact, they gave importance only to women's education, and the fruit of their labour can be seen explicitly today.

Before they came to the northern part of India, no constructive effort had been made in this direction. After the establishment of their educational institutions in different parts of India, they began to emphasize more on the issues and challenges of women than appropriating the conventional system of education. The visionaries strongly believed that educational level of women is important largely because the educational attainment can affect the age of marriage, reproductive behavior, the use of contraceptives, the health and nutritional levels of the family, proper hygienic practices, migration trends and above all, their own status. They also felt that women's education has found to have been a more significant effect in reducing the poverty ratio and promoting sustainable development, influencing family size and women workers.

It is to be noted that almost all developing countries have been focusing on the need for development of women and their active participation in the mainstream development processes. It is also widely recognized that apart from managing the household, and bearing children, women are going out for earning income from different domains as workers, and entrepreneurs. They have also proven that they can be better entrepreneurs and development managers in any kind of human development activities. For JM visionaries, the empowerment of women has been the focus of attention for they considered that education is an active process of enabling women to realize their identity. In fact, this was the predominant objective of the JM sisters when they started the first institution outside Europe, in Agra, India in 1842.

From a very insignificant beginning, the institutions have grown by leaps and bounds not only in terms of infrastructure, but also imparting quality education and discipline, and living up to appreciable values that were most cherished and experienced by St. Claudine Thevenet. For Claudine, the education of young girls was an important task in forming them as free and responsible human beings. She believed that transformative education affirms their dignity, self-respect, and respectability. Claudine believed that it is, especially, the duty and responsibility of her and her followers who were called to serve humanity. The beginnings were obviously humble, the progress gradual, but the achievements of the past 177 years have been marvelous. The results are, therefore, for everyone to see and appreciate, and this has only been possible due to the hard work and dedication of the management, staff, parents, students, and whole-hearted support of the local administration.

They prepare young women with a sound humanistic, scientific, and spiritual training capable of hard, sustained work for society. The JM institutions are imparting quality education to students for nation building by inculcating values such as a balanced view of life, sense of dedication, duty and respect for others and instilling the spirit of love, compassion, forgiveness, justice, transparency, and responsible citizenship. In the midst of indiscipline, strikes and lawlessness prevailing in other educational institutions, JM institutions present a picture of comparative peace and academic excellence. They train young girls to be exemplary women, good wives, and exceptional mothers with a sense of responsibility and commitment. An institution which imparts a good education is a vital service rendered not only to the neighbouring communities and the academic milieu but also to the wider society and to the country. In this perspective, the findings show the typical and significant contributions that the JM institutions are rendering to the country by educating the girl child.

The tremendous inputs put in the institutions on which the study has been made, bore further results in the fast-growing development of other institutions in many of the states. The Delhi Province today is spread over Uttar Pradesh, Uttaranchal, Himachal Pradesh, Haryana, West Bengal, Chhattisgarh, the National Capital Territory of Delhi and southern states of Kerala and Karnataka. Now it also has an establishment in the Philippines. The JM Sisters have extended their mission further by establishing more educational institutions after India's Independence. Taking into account the need of the local people the JM Sisters started Hindi Medium Schools in the northern region: in 1955, St. Agnes' Hindi Medium High School, Dehradun, in 1961, Krista Raja Hindi Medium High School, Delhi, in 1962, St. Lawrence's Hindi Medium High School, Mussoorie, and in 1991, JM Hindi Medium High School, Bhurewala, Haryana.

In 1968, JM Sisters started their much-reputed Jesus and Mary College, Delhi, and in1981, St Joseph's College, Sardhana, Meerut, as the centres of higher learning. The JM Working Women's Hostel in Chalil, Kerala, started in 1982 was yet another attempt to extend their service for working women in the coastal region of Kerala. Another CJM High School was started in 1996, in Ranaghat, West Bengal. In 1997, responding to the request of the local people JM Sisters opened CJM Working Women's Hostel in Mangalore. In the year 2003, JM Sisters opened a Primary School in Tilinga, Chhattisgarh and later in 2006 they started their CJM Social Work Centre in Davavo, Philippines. Apart from the traditional teaching-learning centres, the JM Sisters designed a Women's Cell for the uplift of women and remedial classes for the academically weak students. These institutions and enterprises are in tune with the educational mission of their Foundress, and for the needs of the people.

In spite of all that has been done for women's education, it remains a distant goal. The Indian Constitution requires that primary education be provided for all children between the ages of 6 and 14. Of children between the age of 6 and 11, only 4 out of 5 attend school, and of those between 11 and 14 years only 2 out of 5 attend school. Dropout rates are high. Of every 100 children who enter grade 1, only 25 children reach grade 8 (Catholic Directory, 2007). These average rates do not truly portray the distressing picture of educational deprivation prevalent in the rural areas. The worst affected are underprivileged groups identified in the Indian Constitution as requiring special assistance such as tribals, nomadic tribes, scheduled castes, and other low-income groups. Among them, the educational status of girls is the lowest of all.

In 1976, the Government of India in its primary education survey reported that it had achieved the universal education of the country's boys in the early primary grades. There was, however, a persistent lag in the enrollment of girls; only 63.5 percent of India's girls aged 6-11 were in school, compared to 97.5 percent of the boys. In the higher grades, enrollment dropped precipitously for both sexes, but even more so for girls. The proportion of girls in the upper primary grades is less than half of that of boys (24.5 percent girls, 48.7 percent boys). After Independence, each government has contributed in their own ways to the women education and child welfare.

Despite the growing consensus among development experts that womcn's cducation leads to higher family income and to increase in health, nutrition, and family planning, specific attention was paidto reduce this gap. One can surmise several reasons for this comparative neglect of women's education. One reason is an unwillingness to see girls'access to schools as a distinctive issue that may require special ameliorative measures. The general rise in women's literacy and school attendance during each census decade, prompts an evolutionary perspective from which it is assumed that the problem will be solved in time as the general level of education rises. The proponents of this view point out that there is little evidence of discrimination against girls with respect to school entry or facilities, particularly at the primary level. It is not known, however, how many older girls may be deterred from attending school due to the lack of toilets in rural schools. One must also ask whether the nation can afford to wait for evolutionary progress to bring women to education if the linkages with other developmental goals are so strong.

On the other hand, there is a general sense of ineffectualness about the possibilities of reforming India's women's education. The educational system is mammoth, decentralised, bureaucratised, and part of a status culture that holds itself above rustic villagers and slum dwellers. It is also severely under-funded, particularly at lower levels. The many faceted proposals of the distinguished 1965 Educational Commission of India had done something substantial. Nevertheless, compared to agriculture, where new technology is yielding commendable results, there are only a few apparent mechanisms of change in education. This is largely due to the fact that there is a little political will to create them.

The problems of women's education are made more difficult by the overlay of commonplace assumptions which, added together, make a daunting argument about the impossibility of increasing their school attendance. Families'needs for girls to care for younger siblings, their reluctance to send pre-pubertal girls outside the house, early marriages, and the natal family's unwillingness to invest in girls who will anyway leave for another family's household are the obstacles usually cited. These factors are deeply embedded in the culture's fundamental attitudes toward women that change can only be evolutionary. It is against this background that the educational vision and charism of the Congregation of Jesus and Mary and their challenges in the field of women's education appear so exciting.

In the midst of growing unrest and liberalism in the West, the Catholic visionaries took education as its universal mission. The JM Congregation being French by origin, could appropriate the empowerment-oriented mission of its Foundress Claudine Thevenet amidst challenging socio-political situations both in France and in India. The pain and suffering made her firm in faith and the hardships during her childhood and the authentic Christian witnessing of her family showed her the ephemeral and the transient nature of life. Accompanying the consecrated life of Claudine and her vision of education that has been left as a legacy for the members of her Congregation to follow, it focuses on the major happenings that made her to commit herself for the uplift of the poor women.

In fact, the French Revolution shaped her faith. Consequently, empowering women became the dynamic charisma of her vision throughout her life. It is this authentic vocation the JM Sisters follow through their committed life. The enlightened Catholic visionaries such as bishop Borghi and others made the Indian nation privileged to have the presence of the JM Sisters in North India to empower women through quality and world-class education.

Any visionary organization will definitely have an asset and a driving force called charisma. Similarly, only an efficient and organised organizational structure can ably execute the vision and mission of visionaries. The study reveals that it was the charisma of the Foundress which helped building the educational institutions and the internal mechanism of the administrative policies operate. The structure of the JM Congregation is inextricably related to the structural pattern of the educational institutions, and the Congregation has a well-built structural frame, which provides their educational institutions administrative efficiency, structural stability, and intellectual productivity.

The hierarchical structure has been well presented in the graphical representation, and it gives an understanding of the structure that makes the important policy decisions. It strictly follows the spirit of the constitution of the JM Congregation. Imbued with the indomitable vision, Claudine hoped that the students would act as a 'leaven' in their social set up. If this were to be done effectively the students would need a strong intellectual formation. She did not pioneer any new system of education; instead, she took the best elements in the educational system of her time, catholicized them and organized them so as to achieve her purpose better.The life of the JM Sisters in a community is a part of the preparation and formation for the effective educational mission. These educational institutions mould young women into mature women with the foundational vision of JM congregation. The study affirms the fact that this structural framework of the institutions makes the expansion of its mission possible. An institution which imparts a quality education is a vital service rendered not only to the neighbouring communities and the academic milieu but also to the wider society, country and to the whole world.

For Claudine, education was a means to enable the students to attain the ultimate purpose for which they were created. Her goal was to instill a scientifically established outlook in the society. To be influential in their milieu, the students needed to be proficient in the skills for such a milieu. The educational vision of Claudine was to make students earn a decent livelihood and to live a dignified human life. She offered subjects that helped people specially girls, earn a livelihood and turn out to be good mothers, wives, sisters, leaders in their families and their country. Hence her liberal studies were based predominantly on vocational studies with an inclusive approach.

Education, for Claudine, had a social purpose, namely that its benefits were to be for all, including the poor, disadvantaged and depressed communities. Hence the JM educational institutions have the vision of producing outstanding leaders so that new generations of people, free from hunger, poverty and inequality can be created. Like the earlier humanists she wanted the whole person to be educated namely, body, mind, emotions and crowned by philosophy and theology which provided the reason for a good moral living. She also encouraged excellence in studies.

Claudine also gave a certain direction in the educational work to be carried out by JM Congregation. She believed that personal education together with solid learning and a method of expounding knowledge would be a great help to a better knowledge and service of God. Claudine saw educational work as a means to accomplishing the goal of the society. This goal was to facilitate each individual in the society to realise the ultimate purpose for which they were created. The primary way to fulfill the purpose was an exemplary living of one's life.

Even in the changed circumstances, the JM Sisters feel that they have certain contributions to make through their educational institutions. Being aware of this mission, the JM Sisters have all along endeavored to establish educational institutions, especially for women wherever they were invited. The pictorial presentation of the states along with their educational institutions locates the centres of the JM mission during that period. Starting with St Patrick's School, Agra, as the first of its kind by the JM Sisters, in 1842, this study traces the linear progression of its establishments one after another. Apart from giving the prosaic details of each institution, this study absorbs its wistful moments of trial and tribulations along with each institution's heights of achievement. While times may have changed, the JM spirit has not, though it has been renewed to suit modern times.

The characteristics of JM education provides the inspiration, values, attitudes and style which have marked JM education for centuries and must continue to do so even today. The typical and significant contributions that the JM institutions are rendering to the country through the development of the already established institutions find its expression in this study. The JM Congregation being a religious order with education as its main apostolate, the growth and development of their educational mission is construed as such in terms of the growth and development of the JM Congregation.

After Independence, the JM schools and colleges underwent a lot of change in their infrastructure, academic pattern, co-curricular and extra-curricular activities. For example, St Patrick's Junior College which was started as a little primary school and orphanage, today excels as an English Medium Senior Secondary School with the strength of approximately 1500 students catering to middle class families. The institution is affiliated to the Council of Indian School Certificate (ICSC) offering Arts, Science and Commerce subjects to the students in classes XI and XII. Besides its academic studies, the school encourages their students and instills in them a lot of social, moral, and civic values. St Patrick's stands as one of the best girls, school not only in Agra but in the whole of Uttar Pradesh.

St Joseph's School, Agra is no longer a poor children's orphanage school. It is a Hindi medium Inter College with strength of over 1900 students from pre-primary classes up to Class XII. Most of the students come from families in the low-income group. The institution is affiliated to the Uttar Pradesh State Board and receives grant-in-aid only for classes VI-XII. Arts, Science, Commerce and Computer Science are the subjects offered at the senior secondary level. The institution still accommodates the poor and the orphans, but not in large numbers. The original block that was St. Joseph's Orphanage in the early days remains intact. The new blocks for the senior sections are built and used.

CJM Waverly today is vastly different from the Waverly of a hundred and seventy years ago. Catering to over 500 girls from classes I to X, it has a mix of students from all over the country and abroad. Special mention needs to be made of the Thai girls, daughters of NRI parents in Thailand, who form a sizeable contingent in the school. The majority of the girls are boarders, but the school has now opened its doors to the children of local residents. Well equipped class rooms, science labs, a library with old documents and books as well as modern fiction and periodicals, a needle work room, art room, music room, a computer lab and various courts and playing fields testify to the delicate mix of the old and the new.

The school has changed with the times and prides itself on this change. Today, the schoolworks under the educational pattern of C.B.S.E. The administrative authority is planning to ameliorate the school to class XII due to the pressing demand from the parents and local people. Interestingly, self-defence courses like karate and so on were introduced to train the girls in the art of self-defense. Computer classes are, of course, a compulsory part of the curriculum beginning from class 1, yet the traditional womanly arts of needle work, painting and music have not been forgotten. The annual display of needle work and crafts with its exquisite collection of embroidery, knitting, fabric painting and toy making, bears ample testimony to this fact. The tastefully furnished dormitories, each with its own colour scheme, the Junior Section being especially noticeable with a favourite doll or stuffed toy seated atop each bed, underline the warm and homely atmosphere. With laudable objective of providing an all-round quality education to children of less well-off parents, in 1962, the school authorities opened a branch school St Lawrence within the same campus. This school caters to 600 boys and girls, not only educating them but also supplying them with uniforms and other necessities.

Sardhana has been called "Pearl of the Congregation in India". From its inception CJM Sardhana had worked consistently for the training and education of the poor Indian girls. Today, the village of Sardhana is rapidly developing into a flourishing town. The school has come a long way from its earlier works of education to an Inter-college. St Joseph's Inter-college is a grant-in-aid institution. The school and the college are Hindi medium institutions. Today, the school has about 1800 students from classes 1 to XII. After class XII, the students secure admission to the Degree College. In 1981, St Joseph's Sardhana was raised into a Degree College. It still stands as the first Catholic college and the only Hindi medium grant-in-aid Degree college for women in Uttar Pradesh. It has now a strength of approximately 600 students and offers courses in Arts and commerce subjects. It was promoted into a B. Ed. College very recentlyThe old orphanage which looked after hundreds of girls has been changed to a hostel which accommodates about 100 girls who pay according to their means.

Shimla the 'Queen of Himalayas' has been the summer residence of the Viceroys of India for many years. In 1863, the administrator of the Agra Archdiocese purchased two estates in Shimla for a Catholic orphanage and a school for boys and girls. One was given to the Religious of Jesus and Mary who established CJM School Chelsea in 1864. Today, CJM Chelsea is no more an orphanage but it is an unaided English medium institution with an approximate strength of 1500 girls from nursery classes to class X. The school is affiliated to the Council for Indian School Certificate Board due to the pressing demand from the local students from the hill tops and the valleys. The hostel which accommodated 300 girls from all over the country and outside the country closed down in the year 2000. The old dormitory buildings were converted into classrooms. A new building with 25 classrooms and a multi-purpose hall has been catering to the needs of students.

The CJM School, Dehradun, established in 1880, was at first a temporary school. In 1901, it became officially a permanent day-school entitled St Joseph's School. Today, the school has developed tremendously and has fine modern buildings. It is an unaided English medium institution with an approximate strength of 1500 students, from pre-primary classes to class XII. Affiliated to the Council for Indian School Certificate pattern it offers courses in Arts, Science and Commerce to Classes XI and XII.

St Anthony's School Agra started as a temporary day-school for the Irish girls at Numilah, today is known as St Anthony's Junior College. In 1950, St. Anthony's had undergone some major repairs, constructions, and extensions. As the number of students increased there was need for more accommodation and better facilities. In 1977 a regular community of nuns who lived at St Patrick's came to reside on the premises of St. Anthony's as the needs of the institution grew. Even though the school was started as a co-educational institution, in 1980 St. Anthony's changed from a co-educational to provide education only to the girls. One more block, the Marian block was constructed and added to the existing buildings. It was in 1984 that the school got its affiliation to the I.C.S.E. Board, New Delhi. The institution sent its first batch of I.C.S.E. students and they passed with flying colours. In 1986, St Anthony's became a centre for I.C.S.C. Board Examinations. In 1996, it sent up the first batch of I.C.S.C students. Today, it is an English medium school with an approximate strength of 1500 students, from pre-primary classes to Class XII, and it offers courses in Commerce and Science.

St Bede's College, Shimla, pride of the educational authorities for its high standard of education in India, was founded in 1904 as a Teacher Training College (TTC). It was affiliated to the Anglo-Indian Board of Education. Besides the training of teachers, students were prepared privately for Degrees of the East Punjab University. After partition, there was a great demand for higher education and St Bede's took up the challenge of raising the college up to degree level by providing higher education to young Indian women. Today, St Bede's College, in the state of Himachal Pradesh, is affiliated to the Himachal Pradesh University and receives a grant-in-aid from the government. Apart from having Teacher Training Course, the college offers undergraduate courses in B.A. Programme in various disciplines, B.Sc.in non-medical, B.A. Honours in English, Economics, Geography, B.B.A, B.C.A., B.Sc. Micro-Biology, B.Sc. Biotechnology, B.Com; Post Graduation in M.A. English, Geography, Psychology and M.Com. The college also offers various 'Add-on Courses' under the HP University. The college continues to have a hostel which accommodates approximately 200 girls. Today, there is an increasing governmental involvement that regulates courses, syllabi, examinations, and staff service programmes. Due to the undue intervention of the changing state governments, the college faces a series of difficulties and it affects the effective running and the autonomy of the college. Despite all these challenges, the college administration continues to deliver its best to provide an excellent academic environment.

Since 1842, JM educational work has been largely responsible for preparing an enlightened community which can hold its head high. The JM Sisters did their absolute best to realize the vision of their Foundress St. Claudine. The JM educational mission aims at the formation of an allround person who is intellectually competent, open to growth, religious, loving and committed to justice in generous service to the needy people in society. The impact that the JM Congregation had on the lives of their students through their institutions is the best testimony to the success of their efforts. The success stories of the JM students in terms of achievements display the achievement in the field of women education to the effectiveness of education offered by the JM institutions.

The JM institutions contribution to the building up of individuals in terms of their leadership, commitment to the family, society and nation, responsible citizenship and nation-building, dedication for the general welfare of the people, suggests that the level of achievement and contribution towards women's education is far more deeper that it has been explored so far. These educational institutions focus on eliciting responses in the areas of personal fulfillment and family, educational achievement, occupational intent, economic uplift, and social acceptance.

The JM institutions and its education have made a deep impact on the lives of their students through persistent efforts at realizing the JM vision of education for more than 175 years. Their stress on integral development rather than on mere academics, on all-round excellence rather than mere success in examinations, character development and social outreach, has contributed to producing students well-adjusted to society. The JM institutions, animated by a noble vision and mission of empowering women, are free of prejudice and bias. They create an ethos that is non-discriminatory and respectful of students of all religious backgrounds and communities. This makes for an inclusive and secular outlook where all are treated equally.

Education had undergone a profound change all over the world. The diversified culture and the challenging task ahead widened the scope of education in India. Considering the signs of time, there are various groups of women religious Congregations involved in the ministry of women education. Though CJM was the first group of Sisters pioneered the cause of women education in the North, other religious Congregations also contributed to the cause of women education in India. All these women religious Congregations are working for the same cause and contribute to the women education in India. For them, education greatly consisted in taking care of children by studying the character and potential of each child to direct them on the path of truth and good, and guard them against the allurement of vices.

No matter how educational attainment is conceived in the assessment of other Congregations. In the North, women reap benefits of education because of the exclusive presence of the JM educational tradition. In the changing scenario of the society, JM visionaries passionately believe that the exposure to teaching-learning process alone is not sufficient to assure acceptable educational achievement levels. The academic support and encouragement provided by teachers, peers, and others may be especially important to girl students who face social pressure not to excel in school or career oriented programmes. The undervaluing of women's education is a worldwide phenomenon, expressed both in school and outside, and its effects on girls'attainment are profound. Women's enthusiasm for schooling in India may be hampered by the fact that employment opportunities are lower for women educated above the middle-school level. Therefore, the JM mission of education has to consider the following suggestions in their future educational policies in order to make their apostolate relevant and updated in the North Indian context:

a. Its concerns should be more on the education of poor children in the rural and tribal areas.

b. It should form policies to cater to the needs and concerns of the poor girls in the villages rather than focusing on the elite class in society.

c. It is not a question of the quantitative expansion of the JM institutions but its qualitative reshaping as well.

d. It should strive to provide primary education for children in the age group 6-14 in selected rural areas.

e. It should focus to improve the quality of education in the primary schools in selected underdeveloped areas and relate it more closely to the life and needs of the rural children and with rural development.

f. It should evolve similar programs for primary education in urban slums, to improve its quality, and to make it more relevant to the life and needs of the slum children.

g. It should produce improved educational materials for primary education in rural areas and in urban slums.

h. It should devise improved techniques for producing materials for the effective training of primary teachers.

This study helps to gauge the impact of the JM education imparted by the Catholic visionaries in North India and its effect on those students who come to study in their institutions. It suggests that similar such in-depth studies need to be undertaken to assess specific policies in order to improve the overall quality of the elementary, secondary, and higher education that they offer. The ways in which this critical survey presented, and the questions raised will provide a basis for further research in the area. To the visionaries of the Congregation of Jesus and Mary, women's education has represented a route to national dignity and independence by countering obscurant social practices. This study hopes to capture the great hopes of education and can contribute to the formulation of further policies which will ensure that such hopes are not belied. Despite the fact that the educational institutions undergo a series of challenges and difficulties, these institutions of higher learning stand firmly rooted on the solid foundation of St Claudine's vision, commitment, hard work and dedication without compromising the quality of education.

Going through the annals of educational history of the Congregation of the religious of Jesus and Mary in North India, the JM educational establishments have marked significant role in nation building. Ever since its inception in India in 1842, the JM sisters have been seen by many as women of good will and warriors for the good of the mother country in the field of women's education. As a result of their crucial contributions to education in India, the rulers were delighted to confer different designations to the JM institutions and encouraged the visionaries to impart education to the needy in the country. The JM institutions have journeyed through the vicissitudes of time, with its glorious history of women education, with hopes and daily struggles of life spent in service and fidelity to work. The JM institutions have influenced the society particularly through their family values by which they have helped for developing a moral society based on family values.

The primary purpose of JM institutions has been to create responsive and responsible citizens. The good practices adopted by JM institutions have enabled imparting knowledge to holistic growth. The available records do suggest that the JM students today are placed in the best universities for higher education across the globe and are in positions of responsibilities in both public and private sectors. Many of our students have also become entrepreneurs and generated employment. They have made a mark in all possible fields comprising education, research, social work, sports, fine arts, performing arts, entertainment, mass communication and management. This path breaking transformation ascertains that JM practices have helped them excel in their pursuit of perfection and vision. However, there are several milestones yet to be reached. The autonomous status will enable the higher educational institutions to address the challenges being faced by the institutions. The approach of inclusiveness will help bridge the yawning gaps between castes, class and creed created in the society. The vision of the foundress of the JM Congregation would get fulfilled only when adequate attention is made on strengthening humane values, celebrating the diverse cultural, ideological, ethnic, religious, intellectual richness, and enhancing the team by bonding rather than segregating on the basis of caste, religion and creed.

Endnote

[1] '*Ex Corde Ecclesiae*' is an apostolic constitution issued by Pope John Paul II regarding Catholic colleges and universities. It was promulgated on 15 August 1990.

Works Cited

Agrawal, S.P. and Aggarwal, J.C. Women Education in India. New Delhi: Concept Publishing Company, 1992.

Allender, Tim, *Ruling Through Education: The Politics of Schooling in colonial Punjab*, New Delhi: New Dawn Press Group, 2006.

___________. "Transcending the Centre-Periphery Paradigm: Loreto teaching in India, 1842-2010,"in BarnitaBagchi, Eckhardt Fuchs, and Kate Rousmaniere, Connecting Histories of Education: Transnational and Cross-Cultural Exchanges in (Post-) Colonial Education, Berghahn, New York, 2014, pp. 227-241.

Aiya, Nagam V. *The Travancore State Manual*. Vol. II. Trivandrum: Govt. Press, 1906.

Albert. "One Hundred Years in Sardhana," *Examiner*, 10 January 1959, Archbishop's House Archives, Bombay.

Andrew. "Correspondence of Mother Andrew to Agra."ts. June 1945.

Annan, Kofi. "Best Defence Spending is on Girls."*Women Children and Human Rights*. (2000): April-June, 20-24.

___________. "Two-word Mantra." *Documentation on Women and Children*. (2004): March, 5-9.

Antonio, Javierre and Paloma, M de la Alvarez. *Claudine Educator*. Rome: JM Generalate Publication, 1982.

"A Family Treasure."ts. Jesus and Mary Archives, Rome, 1843.

"A Hundred Years of Service." *The Statesman* [U.P.] 18 Sept. 1945: 6+

Arora, S. and Mathur, D. "The Hunger Project", Vision, Jesus and Mary College, New Delhi, 1989.

Augustine and Balachandran, S. "The Claudine Thevenet Outreach Programme –1984-85", Jesus and Mary College Magazine, 1984-85, New Delhi.

Barrel, Thomas More and Carlos, Marie Theresa. *Positio: A Study and Documentation on the Introduction of the Cause and Virtues.* Ipswich: RJM Publication, 1983.

Batra, Poonam. "Women's Studies and development Centre –A Recapitulation", Spectrum, Jesus and Mary College, New Delhi, 1991.

Bellenoit, Hayden, J.A. "Education, Missionaries and the Indian Nation, c. 1880-1920," in Primal V. Rao (ed.), *New Perspectives in the History of Indian Education*, New Delhi: Orient BlackSwan, New Delhi, 2014.

____________. *Missionary Education and Empire in Late Colonial India, 1860-1920*, London: Routledge, 2007.

Borghi, Antony. "The Second Group of JM Nuns." *Bengal Catholic Herald* (Culcutta), Vol. 5, 23 Nov. 1844: 3+.

____________. "St. Mary's School." *Bengal Catholic Herald* (Culcutta) Vol. 3, 1 Dec. 1842: 2+

____________. "Correspondence of Bishop Borghi."ms. 28 June 1843, Archbishop's House Archives, Agra.

____________. "Missionary Institutions in the Agra Mission in the Nineteenth Century." *Agra Weekly Register.* 3 May, 1862.

Buck. Edward J. *Simla-Past and Present.* Shimla: Minerva Book House, 1989.

Carli. "Women in the Society." *Bengal Catholic Herald* (Calcutta) Vol. 9, 4 March, 1848: 4+.

"Centenary Celebration." *Centenary Souvenir 1903-2003*, St. Bede's College, Shimla, 2003.

Channan, Bhavya Nayna. "Profile: St. Bede's College, Shimla", Hindustan Times, 14 July, 2009; Report on the Administration of the Punjab and Its Dependencies, Civil and Military Gazette Press, Lahore, 1908.

Chaube, S.P. *Some Great Indian Educators.* Agra: Bharat Publications, 1957.

Cherian, C.V. "Kerala Empowerment through Enlightenment". *Indian Christian Dictionary for the New Millennium.* Kottayam: Rashtra Deepika (2000): 120-129.

Chopra, Radhika. *Militant and Migrant: The Politics and Social History of Punjab*, Routledge, New Delhi, 2011.

Chiasson, Laurntine. *Unless a Wheat Grain Dies.* Trans. Evangeline Flynn. London: Willesden Green, 1981.

Chander, Shivani. "The Debating Society", Vision, Jesus and Mary College, New Delhi, 1989.

Christhu Doss, "M. Protestant Missionaries and Depressed Classes in Southern Tamil Nadu, 1813-1947", *Ph.D., Thesis*, submitted to the Center for Historical Studies, School of Social Sciences, Jawaharlal Nehru University, New Delhi, 2009.

Chronicles of St. Patrick's School Agra. ms. 3. St. Patrick's School Archives, Agra, 1845.

Chronicles of St. Anthony's School Agra. ms. 5. Anthony's School Archives, Agra, 1926.

Chronicles of CJM Mother House. ms. 4. CJM Mother House Archives, Rome, 1947.

Chronicles of CJM Waverly. ms.1. CJM School Archives, Waverly, 1845.

Chronicles of CJM Sardhana. ms.7. CJM School Archives, Sardhana, 1857.

Chronicles of CJM Lahore. ms.1. CJM Archives, Lahore, 1876.

Chronicles of Lucknow Cathedral. ms. 12. Bishop's House Archives, Lucknow, 1880.

Chronicles of CJM Delhi.ms. 1. CJM School Archives, Delhi, 1920.

Chronicles of CJM Delhi. ms. 2. CJM School Archives, Delhi, 1923.

Chronicles of CJM Delhi. ms. 4. CJM School Archives, Delhi, 1929.

Chronicles of CJM Hampton Court. ms. 4. CJM School Archives, Hampton Court, 1930.

Chronicles of CJM Dehradoon. ms. 1. CJM School Archives, Dehradoon, 1901.

Chronicles of CJM Dehradoon. ms. 2. CJM School Archives, Dehradoon, 1912.

Chronicles of CJM Dehradoon. ms. 4. CJM School Archives, Dehradoon, 1947.

Chronicles of St. Patrick's School Agra. ms. 55. St. Patrick's School, Archives, Agra, 1901.

Chronicles of CJM Waverly. ms.1. Convent Archives, Waverly, 1845.

Chronicles of CJM, Mother House France, Generalate Archives, France, 1845.

Community Report. ms. 31. RJM Generalate, Rome, 1820.

Cuthbert, Mary. *Echoes of a Century in India*. Ranchi: Catholic Press, 1942.

____________. *A Pioneer: Life of Mother St. Clare of the Congregation of Jesus and Mary*. Ranchi: Catholic Press, 1943.

Dass, R.M. *Women in Manu and his Seven Commentators*. Varanasi: Kanchan Publications, 1961.

De Cesinale, Roch. "The Collection of Writings of Rev. Fr. Roch De Cesinale, Cap. of the College of the Missions at Agra, (1868) concerning the Establishments of the CJM in India."Unpublished essay, Trans. Margaret Mary Lane, Rome: JM Generalate Archives, 1980.

De Rome, Marie Sainte Cecile. *Canticle of Love*. Trans. Mary Saint Stephen, Canada: Quebec Newspapers Ltd., 1945.

Dharchaudhuri, Indira. "A Fair Career,"*Documentation on Women and Children*. (2004): January-March, 1-3.

D'orsey, Alex. *Portuguese Discoveries, Dependencies and Missions in Asia and Africa*. London: W.H. Allen & Co. Ltd., 1893.

D'Rozario, P.S. "Missionary Journey."*Bengal Catholic Herald*. (Calcutta), Vol. 3. Saturday, 2 July, 1842: 3+.

D'Souza, Daniel. *The Growth and Activities of the Catholic Church in North India*, Mangalore: Sharada, 1982.

____________. "Influence of Catholic Women in the Mughal Seraglio."*New Leader* 7 March 1979: 1-7.

Du Jarric, Pierre. *Akbar and the Jesuits*. Trans. C.N. Payne. Delhi: Tulsi UP, 1989.

Elise, Flury. *Practical Hints on Education*. London: R & T, Washbourne Ltd., 1910.

Fernando, Leonard and Sauch, Gispert. *Christianity in India: Two Thousand Years of Faith*. New Delhi: Penguin Books, 2004.

Flannery, Austin. *Documents of Vatican II*. Bombay: St. Paul Publications, 1998.

Franciscan Annals of India. Vol. XXXI, No. 5, 1949.

Funk and Wagnalls, ed. *The Readers Digest Great Encyclopaedic Dictionary*. London: Readers Digest Publication, 1968.

EvangeliNuntiandi of Jesus and Mary. ts. Rome: Religious of Jesus and Mary Generalate Archives, 1983.

"General Summaries about the Houses of the Congregation."ts. RJM Generalate Archives, Rome. 1950.

"Editor's Note." *Echoes*, The College Magazine, St. Bede's College, 1943.

Gibbons, William J. *Seven Great Encyclicals*. New York: Paulist Press, Publications, 1939.

Gonzaga. "Mother Louis Gonzaga's letter to Mother General."ms. RJM, Generalate Archives, Rome, 1851.

____________. "Letters from Mother Louis Gonzaga."ms. May 1845. Archives Rome.

"Great Educationist."*Simla Times*. 20 February, 1936: 6+.

Hartman. "The Works in Agra Mission."*The Examiner*, 4 May, 1849, Bombay.

Herbert H., Risley. *The People of India*, Thacker, Spink & Co.; London: W. Thacker & Co, 1908.

History of the Congregation of the Religious of Jesus and Mary. Gujarat: Anand Press, 1991.

Horny, Jeanne Marie. *Claudine Thevenet-Lyon 1774-1837*. Trans. Thomas More Barrell. Rome: RJM Publication, 1989.

Hyacinth. "History of Agra Mission."*Franciscan Annals*. June, 1910.

Jacopi, Michael Angelo. "Correspondence of Bishop Michael Angelo Jacopi to the Priests in Agra."ms. June 1846. Archbishop's Archives, Agra.

____________. "Correspondence of Bishop Michael Angelo Jacopi."ms. 1855. Sardhana Church Archives, Meerut.

JM Annals. ts. CJM Chelsea, Shimla Archives, 1949.

John, Marina. "Principal's Desk", Hand Book, Jesus and Mary College, New Delhi, 2005.

Johnston, Anna. *Missionary Writing and Empire, 1800-1860*, Cambridge University Press, Cambridge, 2003.

Keegan, W. *Sardhana and its Begum.* Agra: St. Francis'Orphan Press, 1932.

Kottamkombil, Janet. "Annual Report of CJM School." *Souvenir.* Dehradoon, 2001: 4.

Kumar, Krishna and Oesterheld, Joachim (eds), Education and Social Change in South Asia, Delhi: Orient Longman, 2007.

Kumar, Krishna. *Politics of Education in Colonial India*, Routledge, New Delhi, 2014.

Kumbhare, Arun R. *Women of India: Their Status, Since the Vedic Times*, iUniverse, Bloomington, 2009.

Leitner, D.W. *History of Indigenous Education in the Panjab since Annexation and in 1882*, Calcutta: Superintendent of Government Printing, 1882.

Life and Work of Mother Mary St. Ignatius (1774-1837). Dublin: Clonmore and Reynolds Ltd., 1953.

*Lucknow Church Chronicle.*ms. Bishop's House Archives, Lucknow, 1870.

Maghew, Arthur. *Christianity and Government of India.* London: Faber and Gwyer, 1971.

Mali, M.G. *Education of Masses in India.* Delhi: Mittal Publications, 1964.

Maria, Gabriella. *The Life and Times of Claudine Thevenet.* Trans. Catherine M. Dell. Gujarat: Anand Press, 1977.

*Military Records.*ts. The Agra Cantonment Records, Agra, 1902.

Minutes of the RJM General Council. ms. Session of June 27, France, 1823.

"Missionary Institutions in the Agra Mission in the Nineteenth Century."

Agra Weekly Register, 3rd May 1862, Bishop's House Archives, Lucknow.

Mitra, Alicia. *A History of the Congregation of the Religious of Jesus and Mary in India 1842-1993.* Gujarat: Anand Press, 1999.

Mitra, M. and Tripathi,S. "Planning Forum", Jesus and Mary College Magazine, 1984-85, New Delhi.

Motte, Therese. *A Missionary Epic: The Letters of Mother Mary St. Therese.* Ed. Abril, S. Gujarat: Anand Press, 1992.

____________. "Correspondence of Mother Therese to Mother Andrew in France."ms. January 1843, JM Generalate Archives, Rome.

____________. "Correspondence of Mother Theresa."May 1845, ts. *JM Annals*, St. Bede's College Lib., Shimla.

____________. "Correspondence of Mother Theresa". May 1849, ts. *JM Annals*, St. Bede's College Lib., Shimla.

____________. "Mother Theresa's Letter to Mother House in France."ms. RJM Generalate Archives, Rome, 1850.

Murphy, Clementine. "Correspondence of Murphy."ms. Dec. 1845, RJM Provincial House, Pune.

____________. "Correspondence of Mother St. Clementine Murphy." ms. Aug. 1845. RJM Generlate, Rome.

____________. "The First Sixty Years."ts. JM Provincial House Archives, Pune1846.

Nag, Sajal, *The Uprising: Colonial State, Christian Missionaries, and Anti-Slavery Movement in North-East India (1908-1954)*, New Delhi: Oxford University Press, 2016.

Neill, Stephen, *A History of Christianity in India: The Beginnings to AD 1707,* Cambridge: Cambridge University Press, 1984.

Nesfield, J.C. *Brief View of the Caste System of North Western Provinces and Oudh*, Government Press, Allahabad, 1855.

"Our Catholic Schools."*Franciscan Annals,* Archbishop's House Archives, Agra. May 1912.

Pal, Gobindachandra. "Women's Education for a Better Nation."*Documentation on Women's Concerns.* (1993): July-Sept., 5-7.

Panikar, K.M. *Asia and Western Dominance.* London: George Allen & Unwin Ltd. 1953.

____________. *India: Past and Present*, New Delhi: Prentice-Hall International,1964.

Paul, Mary. "Correspondence of St. Mary Paul."ms. Dec. 1940, Jesus and Mary Provincial House, Pune.

Persico, Ignatius. "Our Catholic Mission at Agra."*Fransiscan Annals of India*, Archbishop's House Archives, Agra. July 1914.

Polin, Therese. *Constitutional Texts of the Congregation of the Religious of Jesus Mary.* Rome: Jesus and Mary Publications, 1977.

Pius, Pope XI. "Christian Education of Youth."Ed. Gibbons, William J. *Seven Great Encyclicals.* New York: Paulist Press Publications, 1939. 25-39.

Rao, Parimala V. "Compulsory Education and the Political Leadership in Colonial India, 1840-1947," in Parimala V. Rao (ed.), *New Perspectives in the History of Indian Education*, New Delhi: Orient Black Swan, 2014.

Rodrigues, Melba. "Mother Felix: May She Rest in Peace", Jesus and Mary College Magazine, 1984-85, New Delhi.

Rule Book of 1843. ts. Jesus and Mary Generalate Archives, Rome.

Sarangapani, Padma. "The B.El.Ed. Programme", Dimensions, Jesus and Mary College, New Delhi, 1996-97.

School Admission Register, ms. 4. St. Anthony's School Archives, Agra, 1910.

School Admission Register, ms. 10. St. Anthony's School Archives, Agra, 1926.

School Admission Register, ms. 23. CJM Waverly, Mussoorie School Archives, 1913.

School Admission Register, ms. 26. CJM Waverly, Mussoorie School Archives, 1916.

School Inspection Report St. Joseph's Sardhana. ts. St. Joseph's School Archives, Sardhana, 1886. 2.

School Inspection Report St. Patrick's Agra. ts. St. Patrick's School Archives Agra, 1930. 1-4.

School Inspection Report St. Joseph's Agra. ts. St. Joseph's School, Agra, 1922. 3-4.

School Inspection Report St. Joseph's Agra. ts. St. Joseph's School Archives, Agra, 1928, 2-4.

School Inspection Report CJM Waverly. ts. CJM School Archives, Waverly, 1931, 1-5.

School Inspection Report St. Antony's Agra. ts. St. Anthony's School Archives, Agra, 1926, 4-5.

School Inspection Report CJM Delhi. ts. CJM School Archives, Delhi, 1931, 3-5.

School Inspection Report CJM Hampton Court.ts. CJM School Archives, Hampton Court, 1922, 1-2.

Seth, Sanjay, "Secular Enlightenment and Christian Conversion: Missionaries and Education in Colonial India,"in Krishna Kumar and Joachim Oesterheld (eds), Education and Social Change in South Asia, Delhi: Orient Longman, 2007.

Shardha, K. "Yoga-Sadhana Kendra in JMC", Vision, Jesus and Mary College, New Delhi, 1989.

Smith, N.R. "One Fifty Years of Service."*The Statesman*. Nov. 14, 1991. 5+.

Smith, Sydney. *The Congregation of Jesus and Mary –Cameos from its History*. London: Burnes & Oates Ltd., 1917.

Sores, Aloysius. *Catholic Church in India*. Nagpur: Govt. Press and Book Depot, 1964.

"The Arrival of Six Nuns."*Examiner*. Nov. 1842. 16.

"The Church in North India."*Tribune* (Shimla) 5 August, 2007: 2+.

"The letter of the Agra correspondent." *The Bengal Catholic Herald*. (Culcutta) 15 February 1849: 3+.

Theodora. "Correspondence of Mother. St. Theodora."ms. 12 Aug. 1958, JM Generalate Archives, Rome.

The Funeral Records. ms. 3. Sisters of the Congregation of Jesus and Mary, St. Patrick's Convent Archives, Agra.

The Gazetteers. No. 12. Nov. 1877. Government Archives, Bombay.

The Gazetteers. No.50. July 1862, National Archives, New Delhi.

The New Oxford Annotated Bible. Michael D. Coogan, ed. New York: Oxford, 1987.

Theresa, Mary. Heroes and Heroines Canonized in the Twentieth Century, Book II, 1951-1999, Authorhouse, Bloomington, 2009.

Thomas P. "The Advancement of Christianity in India." *The Clergy Monthly*, Ranchi. Vol. XII (1), Jan-Feb, 1948, 1-3.

Thomas, Susan. "Banish Hunger Project", Spectrum, Jesus and Mary College, New Delhi, 1991-92.

Vani, Evangelist."Speech on the occasion of Centenary." *Souvenir of the Waverly Centenary1845-1945*. JM Provincial House, Delhi, 1945, 8.

Vannini, Fulgentius. *Bishop Hartman*. Alahabad, UP: St. Paul Publication, 1966.

____________. *Hindustan Tibet Mission*. Delhi: Vishal Printers, 1981.

Vicar General and Administrator. *Catholic Calendar and Directory- for the Archdiocese of Agra, Allahabad and Lahore*. Agra: St. Francis Orphan Press, 1908.

www.ingramcontent.com/pod-product-compliance
Ingram Content Group UK Ltd.
Pitfield, Milton Keynes, MK11 3LW, UK
UKHW041857190726
13854UKWH00002B/956